KINDERGARTEN TEACHER'S MONTH-BY-MONTH ACTIVITIES PROGRAM

Elizabeth Crosby Stull   **Carol Lewis Price**

THE CENTER FOR APPLIED RESEARCH IN EDUCATION
West Nyack, New York 10995

Library of Congress Cataloging-in-Publication Data

Stull, Elizabeth Crosby.
    Kindergarten teacher's month-by-month activities program.
    p. cm.
    ISBN 0-87628-497-7 : Spiral   ISBN 0-87628-500-0 : Paper
    1. Kindergarten—United States—Curricula. 2. Kindergarten—United States—
Activity programs. I. Price, Carol Lewis. II. Title.
LB1180.S78   1988   87-15857
372'.218   CIP

Printed in the United States of America

20 19 18 17 16 15 (S)   10 9 8 7 6 5 4 3   (P)

ISBN 0-87628-497-7 (S)   ISBN 0-87628-500-0 (P)

 **THE CENTER FOR APPLIED RESEARCH
IN EDUCATION**
West Nyack, NY 10994
A Simon & Schuster Company

On the World Wide Web at http://www.phdirect.com

Prentice-Hall International (UK) Limited, *London*
Prentice-Hall of Australia Pty. Limited, *Sydney*
Prentice-Hall Canada Inc., *Toronto*
Prentice-Hall Hispanoamericana, S.A., *Mexico*
Prentice-Hall of India Private Limited, *New Delhi*
Prentice-Hall of Japan, Inc., *Tokyo*
Simon & Schuster Asia Pte. Ltd., *Singapore*
Editora Prentice-Hall do Brasil, Ltda., *Rio de Janeiro*

This book is dedicated to those who dedicate themselves to five year olds—the kindergarten teachers who greet boys and girls when they're brand new and shiny and share with them the magic of learning.

We are grateful to Evelyn M. Fazio, our editor; for her vision, encouragement, and support.

I'd like to give special recognition to two New York State Kindergarten Nurturers—Jane Weber (Greece Central) and Wanda Ward (Pittsford Central), as well as E. J. Searl, nurturer-at-large.

E. C. S.

Bear hugs to Bruce and Sharon, my rainy-day friends—and to the Brothers and Sisters of the Irish Kindergarten Society. They all still clap for Tinkerbell!

C. L. P.

ELIZABETH CROSBY STULL, PH.D. (The Ohio State University) began her career as a teacher of grades 1, 2, and 4 in the public schools of Greece Central, Camillus, and Pittsford in upstate New York, and is presently an adjunct professor at The Ohio State University, where she has taught the Kindergarten Methods course as well as courses in Child Development. Dr. Stull has published many articles in such professional publications as *Instructor* and *Teaching K-8* and is affiliated with the National Association for the Education of Young Children and the International Reading Association.

CAROL LEWIS PRICE, M.A. (The Ohio State University) has served as a pre-school director, a kindergarten teacher and first-grade teacher and is currently an elementary school principal in Worthington, Ohio. Mrs. Price has written curriculum and courses of study for handwriting, math, reading, kindergarten assessment, social studies, science, and computer education and has conducted many inservice workshops for elementary teachers. Her professional affiliations include membership in Elementary Kindergarten Nursery Educators, Phi Delta Kappa, Phi Kappa Phi, and Phi Lambda Theta.

DR. STULL AND MRS. PRICE are also the authors of *Science & Math Enrichment Activities for the Primary Grades* published by The Center in 1987.

ABOUT THE AUTHORS

ABOUT THIS BOOK

The *Kindergarten Teacher's Month-by-Month Activities Program* offers over 400 activities and over 100 full-page activity pages to help you plan an effective kindergarten program. When planning your kindergarten curriculum, there are several important elements to keep in mind:

- *Philosophy*—How do I feel about early childhood education and its relationship to the development of the child? How do I believe children learn best? Is my philosophy consistent with the adopted district curriculum?

- *Goals*—What are the educational goals of the school system? What are the needs of the children and their parents? What concepts do I feel are important to teach?

- *Curriculum*—How will I provide an attractive and inviting classroom? How will I arrange the daily schedule of activities? How flexible is the curriculum? Does the program meet the needs of all types of learners?

- *Evaluation*—Is each child learning? Is each child having fun? Is the program broad enough to accomplish the designated general curriculum goals and yet still allow me to address the specific learning strengths and areas of concern of each child?

The activities in the book address each of these four areas. Divided into sections for each month of the school year, the book includes the following skill areas:

1. *Recommended Books*—Each month's listing of recommended books gives a brief description of each book. Read these books to your students during the particular month. The stories relate to the skill areas you will cover.

2. *Reading Skills Activities*—These activities teach and reinforce such basic reading skills as letter recognition, language development, upper- and lowercase letters, colors, and story writing.

3. *Math Skills Activities*—These activities cover such math skills as counting, sets, the calendar, money, shapes, and measuring.

4. *Other Skill Areas Activities*—These activities relate to the particular month of the year. For example, your students will learn about school safety in September, animals' winter habits in January, bird migration in March, and summer safety in May/June.

5. *Reproducible Activity Pages*—At the end of each month are at least ten ready-to-use full-page activity sheets that relate to some of the activities in that particular month. These activity pages can be reproduced as many times as needed for use with your students.

Keep in mind that most educators now agree that kindergarten is one of the most important and influential experiences a child can have. The *Kindergarten Teacher's Month-by-Month Activities Program* will give you an opportunity to work with enthusiastic and curious youngsters at a time in their development when everything is new and exciting!

Elizabeth Crosby Stull
Carol Lewis Price

HOW TO ASSESS KINDERGARTEN STUDENTS

Teachers of young children will find that although students might be nearly the same age chronologically, they may be at very different stages developmentally. There is a wide range of skill levels in the kindergarten classroom and it is necessary to have pertinent information about each child. An ongoing assessment of the students throughout the year will ensure the identification and early diagnosis of possible learning difficulties as well as learning strengths. It will enable you to plan an education program of varied experiences that will encourage the optimal development of all.

By evaluating several times during the school year, you are able to plot each child's capabilities when he or she enters school, what he or she learns during the year, and when the growth occurs. It is important that the skills assessed be consistent with those taught in the classroom and reflected on the reporting form to parents.

Remember that each child is unique and special. A careful evaluation record serves as a diary of the children's accomplishments.

Evaluation Forms

The evaluation sheet of *math and reading readiness skills* shown here lists a sequence of skills in the math and reading areas. The evaluation sheet of *language development, listening, and motor skills* lists important skills in the areas of language, listening, and vocabulary development. The motor area is divided into *gross and fine motor skills.*

These evaluation forms have a space for the child's name and birthdate and are divided into columns for notes about the child's progress at various times during the school year. You might want to check each student at two-month intervals, such as September, November, January, March, and May. You can duplicate the forms so that you have one of each child in the classroom. The copies can be hole punched and kept in a 3-ring binder for easy reference during parent/teacher conferences.

Assessment Charts

The assessment chart for *capital and lowercase letter recognition* is an easy and accessible tool for use in evaluation.

The assessment chart for *numeral, shape, and letter recognition* may be enlarged and kept in the notebook with the individual evaluation forms.

Questionnaire to Parents

The questionnaire may be given to parents at the beginning of the school year. It provides you with important information about each child.

The Calendar

You can fill in this "refrigerator" calendar and distribute copies to parents as a reference to the kindergarten schedule. The sample calendar of January lists the skills and study units to be taught during the month.

The Newsletter

You can reproduce the blank newsletter sheet and fill it in to be used each month to communicate to parents. The sample shown here describes what is happening in the kindergarten classroom in November.

Name	Birthdate	Dates of Evaluation							
Reading Readiness Area									
Recognizes capital letters									
Recognizes lowercase letters									
Given a word, names beginning sound									
Given a word, names ending sound									
Given a letter, names words that begin with letter									
Recognizes color words									
Recognizes number words									
Recognizes sight words									
Identifies rhyming words									
Reproduces rhyming words									
Recognizes blends and digraphs									
Writes words phonetically									
Math Readiness Area									
Recognizes numerals, 1–12									
Recognizes numerals, 0–30									
Counts to….									
Recognizes basic shapes									
Sorts and classifies objects									
Recognizes/reproduces patterns									
Counts objects (1–1 correspondence)									
Adds and subtracts									

Name	Birthdate	Dates of Evaluation			
Language Development/Listening					
Knows full name, address, phone number, birthdate					
Listens attentively to stories					
Identifies sequence of events in stories					
Can follow 3 verbal directions					
Can repeat simple rhymes					
Contributes to large discussions					
Speaks in full sentences					
Uses proper articulation					
Has a good vocabulary					
Motor Skills (Gross)					
Walks balance beam, forward and backward					
Can hop, jump, march, skip					
Can bounce, throw, catch a ball					
Motor Skills (Fine)					
Colors appropriately					
Uses scissors appropriately					
Uses appropriate pencil grip					
Writes own name					
Forms shapes correctly					
Forms numbers correctly					
Forms letters correctly					
Can trace a pattern					

TEACHER ASSESSMENT MATERIALS—CAPITAL LETTER RECOGNITION, LOWERCASE LETTER RECOGNITION

These charts may be enlarged to be used with the children. To evaluate a child's letter recognition skills, point to each letter and ask the child to name it. It is important to ask the letters out of sequence so that you can be sure the child knows the letter.

N	B	Q	P
D	R	W	Z
F	A	S	V
C	E	T	U
G	X	H	K
J	I	L	N
O	M	Y	D

z	w	r	d
p	q	b	n
u	t	e	c
v	s	a	f
n	l	i	j
k	h	x	g
d	m	o	y

TEACHER ASSESSMENT MATERIAL—NUMERAL RECOGNITION, 1-30, SHAPE RECOGNITION, COLOR RECOGNITION

These charts may be enlarged to be used with the children. Color each shape with a different one of the eight basic colors. To evaluate a child's number recognition skills, point to each numeral and ask the child to name it. In checking shapes and colors, point to each shape and ask the student to name the shape and its color.

21	18	6	10	4
11	30	26	14	1
23	19	15	9	16
20	25	17	13	12
3	24	22	29	2
8	28	7	5	27

QUESTIONNAIRE FOR KINDERGARTEN PARENTS

Dear Parents,

Would you please take a few minutes to answer the questions below. This will help me get to know your child better. Thank you!

Child's name _____ (as you want him/her called at school)   Birthday _____
Age _____ (years) _____ (months)

1. Please list the names and ages of your child's brothers and sisters.

2. Has your child had preschool or play-group experience? (Please give name of school and number of years attended.)

3. Does your child have any difficulties with speech?

4. Does your child have any health problems or allergies?

5. Does your child have any special interests?

6. Is your child afraid of anything?

7. What responsibilities does your child have at home?

8. What form of discipline do you use at home?

9. What skills has your child acquired?

_____ Knows address

_____ Knows phone number

_____ Knows birthday

_____ Can say full name

_____ Can print full name

_____ Counts to....(how far?)

_____ Knows the difference between right and left

_____ Knows the names of colors

_____ Can recognize numbers to 12

_____ Recognizes capital letters

_____ Recognizes lowercase letters

_____ Recognizes letter sounds

_____ Likes to listen to stories

_____ Can tie shoes

_____ Can button own clothing

_____ Can zip own clothing

_____ Can tell time

_____ Has experience with crayons

_____ Has experience with scissors

10. If your child is reading, how did he/she learn and how long has he/she been reading?

11. What are your expectations for the kindergarten program? What specific things would you like to see happen this year?

12. Would you be interested in helping in the classroom? Is there a particular day and time that is best for you?

13. Is there anything else that you would like to tell me about your child?

This will be an exciting year! I look forward to getting to know you and your child.

Thank you!

Sunday	Monday	Tuesday	Wednesday	Thursday	Friday	Saturday

January

Sun.	Mon.	Tues.	Wed.	Thurs.	Fri.	Sat.
		Happy New Year! **1**	Back to School! AM-Music **2**	AM-Library PM-Gym **3**	PM-Music **4**	**5**
letter - Bb Mr. Beautiful Buttons • Snow • Graphing **6**	PM-Library **7**	AM-Gym **8**	AM-Music **9**	AM-Library PM-Gym **10**	PM-Music **11**	**12**
letter - Ww Mr. Wonderful Wink • Mexico • Graphing **13**	PM-Library **14**	AM-Gym **15**	AM-Music **16**	AM-Library PM-Gym **17**	No School Teacher Work Day **18**	**19**
letter - Ss Mr. Super Socks • Mexico • Leo Lionni (author) • Graphing **20**	No School Martin Luther King Day **21**	Report Cards are sent home. PM-Music **22**	PM-Library **23**	AM-Gym **24**	AM-Music **25**	**26**
letter - Tt Mr. Tall Teeth • Fairy Tales • Rhyming Words • Graphing **27**	AM-Library PM-Gym **28**	PM-Music **29**	PM-Library **30**	AM-Gym **31**	AM-Music Feb. 1	Feb. 2

NOVEMBER KINDERGARTEN NEWS

Dear Parents,

The holidays are near and the kindergarten children are busy as we plan for the festivities. Our study of the Pilgrims and Indians will culminate in a celebration feast on Wednesday. Tuesday will be cooking day and we'll mix and bake cornbread and pumpkin cake. Our reading readiness and math work for the week will be centered around our preparation for Thanksgiving.

We have been working on recognizing the letters of the alphabet, both capital and lowercase. Now we will spend a week learning about each letter. We have just completed Ff week—learning how to form that letter and how the letter sounds at the beginning and end of words. The boys and girls should bring in magazine pictures that begin with the letter for our experience chart. The letter schedule is:

November 29-December 3	letter Dd
December 6-December 10	letter Mm
December 13-December 17	letter Gg

In math, we continue to work on numbers to 12—their formation and the concept of "how many." We are learning number words, also. Being able to know how many objects are in a set of 0 to 5 objects without counting is an important concept and one that takes practice. You can help your child by creating sets of up to five objects (silverware, pennies, marbles, bottle caps, etc.) and asking your child to decide "how many" quickly, without counting.

Our other skill areas for the next three weeks will include Maurice Sendak (the author and illustrator of children's books), Hanukkah, and holiday traditions.

At this special time of year as we reflect upon our good fortunes, I thank you for sharing your child with me. I hope each family enjoys a wonderful celebration together.

Sincerely,

_____

Teacher

CONTENTS

OCTOBER

Scaring Up an Exciting Month

NOVEMBER

A Harvest of Good Ideas

DECEMBER

A Festive Atmosphere

JANUARY

A Blizzard of Winter Experience

FEBRUARY

A Sweetheart of a Month

MARCH

Lions, Lambs, and Learning

APRIL

A Cloudburst of Classroom Creativity

MAY AND JUNE

My, How You've Grown!

SEPTEMBER

WE'RE "BEARY" GLAD TO SEE YOU

Welcome to the beginning of a new year in kindergarten. As you prepare your classroom and your thoughts for the days ahead, why not choose a theme to carry through the activities and experiences you have planned for the children. The learning theme of this month is "teddy bears." As you read through the reading, math, and other activity suggestions and look through the reproducible activity pages for September found at the end of the chapter, you will find many ideas for inviting teddy bears to be an intriguing and creative part of learning. Bears in the classroom can truly be "beary" exciting!

Recommended Children's Books for September

First Day in School by Bill Binzen (New York: Doubleday & Company, 1972). It's the first day of kindergarten. All summer the classroom has been empty and now the children are beginning to arrive. They wonder what school will be like. As their parents bring them to the classroom door, the boys and girls look confused and frightened. Carmen and Luis want to go home. As the teacher shows the students around the room, they become interested in the many games and toys. By the time her mother comes to pick her up, Maria even says, "School was fun." The photographs in this book are lovely and sure to help any new kindergartener feel at ease.

The Most Amazing Hide-and-Seek Alphabet Book by Robert Crowther (New York: The Viking Press, 1977). This alphabet book is done in large black letters on a white background. The letters turn, twist, fold, pull, and move to reveal a colorful object that begins with each letter. Letter recognition is reinforced by capital and lowercase letters on each page. The format of the book is striking and children love guessing what special surprise is hidden behind each letter.

Corduroy by Don Freeman (New York: The Viking Press, 1968). Corduroy is a bear who has lived in a department store all of his life. He waits for someone to come along and take him home. One day a little girl notices him and asks her mother to buy him. Mother says that she doesn't have enough money and, besides, the bear has lost a button on one of his shoulder straps. Poor Corduroy! He didn't realize that his button was gone and so he begins a journey through the department store to look for it. A night watchman finds him and carries him back to the shelf in the toy department. The next day, there is a wonderful surprise waiting for Corduroy. The little girl has come back to take him home. Children will love the adventures of this lovable bear.

Willy Bear by Mildred Kantrowitz, illustrated by Nancy Winslow Parker (New York: Parents' Magazine Press, 1976). This simple book tells the story of a little boy who is getting ready for his first day at school. He eases his own fears by telling his bear, Willy, about what the day will be like. He assures Willy that he is indeed old enough and grown up enough to go to school. When it comes time to leave, however, Willy is not dressed so the little boy tells him that he will go to school first and meet the teacher and the new friends. What wonderful reas-

surances this book gives to anyone, child or bear, who is beginning something new.

The Teddy Bears' Picnic by Jimmy Kennedy, illustrated by Alexander Day (La Jolla, CA: Green Tiger Press, 1983). The words to the old song "The Teddy Bears' Picnic" are the text for this fanciful tale of teddy bears who go to the woods for the annual teddy bear picnic. A record of the song is included, with a rendition by Bing Crosby and another by The Bearcats.

All for Fall by Ethel and Leonard Kessler (New York: Parents' Magazine Press, 1974). This story begins with the question "What are the colors of fall?" Perceptions of fall are described in terms of colors, sounds, events, food, animals, changes, play, holidays, weather, and seasons. The illustrations reinforce the images of the words and create a sense of the arrival of fall. Your students will enjoy the sing-song sentences and rhymes.

Brown Bear, Brown Bear, What Do You See? by Bill Martin, Jr., illustrated by Eric Carle (New York: Holt, Rinehart and Winston, 1967). The repetition of the phrases in this book enable children to "read" the story instantly. The rhyme, "Brown bear, brown bear, what do you see?" leads to a chain of animals, all looking at one another. The pictures of the animals are large and colorful and are immediate attention-getters for the children. It's a story to be read over and over and remembered always.

Blueberries for Sal by Robert McCloskey (New York: The Viking Press, 1948). This story is really the parallel tale of a little girl and a bear cub who each wander away from their blueberry-picking mothers and mistake the other's mother for their own. The setting is the Maine countryside on a summer day. The dark blue and white illustrations are captivating. Little children love the suspense of this story—will the little girl and the cub find their own mothers?

Here I Come, Ready or Not by Jean Merrill and Frances Gruse Scott (Chicago: Albert Whitman & Company, 1975). Every child can identify with the game of hide and seek. This book is a game of hide and seek, with the reader involved in every hiding place. The children in this book live on a farm, and as they tuck themselves away in all kinds of secret places, we also get a good look at farm life in the fall. There are apples being sorted and crated and hay being lifted into the haymow. Kate and Tony finish their hide and seek game just in time to be really ready for lunch.

Ira Sleeps Over by Bernard Waber (Boston: Houghton Mifflin Company, 1972). The little boy in this story is thrilled that he has been asked to sleep over at his friend Reggie's house. But he's never slept without his teddy bear before and he's not sure whether Reggie will laugh at him if he brings the teddy bear to spend the night. His mother and father assure him that it will be perfectly fine to take the bear along but his sister assures him that Reggie will laugh. What happens at Reggie's house is proof positive that everyone needs something to help them feel safe and secure—and that teddy bears are special friends, even if their names are Tah Tah and Foo Foo.

Reading Skills Activities

Letter Recognition

Children come to school with a variety of skill levels. Some of the boys and girls will probably be able to recognize and name all of the letters of the alphabet. Others will know many of the letters and there will be yet another group that is only familiar with a few of the letters or none at all. A letter review will be helpful to everyone. As you engage the boys and girls in a variety of letter activities and have the opportunity to assess each one individually, you will have a clearer idea of those students who are going to need reinforcement and those who are ready for extension experiences.

Alphie, the Alphabet Worm. Alphie is a versatile teaching tool and a fun way for kindergarteners to work on alphabet letters. He is constructed of oaktag circles covered with different colors of felt. The size of the circles will depend on the space you have available for displaying the worm. For use on a large bulletin board or the chalkboard, the circles could be six inches in diameter. Cut twenty-seven circles, one for each alphabet letter and one for Alphie's head. Cut twenty-seven circles of felt in a variety of colors or twenty-seven circles of wallpaper in different patterns and glue these on the pieces of oaktag. Cut a set of capital letters from felt in different colors. Glue a different letter on each felt circle or wallpaper circle. Next, cut a set of lowercase letters from the corresponding color of the capital letters and another set of lowercase letters from one color of felt not used for a body part. Do *not* glue the lowercase letters on Alphie's body parts. If the worm is to be used on the chalkboard, glue small pieces of magnetic tape on the back of each circle. To complete the head, add felt eyes, a fuzzy pom-pom nose, a red felt smile, and antennae fashioned from two pipe cleaners with pom-poms glued to one end. Tape the other ends to the back of the head.

Alphie can visit the classroom for as long as the boys and girls need help with letter recognition and then can be used for letter/sound association games.

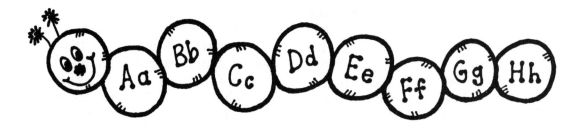

Some ideas for using Alphie include:

- Have the children sit in a semicircle, facing Alphie. Explain that he is a worm that has come to live in the classroom while they learn more about letters. Point to each of the body parts as the children say each letter. They might also sing the alphabet song ("A–B–C–D–E–F–G," etc.) as the teacher or a child points to the letters. Pass out the lowercase letters to the boys and girls and have them look carefully at their letters. If anyone is unsure about the name of their letters, they may ask a friend. As the teacher calls out a letter, the child with that letter comes forward and places it on the correct body part. (The felt letters will stick to the felt circles. If using wallpaper circles, add a small piece of sewing tape to the wallpaper so that the felt letters will adhere.) Use the set of multicolor lowercase letters when you are teaching recognition so the students can match colors as well as letters. Give the children the set of letters that are all one color as they become more skilled.

- Throw all of the body parts, except the head, in the middle of the circle and tell the children that when Alphie woke up that morning and shook himself, his body fell apart! "Can you help put our friend, Alphie, back together again?" "Does anyone see the first letter of the alphabet?" "Does anyone see the letter that comes next?" "What letter comes before F?" "What letter comes after T?"

- Mix up the body parts on the chalkboard or bulletin board and have the students put them in the right order.

- After the class is familiar with the alphabet, take away all of the letters except A, B, C, and D. Talk about those letters for a few days, concentrating on likenesses and differences between the capital and lowercase letters and the sequence of the letters. Discuss words that begin with each of the letters and how to write the letters. "Whose name begins with the letter B?" "Who has the letter B in their name?" "What food can you think of that begins with the letter D?" Gradually add the rest of the body parts, three or four at a time, until Alphie the Slug becomes Alphie the Worm again.

- A child can choose his/her favorite letter and take that body part to the art table where he or she can draw pictures of things that begin with the letter.

- Talk with the children about how they might "check out" an Alphie body part. They must sign their name and chosen letter on a large sheet of chart paper and take that letter home to share with their family overnight. When they return the letter, they might talk about what they found in their house that started with the letter or what letter games they played with their families.

- Make a paper Alphie that the children can work with during free choice time. Each child can make a paper Alphie to take home by tracing an oaktag circle pattern on different colors of construction paper. The students can also practice letter formation by writing the letters on the body parts. The worm can be kept in an envelope with the child's name written on the front.

- Make a human Alphie. Give each child a large paper circle with a letter printed on it and ask the children to arrange themselves in alphabetical order. ("The person with the A should start the line over here. The person with the B should come and stand next.") The person who is the "head" can wear a headband made from a strip of paper with two pipe cleaner antennae sticking up at the top...and a big smile! The class can sing the alphabet song and each child can sit down (or stand up, or jump, or bounce, or stand on one foot, or lie down, etc.) as their letter is sung.

Milk Carton Letter Train. This alphabet train is constructed from half-pint milk cartons. These probably can be obtained from the school lunchroom. Use a knife or sharp scissors to cut off the pointed top of each carton, leaving an open box. Cover twenty-six boxes with prepasted paper or brightly colored wrapping paper. Attach cardboard wheels to two opposite sides of the carton with paper fasteners. To label the train cars, either print or glue construction paper letters on the sides of the cartons. The engine is another milk carton, laying on its side, wheels attached, and a paper smokestack on top. The children can cut pictures from magazines and place them in the car with the appropriate beginning letter. They might also bring small objects from home to place in the train. The boys and girls enjoy playing "engineer" and trying to remember what objects or pictures belong with each letter. It's fun to bring in an engineer's cap to be worn by those working with the train.

Tennis Ball Alphabet. This is a good circle game and an excellent way for boys and girls to match capital and lowercase letters. Collect twenty-six tennis ball cans and lids. (Tennis clubs are usually willing to save them for teachers.) Cover the cans with prepasted paper and use a wide-tip permanent marker to print a capital letter on the side of each can. Gather twenty-six old tennis balls (you might ask the tennis club for these, also) and print a lowercase letter on each one. The children are to match each lowercase tennis ball with the corresponding capital letter can and drop the ball inside. Lined up in a row against a wall, under a chalkboard, the cans take up little room. As the students sit in a circle, roll a ball to each. The child must identify the letter and place it in the appropriate can when the letter is called.

Alphabet Toss. Print a set of capital and a set of lowercase letters on 9″ × 12″ sheets of construction paper. During a circle time, toss the letters into the middle of the group of children. When the teacher claps his/her hands together three times, the boys and girls should get up and WALK to a letter, pick it up and take it back to their places. There are several variations for this game:

- Have the class sing the alphabet song and hold up each letter as it is sung.
- The "A" person can lay down his or her letter to start a line and then every other child can lay his or her letter down in turn.
- Ask the children with lowercase cards to stand up so that their classmates can see what letter they are holding. They should sit down and then the capital letters should stand. After everyone is again seated, encourage the group to look around and see if they can spot the capital or lowercase letter that matches their own. The child should get up and go and sit by that person. (Be sure to give the direction for either all of the capital or all of the lowercase people to get up and do the moving.)

Alphabet Hunt. Use the same alphabet cards as those described in the Alphabet Toss to hide in various places in the school building. Lead the children on a tour through the building, cautioning them to look closely because there will be letters hidden along the way. This is a good way to acquaint the children with this large facility that will be their school home for many years. At a central point in the building, disperse small groups of boys and girls to go and bring back letter cards that they spotted along the tour route. When everyone has returned from the hunt, have them line up in alphabetical order to make sure that all of the letters have been rescued. You may need to send out the "letter squad" to find any that are missing.

Alphabet Bulletin Board. Cover a bulletin board with bright yellow paper. Cut the words, "We're 'Beary' Glad to See You!," from red construction paper. From red and blue paper, cut simple silhouettes of boys and girls, one for each letter of the alphabet. Print a capital letter on each child and attach the silhouettes to the bulletin board in two or three rows. Stick a pushpin in the outstretched hand of each child. Cut twenty-six simple teddy bears from brown paper and print a lowercase letter on each. Use a paper punch to make holes in the top of each teddy so that they will fit over the pins. The boys and girls can match capital to lowercase letters by hanging each bear on the arm of the correct child.

Name Recognition

What a thrill it is for children to be able to recognize and write their own names. It is an important skill and should be one of the first learned in kindergarten.

Name Puzzles. Print each child's name on a 3″ × 5″ card. Cut the puzzle into three pieces, using jagged puzzle-like cuts. Put each puzzle in an envelope with the child's name on the front. Arrange the envelopes in a circle on the floor and ask the boys and girls to find theirs as they arrive at school, sit in back of it, and see if they can figure out what the puzzles say.

Name Slates. Fill flat box lids with oatmeal and sand. The children can practice writing their names in these materials.

Wet Letters. Fill an empty deodorant bottle (with a rolling ball top) with water. The children can write their names on the chalkboard and watch them dry and disappear.

Scratch and Sniff Names. On pieces of 9″ × 12″ drawing paper, write each child's name in glue. Hold the papers over a pan and have each child sprinkle his/her name with gelatin and then shake the excess into the pan. This leftover gelatin can be scooped with a spoon and used to sprinkle another name. Set the papers aside to dry completely. These name cards provide a kinesthetic approach to learning names, allowing the children to trace the letters and feel their shapes. The different flavors of gelatin smell wonderful when the boys and girls scratch and sniff!

Chart Names. Write the name of each child on a sheet of chart paper. Call each child to come to the chart and find his/her own name. They can circle their name with a crayon and circle only certain letters requested by the teacher. Ask each child to spell his/her name aloud as he/she points to each letter.

Name Labels. Write the names of objects in the classroom on 3″ × 5″ cards and attach these labels to the corresponding object. Some suggestions would be: desk, table, chair, chalkboard, door, window, clock, cupboard, playhouse, counter, sink, restroom, bookcase, listening center, math center, reading center, flag, computer, block corner, puppet theater. As the children see these labels each day, they begin to "read" them. As a surprise, change the labels one day and see if any of the children notice. For instance, attach the restroom label to the chalkboard. Can they return the labels to the proper spots?

Listening

So many classroom activities depend on the ability to listen—following directions, language development, auditory discrimination and memory, story comprehension and sequencing. Research suggests that those children who are not good listeners are usually not good students. The boys and girls need to know that there will be certain times during the school day when they will need to pay close attention. You can work out your own special signal with them. It might be a few notes on the piano, turning out the lights, ringing a bell, hitting a drum, playing a music box, or holding an arm in the air with the first two fingers up to make "bunny ears." Practice the signal many times each day during the first few weeks of school until the children react instantly and become very quiet, waiting for your directions as to what they will do next.

Cutting

Many children have had little experience with scissors when they come to school. Instead of frustrating them by asking them to cut on lines, give them many opportunities to just cut. A sheet of paper and a pair of scissors will do. Give these items to each child as they sit in a circle. Show them the proper way to hold the scissors and how to cut the paper into strips by just cutting straight across. It is easy to watch the boys and girls in the circle and see who needs help with the skill. As the students finish cutting a paper, they can put their strips in a pile in the center of the circle and get another piece of paper to cut. It's fun to see how high the pile of scraps will be! Ask a helper to bring the wastebasket to the center of the circle and to pick up the strips, one at a time, and drop them in the trashcan. The class can count each strip as it is dropped. Write the number of scraps (usually a LARGE number!) on the chalkboard.

Math Skills Activities

Mathematics is based on patterns and symbols. Small children are not always developmentally capable of understanding these abstract areas. The early childhood program should substitute *real* materials for these patterns and symbols so that kindergarteners can *touch* and *explore* and *understand*. Manipulation is the key to enjoying numbers and their meaning. We want to make the *concepts* rather than the numerical symbols important and logical. In all math activities, young children (and even older ones!) should work with concrete objects before ever working on paper.

Counting

Counting Chart. Prepare a counting chart to be displayed in the classroom. Divide a large sheet of cardboard in squares, ten rows of ten squares each. Write a number in each box, beginning with 1 and ending with 100. As the boys and girls practice rote counting, point to each number as they say it so that they are also becoming familiar with the visual image of the number. Start with only the numbers in the first row, 1–10, and be sure these numbers are familiar before moving to the "teen" numbers.

Counting Objects. Counting objects involves the understanding that each object equals one number. If a child is counting crayons, he/she should say "one" when touching the first crayon, "two" when touching the second crayon, and so on. A child does not understand the concept if he/she says "one, two" when touching the first crayon. Practice counting during circle time. You might

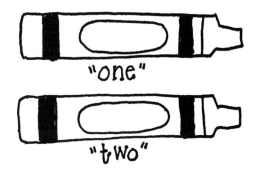

count: the number of boys and the number of girls, the number of tables in the room, the number of chairs in the room, the number of people wearing tennis shoes, the number of people wearing blue pants, the number of people with a tooth missing, the number of people who have babies at home, the number of people who have pets, the number of people with brown eyes, the number of people who walk to school, the number of people who have zippers, the number of people who know how to tie shoes, etc. As the children become familiar with this exercise, ask more difficult questions, for instance, "Are there more people with tennis shoes or more people with tie shoes?" "Are there more boys or more girls here today?" and "Are there more children in our class with brown eyes or blue eyes?" Have a group of boys stand in one part of the circle and a group of girls stand in another. Ask the students to tell which group has "more than" and which group has "less than." Gradually introduce the word "set." "We have a set of boys and a set of girls. Which set has the most children and which set has the least children?"

Graphing

Making a Floor Graph. Working with counting, sets, and "more than" and "less than" leads naturally into graphing. This concept would also be introduced with concrete materials. A large floor graph can be made from a six-foot piece of oilcloth or kraft paper. Use a permanent marker to divide the oilcloth or paper into three columns with six squares in each column. The other side of the oilcloth or paper should be divided into smaller squares, for instance, six columns of twelve squares. The floor graph can be used for making comparisons with concrete objects. Boys and girls can stand on the graph when the class is comparing tennis shoes and tie shoes or brown eyes and blue eyes. If the students have brought a piece of fruit for snack time, they can lay their fruits in appropriate columns (apples, oranges, grapes, strawberries, etc.) and make judgments about "more apples than oranges," "more peaches than plums," or "the most tangelos." You can make labels to put at the head of each column by folding a 3 × 5 card in half and drawing a picture of the object to be placed in that column. These can be laminated and saved for another graphing time. In placing the objects on the graphing squares, the students are also practicing sorting and classifying.

Sets of 1 to 5 Objects

Learning to recognize sets of 1 to 5 objects without counting is a difficult concept and one that takes much practice.

Sets of Real Objects. As the children sit in a circle, lay out five sheets of paper on the floor. On each paper, lay a set of from 1 to 5 objects, with each number represented. Objects might include crayons, erasers, marbles, keys, cookies, nuts, etc. Also, lay out five 3″ × 5″ cards with the numerals 1 through 5 printed on them. Select different children to count the number of objects on the papers and place the correct numeral next to each. Do this several times, talking about the differences in the sizes of the sets and urging the children to make their "best guess" as to how many objects are on each paper without taking the time to count each one. The boys and girls will soon be shouting out the numbers quickly.

Sets on the Overhead Projector. Use an overhead projector and plastic counters for a variation of this game. While the children are sitting in a circle, turn out the lights and turn on the projector. Put five counters on the overhead so that image appears on the screen. One at a time, take away a counter and ask the children how many plastic pieces there are then. Have the children watch the screen as you cover part of the counters and ask them "how many." Each time cover a different number of counters, including covering none (5 counters). At one point, cover all of the counters and ask "how many." The children will probably say "none" and this will be a good time to introduce the word "zero."

Zero

The Empty Set. Pose questions to the children that will require the answer "zero." ("How many horses do we have in our room?" "How many tractors are parked on that table?" "How many cats are sitting on my desk?") Ask them to think of their own questions that could be answered with the word "zero." Explain that "zero" means that the set is empty. Show them some concrete examples: an empty purse, a can with nothing in it, an empty basket, a trashcan with nothing in it, etc.

Shapes

Shapes in the Classroom. Young children have had many experiences with shapes by the time they come to school. They can identify and compare circles, squares, triangles, and rectangles. Informally call attention to shapes in the classroom and use words describing those shapes when referring to those objects. For example, instead of saying, "Look at the clock," say "Look at the round clock." Ask the children to find as many items as possible that resemble the shapes that they are talking about.

Shapes and Directions. Cut shapes from construction paper and give one to each child. When you call the name of a shape and give a direction, the children should respond. ("Put your circle on your head." "Put your square under your left leg." "Put your triangle on top of your right knee." This is also a good way to practice directional words.) The children can trade shapes and play the game again.

Shapes—Alike and Different. Have the children sort through cards containing pairs of geometric figures—some matched and some not matched—and decide whether the pairs are alike or different. If they are the same, the children can place them in one pile and if they are different, in another pile.

Shape Collages. Give the children magazines that have an abundance of pictures and ask them to cut out pictures of objects that are circles, squares, triangles, or rectangles. They can paste these on huge shapes cut from kraft paper and hang the shape collages in the classroom or the hallway.

Stuffed Shapes. Make huge stuffed shapes by taking various colors of kraft paper and cutting two huge squares, two huge circles, two huge rectangles, and two huge triangles. Put the two matching shapes together and staple around the edges, leaving about a foot of space for stuffing. Give the boys and girls pages

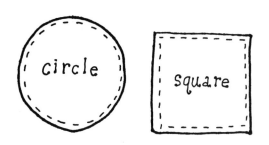

of newspaper and ask them to wad it up and push it into one of the shapes. Keep stuffing until the shapes are plump and then staple the opening shut. A child can write "square" on the side of the square, "circle" on the side of the circle, "rectangle" on the side of the rectangle, and "triangle" on the side of the triangle. The stuffed shapes can be hung in the classroom or in the hallway.

Calendar

An attractive monthly calendar can also be a tool for teaching many math skills.

Calendar Cutouts. Make special cutouts for each month that the children can attach to the calendar on the correct day. Apples would be appropriate for September, pumpkins for October, leaves for November, pine trees for December, snowmen for January, hearts for February, shamrocks for March, umbrellas for April, butterflies for May, and suns for June. The children have to identify the number before they attach it to the calendar. Ask the boys and girls to tell the date and day for today, the date and day for yesterday, and the date and day for tomorrow.

Calendar Graphing. Graph the months that have only 28 days, those that have only 30 days, and those that have 31 days. Talk about Leap Year—when it happens, what it symbolizes. "How would you feel if you only had a birthday every four years? Does that mean you'd only be one year older every four years?"

Other Skill Areas Activities

School Orientation

Here Come the Teddy Bears. Everyone has a favorite teddy and somehow bringing that special friend to school with you on the first day makes you feel a lot braver. About a week before school begins, send each child a short note telling them how excited you are that he/she will be a member of the class and to please bring a favorite teddy bear the first week of school. Plan many get-acquainted and learning activities around the bears.

Graphing Bears. Graph the different kind of bears that the children bring to school on the floor graph (Pooh bears, brown bears, little bears, big bears, panda bears, polar bears, Care Bears, bears with clothes, bears with bows, black bears, or any other kind of bears that come to school!). Talk about which kind of bears have the most, which have the least, or if any have equal numbers of bears. "Which kind of bears could be real?" (brown, black, polar, panda) "Which kind of bears are imaginary?" (Pooh, Care Bears, Yogi Bear, BooBoo Bear).

Bear Words. Use chart paper to write bear words: growl, paw, furry, fuzzy, brown, black, polar, panda, cave, claws, cub, Corduroy, Yogi, Pooh, forest, honey, fish, sharp teeth.

A Bear Collage. The children can look for pictures of bears in magazines. Children's science magazines are especially good for locating pictures of animals. Paste the pictures on a big bear shape cut from a large piece of kraft paper.

About My Bear. To encourage language development, ask each child to tell the class about his/her bear. They might mention the bear's name, where they got it, when they play with it, whether or not they sleep with it, if they've ever left it anywhere by mistake, what they'll do with it when they're older.

Stuffed Bears. Make big stuffed bears by cutting bear shapes from kraft paper, stapling them together, and having the children stuff them with newspaper.

The Three Bears. The story of *The Three Bears* is a favorite! Tell the story and then ask the children to tell what happened first, next, etc. Make the story characters from flannel and encourage the boys and girls to tell the story using a flannelboard. It's interesting to stand close by and hear the special additions to the story line that the children make. Make bear headbands from a strip of paper and paper ears and have the children act out the story. One student could be the storyteller. It would be great fun to videotape the play and then let the children see themselves on television.

Bear Bodies. Talk with the children about bear bodies—how many legs, how many ears, is there a tail, are there claws. Then give each child a ball of clay and ask them to make a bear. These can live in a tabletop forest of tissue paper grass and cardboard trees.

A Bear Booklet. Prepare a booklet for each child to "write" the first week of school. The pages ask the children to draw pictures of such things as: My Bear at School, My Bear at My Seat, My Bear Likes to Eat..., My Bear Likes to Play With..., My Bear in a Forest, and My Bear's Favorite Summer Thing. As the boys and girls work in their books it will give you the opportunity to assess coloring skills, ability to follow

directions, creativity, and independence. The students can take the booklet home at the end of the week.

Bear Ears. The boys and girls can make individual bear ears by cutting round circles from squares of brown paper ("Round the corners of the squares to make circles") and attaching them (staples or glue) to a strip of brown paper that is long enough to fit around the head. Small pink circles can be added to the larger brown ones to make "listeners."

The Bear Class. Take a picture of the "bear class." Arrange the bears the way you would arrange children for a class picture. Use black and white film and snap a photograph of the bear friends sitting on the floor or against a wall. Help the class write a language experience story about bear week on chart paper. Glue the developed bear picture to the top of a sheet of typing paper and type the class story beneath it. Make photocopies of the sheet for each member of the class. The children will treasure them all year!

Bear Songs. Look for bear storybooks, bear fingerplays, and bear songs for the week. Suggested bear books: *Corduroy* (Freeman); *A Pocket for Corduroy* (Freeman); *Ask Mr. Bear* (Flack); *The Biggest Bear* (Ward); *The Big Honey Hunt* (Berenstein); *Blackboard Bear* (Alexander); *Blueberries for Sal* (McCloskey); *Brown Bear, Brown Bear* (Martin); and *Teddy Bears 1–10* (Gretz). Songs might include "The Bear Went Over the Mountain" and the following:

(to the tune of "One Little, Two Little, Three Little Indians")

One little, two little, three little brown bears,

Four little, five little, six little brown bears,

Seven little, eight little, nine little brown bears,

Ten little brown, brown bears.

The children can make up other verses for other kinds of bears, for example, "One little, two little, three little black bears"; polar bears; Pooh bears, etc.

The Picnic Basket: Special Letter Days (D, B, M, S). Introduce the children to the teddy bears' picnic basket. Use a real basket with a cloth napkin at the bottom. The basket will become a permanent fixture in the classroom and will be used for many learning activities. There will be special alphabet letters in the basket each month, for example. This month's letters are D, B, M, and S. Put cards with these letters on them in the basket along with magazine pictures of objects that begin with the letters. During circle time each day, play a matching game by asking children to match the correct letter with each of the pictures. The boys and girls may bring in pictures to add to the basket. Discuss with the children how each of the special letters would sound at the beginning of a word and at the end of a word. Write down words that begin or end with the letters and cut them apart. The children can sort them by beginning and ending letters. Teach the children how to form the special letters correctly. At this time of the school year, it is best for the children to write with crayons on unlined paper rather than trying to place the letters on a line.

Setting the Table. Place a set of play dishes in the basket—three plates, three cups, three napkins, and three sets of utensils. Tuck three bears in the basket also—a papa bear, a mama bear, and a baby bear. Teach the children the proper way to set the table and have them practice with the dishes and bears. Glue construction paper place setting pieces on a sheet of paper so the children will have a model to follow.

The Teddy Bears' Picnic. To culminate bear week, the children enjoy having a surprise teddy bear picnic. When the children arrive at school on the last day of bear week, they should discover that the teacher's bears that have been visiting all week have suddenly disappeared! Poor teacher can't find them and is so worried! The boys and girls will search the room and offer a multitude of explanations as to the whereabouts of the rascal bears. Encourage all of their speculations and pretend to be very worried about the bear friends. Later in the day, read the story of *The Teddy Bears' Picnic* (see recommended books for September). If you are unable to locate the book in a bookstore or library, then simply tell the story that parallels "The Teddy Bears' Picnic" song—about the bears who went to the woods for a picnic. After reading or telling the story, excitedly tell the children that you have an idea—you're sure that the classroom bears have gone on a picnic. As you look for the picnic basket, you'll find that it is gone along with the bears! Ask the children if they'd like to look for the bears. This "bear hunt" will provide an opportunity for the new kindergarteners to take a tour of the big school that will be their home away from home for the next few years. Before school begins that day, hang Teddy Bears' Picnic signs next to the rooms of the important school helpers that you want the children to meet—the nurse, the principal, the cook, the janitor, the secretary, the music teacher, the art teacher, the physical education teacher, the tutor. As you introduce these people to the children and they tell about their jobs at the school, they can also talk about hearing the footsteps of bears go by their doorways and hearing the bear voices singing a song about a picnic in the woods. At each stop the excitement will build because more and more people are involved in the hunt for the teddy bears. After the tour of the school is completed and there is still no sign of the bears, suggest that the children look outside. Sure enough, there the bears will be—having a picnic on the school lawn. (The classroom aide or a mother helper can set up the picnic while you're on the tour.) The bears are seated on the grass around tablecloths filled with jugs of punch and plates of biscuits and honey. The boys and girls and their bears can join the runaway group for a treat. Back in the classroom, write a group experience story about the teddy bear picnic and duplicate it for the children to take home ("My mom won't believe it unless you write it down!"). The next day you can help the children bake biscuits (a good way to practice measuring!) and discuss the sequence of events that led to finding the bears and joining the picnic.

DROP BISCUITS

Heat oven to 450°. Grease a baking sheet.

Stir together in a bowl: 2 cups flour

3 teaspoons baking powder

1 teaspoon salt

Cut into flour mixture with a pastry blender or two knives: 1/4 cup shortening

Mixture should be crumbly.

Stir in with a fork: 1 cup milk

Stir just until mixture holds together and forms a ball. Drop tablespoons full of dough onto prepared baking sheet. Leave 2-inch space between biscuits so they will brown nicely. Bake 10 to 12 minutes, or until golden brown.

Makes about 20 biscuits.

School Helpers. After the children have met the school helpers, set aside a time each week for one of them to come and visit the classroom. Make a bear headband with the words "Helper of the Week" printed on it for the guest to wear as he/she talks about his/her job at the school. The visitor can bring along tools that are used in the job every day; for example, the cook might bring along pans and measuring spoons, the secretary might bring along a notepad and a toy telephone, the custodian might bring along a hammer and a mop, the principal might bring along lists of children in the school and a calendar with appointments. He/she might also bring along favorite children's books to share with the class. Take a picture of each of the school helpers and help the class write a short story about each to put in a scrapbook for the children to look at.

School Safety

Rules. During the first few days of school, it is important for the children to learn the safety rules for the classroom, school, and playground. It is better to have a few simple rules that the children can remember than to have an overwhelming number of regulations. Discuss with the children some of the things that they think would be important if they are to keep themselves safe and not harm anyone else. Try to help them state these ideas positively as you write them on chart paper. Some examples might be:

It is easier for children to understand the playground rules if you take a "field trip" to the play area and explain how to play safely on each of the pieces of equipment.

Safety Signs. Talk about safety signs that the boys and girls might encounter on their way to school: stop signs, yield signs, children at play signs. Ask a safety patrol person from the school safety squad to escort the children to a corner near the school and instruct them in how to cross the street within the crosswalk lines. There are many filmstrips available from the library or your local automobile association that reinforce pedestrian safety.

Bus Safety. Invite the school bus driver to come and talk with the children about bus safety (talking quietly, having backs against the back of the seat, never putting arms out the window, etc.). "Practice" riding on a bus by having the children sit in two rows, one child behind the next and designating a child to be the "driver." Ask them to practice the safety rules as you "make a pretend trip to school." Give the children a simple bus pattern to trace on yellow paper. They can cut out the bus, add windows and people, write the word "BUS," and attach black paper wheels with paper fasteners.

Beginning of Fall

The month of September signals the change of seasons. Depending on where you live in the country, leaves will start to change colors and fall from the trees and the days will be shorter and the weather cooler. Farmers also harvest crops in the fall, including apples, pumpkins, Indian corn, gourds, and nuts.

Fall Collections. If you live in a part of the country where there is seasonal change, ask the boys and girls to look for fall things—leaves, acorns, pine cones, buckeyes, walnuts, hickory nuts—and bring these to school for a fall collection. These nature items can be used for counting, sorting and classifying, patterning, and labeling. Working on a large piece of kraft paper, it is enjoyable for a child to sort a large group of nuts into sets of nuts that are alike in some way. These can be counted and labeled. If there are no fall signs in your area, use 3″ × 5″ cards to create a "fall signs" matching game. On each card draw a fall sign—leaf, nut, acorn, squirrel, pine cone—and ask the children to match the cards that are alike.

A Fall Song. Sing this song to the tune of "She'll Be Comin' Round the Mountain When She Comes."

Oh, the leaves are red and yellow in the fall. (clap, clap)
Oh, the leaves are red and yellow in the fall. (clap, clap)
Oh, the leaves are red and yellow and the apples taste so MELLOW.
Oh, the leaves are red and yellow in the fall. (clap, clap)

Orange pumpkins lay a-gleaming in the sun. (clap, clap)
Orange pumpkins lay a-gleaming in the sun. (clap, clap)
Orange pumpkins lay a-gleaming, they'll be jack-o-lanterns BEAMING.
Orange pumpkins lay a-gleaming in the sun. (clap, clap)

Oh, the air is crisper, colder in the fall. (clap, clap)
Oh, the air is crisper, colder in the fall. (clap, clp)
Oh, the air is crisper, colder and the wind is STRONGER, BOLDER.
Oh, the air is crisper, colder in the fall. (clap, clap).

Making Applesauce. Plan a day to make applesauce in the classroom. Ask each child to bring an apple to school. Core and peel the apples as you talk about the parts of the fruit—the stem, peel, meat, core, seeds. Cut the apples into chunks and put them in a slow cooker or electric skillet. Add a little water and cook until the apples are soft. Mash them with the back of a large spoon or a spatula. Add cinnamon, sugar, and ground cloves to taste. Spoon the delicious applesauce into small paper cups and give each child a plastic spoon. Yummy!

Apple Prints. To make apple prints, cut the apples in half across the apple. By slicing the fruit in this way, the children will be able to see the "star" inside the apple. Dip the apple half in red tempera paint (pour a thin layer in the bottom of a foil pie pan) and print on yellow construction paper. Use green markers to add leaves to the apples.

APPLE CRISP

Heat oven to 350°. In a square pan, 8 × 8 × 2 inches, spread 4 cups of sliced, pared apples.
Sprinkle with 1/4 cup water, 1 teaspoon cinnamon, and 1/2 teaspoon salt.

With a pastry blender, mix until crumbly, 1 cup sugar, 3/4 cup flour, 1/3 cup butter.

Spread the mixture over the apples. Bake, uncovered, about 40 minutes. Serve warm with milk or cream.

WE'RE BEARY GLAD TO SEE YOU!

It's "beary" exciting to come to kindergarten. This bear can be your nametag. Color it and cut it out on the black line. Write your name on the bear's tummy with a black crayon. Ask the teacher to punch a hole in the bear's head and put a piece of yarn through it so that you can wear the bear around your neck. This bear could also be used to make bear centers and games.

Name _____

WHAT COMES NEXT?

The objects in the boxes below are in patterns. For example, the first box has the pattern of square, circle, triangle. The pattern continues with a square and a circle. What do you need to draw to complete the pattern? Finish the apple-worm pattern and the honey jar-spoon pattern also. Color the patterns in this way:

☐ - blue   ◯ - red   △ - yellow

🍎 - red   〰 - green

🍯 - orange   ⟋⟍ - purple

Name _____

ALPHIE, THE ALPHABET WORM

This page should be used with ALPHIE'S OTHER HALF. Alphie is glad to see you! As you look at each one of Alphie's body parts, either trace over the letters that are there or write in the correct letters. Color the body parts. Then use plastic tape to put both sheets together so that Alphie has all of his body parts.

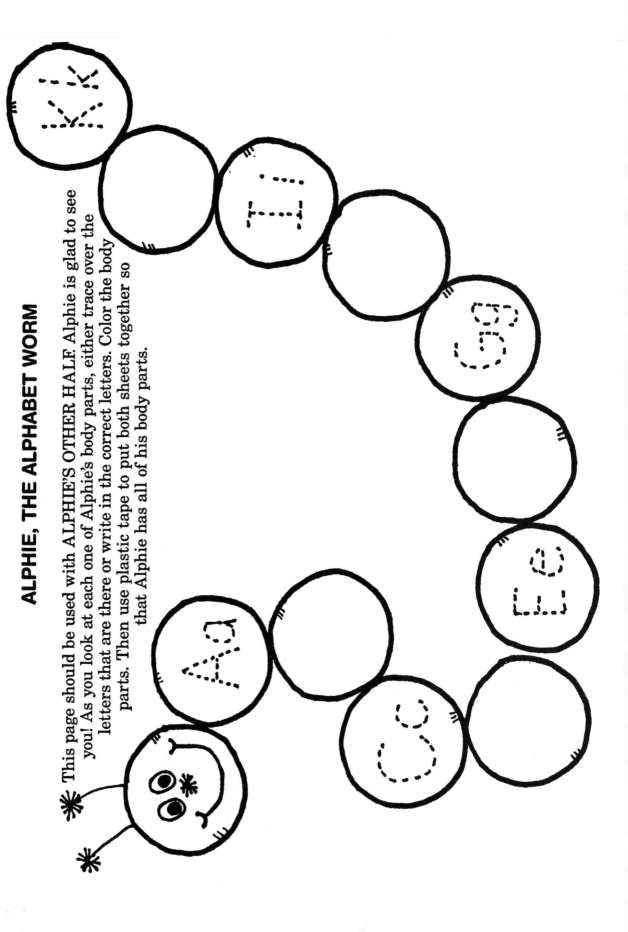

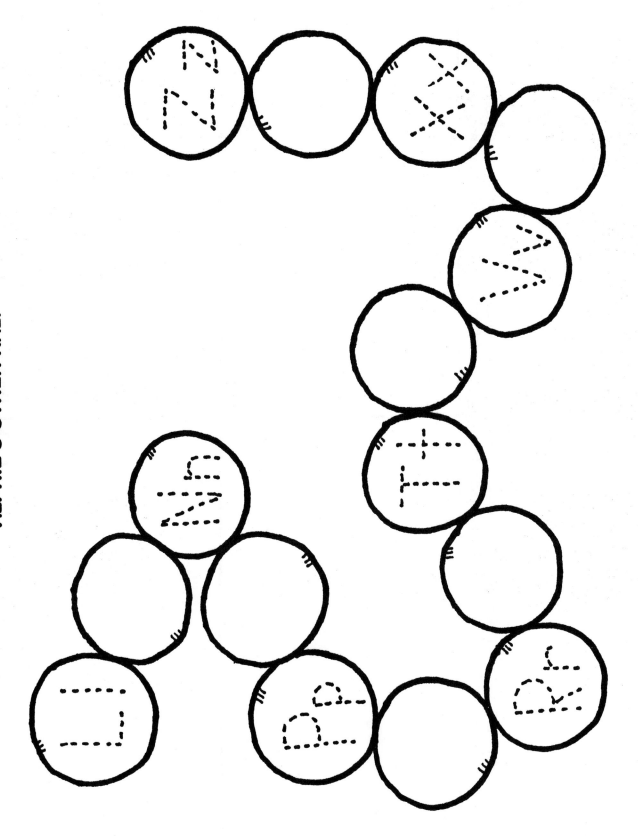

Name _____

CAN YOU SEE A SHAPE?

You've been learning about shapes—squares, circles, triangles, and rectangles. Look around your classroom and see if you can spot objects that are in the shape of a square, circle, triangle, and rectangle. Draw an object in each of the boxes below.

Draw an object that has a square shape.	Draw an object that has a circle shape.
Draw an object that has a triangle shape.	Draw an object that has a rectangle shape.

APPLE—WORM MATCH

Draw a line to match the capital letter on each apple with the lowercase letter on the worm's leaf.

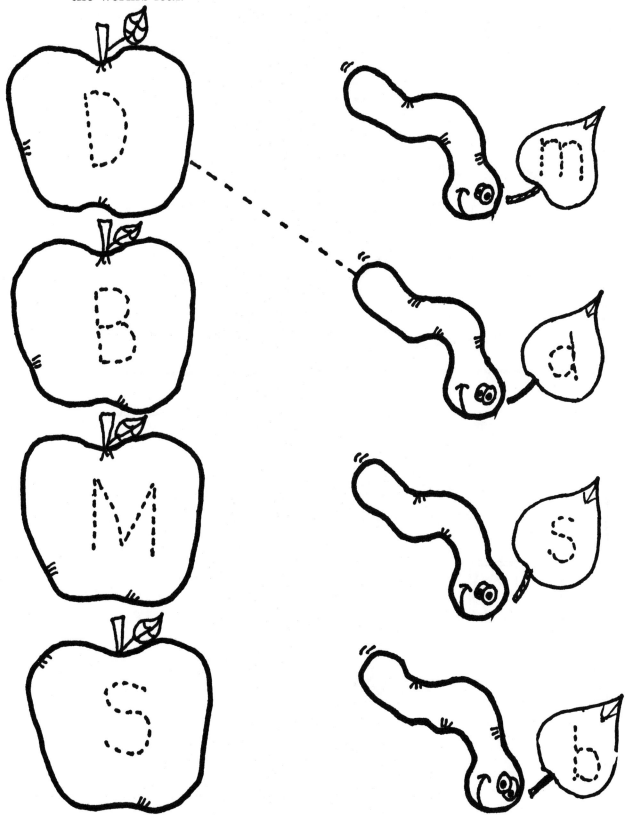

Name _____

DO YOU KNOW…?

Do you know your telephone number and address? Ask an adult to help you write them in the boxes below. Color the pictures. Make the house look like your house. Cut the boxes out on the black lines. Hang the boxes on your refrigerator or in a special place at home and practice saying your phone number and address.

Name _____

LOOK-ALIKE BEARS

These bears have letters on their tummies that look very much alike. Trace over the dotted letters on the bears in the bottom row. Draw a line from the bear in the top row to the bear in the bottom row that has a matching letter. Say the name of the letter as you draw the line. Color the bears that have matching letters alike.

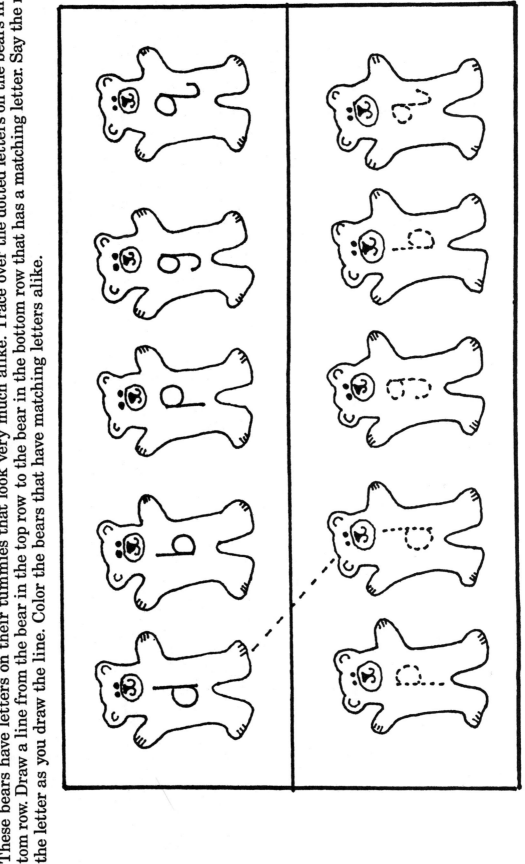

Name _____

HOW MANY WORMS?

These apples are full of worms! Count the number of worms in each apple and write that numeral in the little box next to the apple. The first one is done for you. Color the apples and the worms. The numbers you will use are 0 1 2 3 4 5.

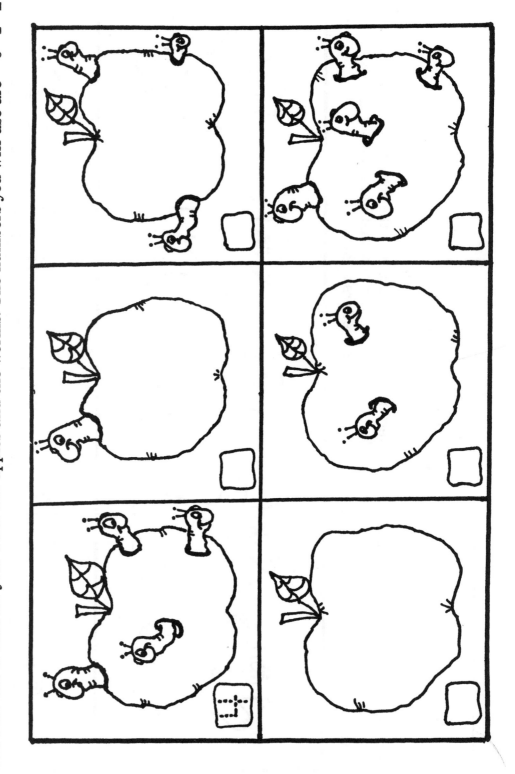

Name _____

HONEY JAR SPOONS

This page is to be used with HONEY JARS. The spoons below have color words printed on them. Cut them out on the black lines and put them in a pile so you'll know where they are when you're ready for them. On the HONEY JARS page, color each honey jar a different color—red, blue, yellow, green, orange, purple, brown, and black. Now, lay the correct spoon on the matching color honey jar. Keep the spoons in an envelope with your name on it so you can play the game again and again.

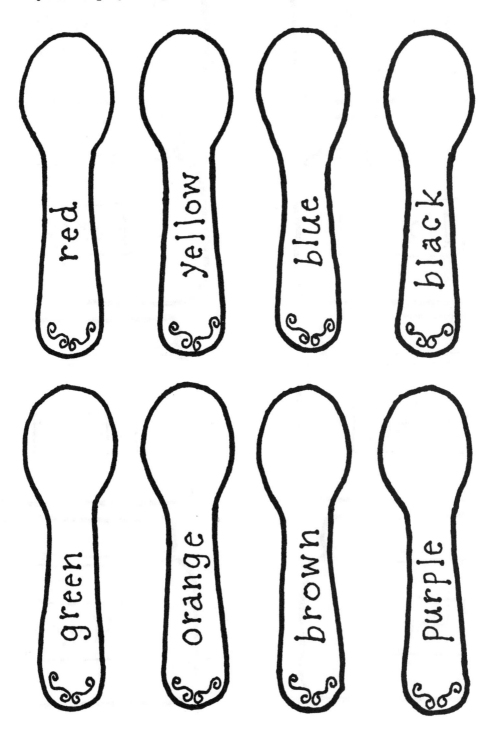

Name _____

HONEY JARS

A TEDDY BEAR PICNIC

This teddy bear would love to go on a picnic but first he has to find his picnic basket. Draw a line through the maze to show teddy the way. Remember not to cross any lines. Happy lunch!

AN APPLE PUZZLE

Apples ripen in the fall and are delicious to eat. Trace over the color word on this apple. Can you read the word? Color the apple the correct color. Now cut the apple apart on the black lines. Be sure to hold your scissors correctly. Look at the apple pieces carefully and see if you can put the puzzle together.

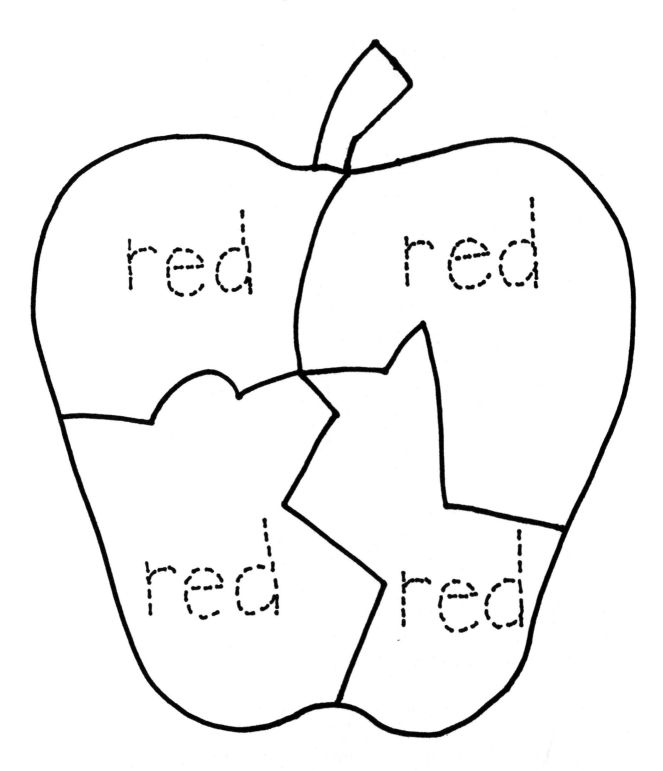

GET READY FOR SCHOOL

It's time to get ready to go to school! What kinds of things are you taking with you on the first day? Trace over the letters and say them aloud. The letters spell the word that names the picture. In the boxes below, trace the letters and then draw an object in each box that begins with the letters and is something that you might bring to school.

A SEPTEMBER CONCENTRATION GAME

Each of the boxes below contains a September picture. Color each picture and cut the boxes apart on the lines. To play the September memory game, lay the cards face down and turn over two cards at a time. If the cards match, you may keep them. If the cards don't match, turn them back over. Your turn is over. Try to remember where each picture is hidden as the other players take their turns. The person with the most matches wins the game.

OCTOBER

SCARING UP AN EXCITING MONTH

By October, when most kindergarteners have settled into the daily school routine, there's magic in the air! As you examine the October reading, math, and other special activities, you'll find many ideas for "scaring up an exciting month" that includes pumpkins, ghosts, and witches. You can sail the ocean with Christopher Columbus, celebrate National Popcorn Week, and create a stimulating environment that magically translates into learning.

Recommended Children's Books for October

Wobble the Witch Cat by Mary Calhoun, illustrated by Roger Duvoisin (New York: William Morrow & Co., 1958). It's time for Halloween and Maggie the witch is making preparations. Her cat, Wobble, is not looking forward to Halloween this year because Maggie has a new broom and he's afraid that he will fall off. Wobble does everything he can to thwart Maggie's preparations and finally, driven by panic, he hides her broom. What's a witch without a broom? The witch, determined to fly, finds a solution that satisfies everyone.

1, 2, 3, to the Zoo by Eric Carle (New York: Collins World Publishing Co., 1968). A good beginning number book that deals with 1 through 10. Pictures are large, with bright bold colors. A train is taking the animals to the zoo, and a little mouse is pictured going through each train car that houses the animals. Children can count the animals. The numeral appears on the page, as well as a drawing showing a visual record of each car that we have visited to that point. When the train reaches its destination, the appealing zoo animals are let out of the train cars, and we can count them all over again on a three-page spread.

When Will I Read? by Miriam Cohen, pictures by Lillian Hoban (New York: Greenwillow Books, 1977). This question often concerns kindergarteners. In this classroom setting, Jim is just not satisfied that he can't read. He is somewhat reassured by an understanding teacher that it will happen eventually, but he's eager right now. Find out how the classroom pet hamsters help Jim to learn about reading.

Truck by Donald Crews (New York: Greenwillow Books, 1980). This picture book is on the move. Trucks are seen from all angles and directions during the day and night and in all kinds of weather. Road signs, directional signs, and many other signs are included for "reading." A Caldecott Honor Book.

Strega Nona by Tomie dePaola (Englewood Cliffs, NJ: Prentice-Hall, Inc., 1975). Strega Nona, which means "Grandma Witch," is a good witch with a magic pot. She sings and chants and the pot bubbles and boils with lots of pasta. All goes well until Strega Nona hires Big Anthony to help with the chores. He overhears part, but not all, of her chanting and when she goes away for the day the temptation to try his hand at magic is too much to resist. The house, street, and town begin to overflow with pasta. Look for an amusing ending.

Green Says Go by Ed Emberly (Boston: Little, Brown & Co., 1968). Good explanations and illustrations to show primary and secondary colors. The large pictures, with a small amount of written text, show how colors are useful to us. "Colors talk" is the message—and the book encourages us to think about colors all around us.

On Market Street by Arnold Lobel and Anita Lobel (New York: Scholastic Books, 1981). The reader goes through this ABC book as though he or she is traveling down Market Street, which is filled with one shop after another. Each alphabet person represents a shop and is designed to reveal whatever it is that the shop is selling. Children can have fun guessing. Go through the ABCs on a shopping spree. A Caldecott Medal winner.

There's a Nightmare in My Closet by Mercer Mayer (New York: The Dial Press, 1968). A little boy goes to bed afraid each night because he thinks there is a nightmare in his closet. One night he confronts the nightmare (which appears in the form of a monster) and the nightmare begins to cry. The boy is sympathetic and takes it by the hand, tucks in into bed, climbs into bed himself, and finally gets a good night's sleep.

Where the Wild Things Are by Maurice Sendak (New York: Harper and Row, 1963). An all-time favorite with young children! Max gets into mischief, is sent to his room and has a monster of a temper tantrum. As he gets more and more angry, the pictures get larger and larger until his rage fills the page. Max begins to simmer down and as his anger recedes, so too do the monster illustrations. Finally, Max is in control again. A Caldecott Medal winner.

Sylvester and the Magic Pebble **by William Steig (New York: The Windmill Paperback Library, 1968).** This story contains the elements of magic that children love. Sylvester, a donkey, collects rocks and finds a magic red pebble. It's fun to have magic at your fingertips, but what happens if you don't make good choices when you state your wishes? Find out with Sylvester what can go wrong! A Caldecott Medal winner.

Reading Skills Activities

Colors (Red, Orange, Yellow, Green, Blue, Purple, Black, Brown)

Children come to school with a variety of skill levels. Some of the boys and girls will probably be able to recognize and name all the colors. Others will know many of the colors and there will be yet another group that is only familiar with a few of the colors or none at all. A color review will be helpful to everyone. As you engage the children in a variety of color activities and have the opportunity to assess each one individually, you will have a clearer idea of those students who are going to need reinforcement and those who are ready for extension experiences.

Sorting Counting Beads. Sort counting beads by color. Store all the beads in a large laminated can covered with rainbow-colored paper. Make little color containers by painting the outside of small juice cans.

Celebrate the "Color Days." (A letter home in advance will help with this activity). Example: ORANGE DAY! How many orange items in the room? Touch them, count them. Ask who is wearing orange? Have children stand together so that you can see the different shades and tones of orange. Then ask the children to try to remember to wear something orange the next day.

With the children, set up a Color Table and encourage them to bring in items during your celebration. On the table, section off areas for the different colors by using different colored material. Put all red items on the red corduroy, all blue items on the blue denim, etc.

Eat a favorite food to celebrate the color day. Some choices include:

RED   – apples, cherries, tomatoes, watermelon

ORANGE – orange slices, carrots, cantaloupe, pumpkin

YELLOW – gumdrops, cheese, lemon pudding

GREEN	– lime gelatin, celery, lettuce, beans
BLUE	– blueberry muffins, blueberry jam, jelly beans
PURPLE	– grapes, plums, grape juice
BROWN	– cookies, cake, chocolate
BLACK	– jelly beans, poppy seed cake (black dots)

Talk about the food you are eating. Children can help print the color word on the board. (For example, the teacher can begin with "r" and ask which letter comes next, and who would like to print it, etc.). Keep a Color Chart record of the food you have eaten (rebus style).

Color Cookies. Make sugar cookies from a simple recipe or buy a large box of vanilla wafers. Mix up a batch of frosting using confectioners sugar and water. Separate the frosting into different containers, add food coloring, and have children put colored frosting on the wafer for a cookie color treat. This can be done with only one color, or more than one at a time.

Animals Change Color in Winter. Show pictures of animals in their summer and winter coats. The rabbit is an excellent example with its change from brown tones to white. What other animals look different in winter? Note that the landscape changes colors too and guide children to discover this relationship that nature has "arranged" for survival. Make "before" and "after" pictures of several of the animals.

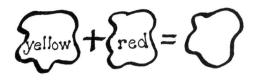

Look Up! For this activity, you will need the overhead projector. Children observe the changes taking place ON THE CEILING. Teacher can wear a crown and use a magic wand, and even sing or chant! On a piece of plastic wrap placed on the overhead projector, put a dab of red tempera paint, a dab of yellow, and a drop of water. Mix and...KA-BOOM! What color do we have now? In this way, mix red and blue (purple), blue and yellow (green), red and yellow (orange), red, yellow, blue (brown). The RECIPE can be printed on the board so that your lesson follows a print format. Children can color in the results. Some may be able to make predictions.

VARIATION: This same activity could be done using pieces of colored cellophane. Have the cellophane available later on the Color Table so that children can produce the different colors, and also peek through the cellophane to see how the color affects the objects in the room.

Color Printing. For each child, you will need two baggies that zip lock. Using fingerpaint, put two colors in the first baggie (1 tablespoon of each). Insert this baggie (zip-lock end first) into the second baggie, and zip lock. It is double-bagged now to prevent leakage. Each child receives a baggie, can flatten it, gently squeeze the colors together to make their secondary color, and practice making letters over and over again with the paint.

Colored Pasta. Pasta can be purchased in a variety of colors. OR, you can color your own with tempera paint, spray paint, or food coloring and lay them out on waxed paper to dry. Make a huge tub full of macaroni wheels, bow ties, elbows, tubes, swirls, etc. Children can count, classify, and pattern with them. They can make giant alphabet letters or words.

Holiday Colors. Colors can be tied in with the traditional colors used on holidays. During this month, HALLOWEEN is a good time to focus upon black, orange and yellow. [Other traditional holiday colors are: Christmas (red/green), Easter (purple, pink, green), St. Patrick's Day (kelly green), Valentine's Day (red, pink, white), May Day (pastels and spring green), 4th of July (red, white and blue).] Does the witch always have to be in black, orange, and yellow? NO. Children might want to experiment with different color arrangements.

My Rainbow Book. Make color books with the children. You can do a page each day. Use white for the background color, make a picture for each page, and print the color name at the bottom of the sheet using a marker of the same color. Some creative suggestions for the book:

ORANGE—Give each child an orange square. They can cut around the edges to make a circle. With crayons or felt-tip markers, they can make this into a jack-o'lantern, and paste it onto the white paper. Using an orange marker, have them print the color word "orange" at the bottom of the page.

YELLOW—From a yellow square, children can cut a circle for the sun. With their markers, have them make a face on the sun and put the lines sticking out around the circle for the sun rays. Print "yellow" at bottom of the page.

PURPLE—From purple paper, gently tear grapes, enough for a whole bunch. Paste on white paper. Print "purple" on page.

BLUE—Draw two big brown muffins on the page. Tear two blue paper berries and paste them on the muffins. (You can bake blueberry muffins today, too!) Print "blue" on page.

RED—Draw a tree with crayons. Put big red apples on the tree with a red felt pen. Print "red" on page. (Eat a big red apple today.)

GREEN—From triangles and circles, make Kermit the Frog. Print "green" underneath Kermit.

BROWN—Trace around a circular pattern twice, for two cookies. Now you have a pair! Draw an equal number of chips on each cookie. Paste, and print "brown" on page. (This can be tied into math by using the terms "pair" and "equal." Also, you can measure, mix, and bake chocolate chip cookies today.)

Language Development

Similes. After the children have been exposed to many colors and many color experiences, they can begin to formulate similes such as:

As red as _____

As orange as _____

As yellow as _____

As green as _____

As blue as _____

As purple as _____

As black as _____

As white as _____

Then, as pink as _____

As aqua as _____

As violet as _____

Halloween Words. Elicit from the children the names of things that we associate with Halloween (for example, ghost, haunted house, cat, witch). Write the words on a chart. With the children, write a Halloween story tying all of the words together. Circle special letters in black, orange, or purple.

Make huge shapes of the following: ghost, pumpkin, witch, cat, and hang them up. Later, print stories on them that are made up by the group. From Halloween stories that children are listening to, and from songs that they are singing, children are forming impressions. Collectively, write a story ON THE CAT about the cat who was afraid to go out on Halloween. Write a story ON THE PUMPKIN about the pumpkin who is visiting the classroom and what it is seeing, hearing, learning. Have the children make up a recipe for witches brew and print it on the WITCH. What will you print on the GHOST?

Halloween Messages. Using the tape recorder, have the children do the following:

Tell their own version of a Halloween tale.

Contact the witch, and have her give out tips for a safe Halloween.

Interview a witch: What is her favorite color? food? scream?

Make up a story about the Ghost Who Wanted to Be a Boy.

Listen to a recording of creaks and groans, and then draw the
picture of the haunted house that made these sounds.

Children like to make their own eerie sound tapes, and these can be used as background sounds for Halloween stories, or for creative movement with the lights out.

The Halloween creatures can leave messages for the children:

GHOST TOAST—If you want to see me, do this:

>Toast a slice of bread
>
>Spread with cream cheese
>
>Put in two raisins for eyes. BOO!

MRS. GOOD WITCH—Share your goodies!

>1 scoop green ice cream
>
>licorice for hair
>
>raisin eyes, nose, mouth
>
>ice cream cone hat   EEEEEKKKK!

Upper- and Lowercase Letters

Special Letter Days (R, H, K, W). As you introduce each letter and sound for this month, have three items in the letter basket. (You can use the picnic basket from September.) Suggest that the children bring in items that begin with the sound you are working with. Your goal for the month could be to have children identify the beginning letter and sound of from 5 to 10 items in the basket. Some item suggestions are:

R—rubber bands, ruler, ring, rope

H—hammer, hinge, handkerchief, hotrod (model)

K—kite, ketchup, keys, kettle

W—witch, wig, wand, wheel

Print the upper-and lowercase letters on the chalkboard as you introduce the special letters for the month. Ask children to check the name of the month, October, to locate one of the special letters. On the calendar, have children check the names of the week days and circle the special letters for the month.

Make upper-and lowercase letter cards and distribute them to the group. Have the children with capital letters stand and form a line. Then have their partners with the lowercase letters join them, one by one.

Place all of the cards with capital letters along the chalkboard and just distribute the lowercase cards. One by one, children can identify and match the upper-and lowercase letters. (This can be in the form of a game: "I am Capital K and I'm looking for my partner.")

Keep several of the upper-and lowercase cards, side by side, on the chalkboard ledge. Have children close their eyes. Teacher, or a child, can mix up two of the letter cards. Then, children can open their eyes and try to find out "who lost their partner." Children can move them back again.

Cut out different leaf shapes. Print an equal number of capital and lowercase letters on them. The children can match them. Or, cut out different

Halloween shapes (witch, ghost, broom, cat, and so on) and place upper- and lowercase letters on the shapes and have the children match them.

Kinesthetic Letter Formation

Pretzel Dough Recipe. Let the children make letters from the following pretzel dough recipe:

1 pkg. yeast
4 cups flour
1 tsp. sugar
1 tsp. salt
1½ cups warm water

Dissolve yeast in warm water. Add dry ingredients. Mix.
Form dough into flat shapes. Brush with egg white. Sprinkle with salt. Bake at 425° for 10 to 15 minutes.

Children can make coils from clay, and form them into letters and words. Letters can also be formed with a stick, in a box or tub of sand. Children can trace around oaktag letters, and cut them out. Make a set of letters from sandpaper, so children can trace around them with the finger and "feel" the shape.

Two or three children can lie down on the floor to form letters.

Math Skills Activities

Sizes

Big, Little, Medium. Use three real pumpkins and have children put them in order, from left to right, by size. Then give directions to the children, such as: "Put the little pumpkin on the counter," "Put the medium-size pumpkin on the rug," "Put the big pumpkin under the sink." Or, place the pumpkins in various places around the room, and have children point to the big pumpkin, stand by the little pumpkin, sit next to the medium-size pumpkin.

Put in Order. Use ordinal number terms when working with the real pumpkins in the classroom. Have the children put the pumpkins in a row so that the FIRST is the largest, the SECOND is the medium size, and the THIRD one is the smallest. Children can follow verbal directions such as, "Now put the smallest pumpkin FIRST," etc.

Smaller Than, Larger Than. This can be done with actual items (concrete) or pictures (semi-concrete). Begin with 2 items and ask: "Is the stapler smaller than or larger than the paper clip?" "Is the clock smaller than or larger than the table?"

"Joey, show us something that is larger than this shoe." "Mary, show us something in the room that is smaller than this book." "Chris, show us something in the room that is smaller than this ___ but larger than this ___."

Have Frank stand up nice and tall. Ask the children to think about the following: "If you think you are smaller than Frank, put up one finger." "If you think you are bigger than Frank, put up your hand." Then ask the children to physically move. "If you think you are smaller than Frank, go on this side of him." (Point). "If you think you are larger than Frank, go on this side of him." Measure Frank, then measure child to child to determine if they are "smaller than, or larger than" Frank (or Bill, or Joan, etc.).

Concepts of Over, Under, High, Low, Tall, Short

Pumpkins on the Fence. You need 9″ × 12″ white paper, three long and three short strips of black paper, and real pumpkin candy pieces. Children can make a rail fence from the long and short strips, and paste them onto the white paper. Give each child the same amount of candy pumpkin pieces to work with, and give the following directions:

Put your pumpkins in a row on the top rail.

Put two up high and three down low.

Put a pair of pumpkins on the right side of the fence.

Put an equal number on the right and on the left.

Put more on the right, and fewer on the left.

Put two on the middle rail, and two under.

Put four on the bottom rail, and three under.

Put one on each rail.

Put five pumpkins on the fence.

Distribute orange paper, scissors, and paste. Children can cut out five pumpkins to the tune of "Five Little Pumpkins," and they can paste them on the fence, according to the directions given. During this time, they can be enjoying the real candy!

High, Low Circle Time. Ask children to come to the circle with their chair. Ask them to listen carefully to the directions, to see if they can establish the pattern. Going from left to right around the circle, say: "Mary, please stand behind your chair. Fred, please sit in your chair. Billy, please stand behind your chair. Bobby, please sit in your chair." (The pattern is stand/sit, stand/sit.) See if children can tell from the information received so far, what the next person is supposed to do. When the pattern is complete, point out that in this pattern, some children are LOW and some are HIGH, some are TALL and some are SHORT. (Children can go around the circle and call out: "Tall/Short" or "High/ Low.")

Circle Time Pattern. Have one child sit on the chair and the next child sit on the floor. Or children can stand behind the chairs and one child can put his or her hand under the chair while another child puts his or her hand over the chair.

Counting

Counting Rhymes. Use a wide variety of number books from the library for counting rhymes. Count forward and backward with the familiar nursery rhymes, such as "One, two, buckle my shoe..." "One little, two little, three little Indians..."

Count and Classify. Count all of the items in the room that have wheels. Count all of the items that make a sound. Count all of the items that have moving parts. Count all of the soft items, hard items, color items. You can graph any of these items.

Children can help during snack time by counting straws, counting crackers and juice. ("If we have six children at this table, how many napkins will we need? That's right! Six! Good! Bill, will you please get them for us? Thank you!") Or ("If we have five people at this table, and we only have four napkins, how many more napkins will we need? I hear four, I hear three. Katy, will you please pass them out and we'll make sure.")

Counting with the Calendar. How many days in this month? How many days in each week? What day is this? Is that the third or fourth day of the week? How many more days until _____? How many days have we been in school?

A Pumpkin Seed Count. During this month, you can have a real pumpkin in the room that can be made into a jack-o'lantern. Have children decide what shape for the eyes and nose (circle, square, triangle?). How many want a happy mouth? A sad mouth? (Count the results.) When you carve the pumpkin together (teacher is the only one to handle the knife), children can scoop out the seeds.

They can wash them and lay them out on paper towels to dry. When dry, place the seeds in a container. Let children sift through them and count out ten, and then "estimate" how many there are altogether. Children can verify the number by making little piles of seeds that have a total of five or ten, for easier counting. Continue to use the seeds for counters. (A small flashlight can be placed inside the jack-o'lantern and it can gleam for storytime.)

Number Recognition (6 to 10)

Treasure Boxes. Make several treasure boxes for the classroom using shoe boxes, school boxes, cigar boxes, etc., that have been covered with colorful paper or painted. The inside of the boxes can contain an array of: marbles, old keys, nuts, feathers, stones, pebbles, bottle caps, colored paper clips, tile samples, corks, tiny lids, nuts and bolts, hinges. Students can work in a defined area, and it can be arranged so that three children work together with one treasure box. In these small groups children are listening for and following directions, such as: make a row of six marbles; take ten paper clips and put them into the shape of a circle, (or triangle, or rectangle); count out eight keys and put them in order from largest, on the left, to smallest on the right.

Children can work with sets. "Put three pebbles in a row. We want six altogether. Take out as many more pebbles as you need to make six." These can be put in two rows of three, or two and four, or four and two, or one and five, or five and one. This can be done with all of the numerals from six to ten. Children need repeated practice with this type of activity. One large treasure box could be made available during playtime for children who select this as a choice.

Months of the Year, 6 Through 10. Children are learning the months or are familiar with them because of their birthdays and other important events. Count from the beginning of the calendar year to find the sixth month—through the tenth month. (June, July, August, September, October). While we're at it, let's give all of the months a number from 1 to 12. Make a large graph of birthdays by month. Make a graph using each birthdate IN the month.

Let's Investigate 6, 7, 8, 9, 10. These numerals keep appearing and reappearing for so many things. Go through these numerals one at a time and keep a tally—find out how many children have one of these numerals in their home address, apartment number, telephone number.

Other Skill Areas Activities

Columbus Day

Sailing the Ocean. Children can make a bright blue fingerpainting of Christopher Columbus sailing the ocean. Encourage lots of wavy lines for the sea.

Sailing, Sailing. Using large building blocks, children can construct the Nina, Pinta, and Santa Maria (or just one boat). Have old sheets sent in by parents to be cut up and used as the sails.

Columbus Storybook. Find storybooks to read to the children and encourage discussion of Columbus, since this information will enrich the role playing. What kinds of sea life would he encounter on the high seas—giant whales, porpoises, sea turtles, octopus, sharks, etc.? Would he see pirates? Other ships? This information is important when Columbus sets sail and looks through his telescope (paper towel holder).

Visual Closure. Select several colorful pictures from magazines of things that Columbus might have seen (flock of birds, whale, sea, sky at night and day, sun, moon, etc.). Cover up most of the picture and see if children can guess what Columbus might be seeing through that telescope!

A Celebration. Is there a parade to celebrate Columbus Day in your town? Who usually marches in the local Columbus Day parade? Who provides the music? To a marching band recording, children can have their own parade with the drum major and majorette, the mayor, the Boy Scouts and the Girl Scouts, and the "band" with the drum (wrist motions), trombones (arm movement), and flutes (fingers flying).

Fire Prevention Week

Fire Drills. Have a practice fire drill several times this month. Establish an alternate route if one of the doorways should be blocked. Also have the children establish a fire escape route for their families at home. (A note sent to parents would be extremely helpful.)

Stop, Drop, Roll. Review the "Stop, Drop, Roll" method of putting out a fire if your clothing should catch on fire. Running will "fan the flames," whereas the method of rolling is similar to trying to put the fire out with a blanket.

The Fire Department. Learn the number of the local fire department. Dial it on a play telephone. Also punch the numbers in on a play telephone. In this way, children know that they can call for help if needed.

Firefighting Equipment. Invite a firefighter to come to class to show the clothing and some of the equipment used for fighting fires. Perhaps your class can visit the big truck at the fire station if it cannot be spared for a visit to school.

Let's Pretend to Be Firefighters. Get a large box from the grocery store and have the children paint it with red tempera paint. Put paper plate wheels on the sides. Inside of this red fire truck put a rope, garden hose, boots, two slickers, gloves, and hats. A bell could be included. Children could answer the call, drive to the scene of the fire, and with the help of the hoses, put out the fire. Then it's back to the station, and everything has to be returned to the same place! See if you can remember how you found it.

Help Prevent Fires. Make Smokey the Bear puppets from brown paper bags and felt pens. His "Prevent Forest Fires" message bears repeating, especially in areas of the country where campers are plentiful at this time of year and leaves are becoming dry. These brown lunch bags could be taken home and used as litter bags in the family car.

Autumn Harvest

Squash and Gourds. Squash and gourds are durable and can be handled by the children. Along with Indian corn, they add a nice autumn touch to your classroom. Check the gourds for the variety of shapes and colors. Also, note the shapes and colors of the squash (turban, acorn, butternut, hubbard, spaghetti, etc.). Although we don't eat gourds, they were once carved out and used at night as candle holders. Today, some people make birdhouses from large gourds by allowing them to dry out and cutting a circle for a "bird door."

A Pumpkin Farm. Arrange to visit a pumpkin farm if you live in an area where it is possible. Some farmers allow each child to take a pumpkin home. Gourds and Indian corn can be gathered at this time by the children if permitted by the host family.

Pumpkin Recipes. "Pumpkin" comes from the Greek word *pepon,* which means a large melon. At one time, pumpkins were hollowed out, turned upside down and put on the head for cutting hair around the edge. That's where the expression "pumpkin head" originated. Early American settlers ate a lot of pumpkin because it's rich in calcium, phosphorus, iron, and vitamins A and C. Here are some pumpkin recipes to try:

ROASTED PUMPKIN SEEDS

Preheat oven to 250°. Wash 2 cups of seeds. Mix seeds with 1 teaspoon salt, and 1½ tablespoons vegetable oil. Spread seeds on cookie sheet. Bake 30 minutes until crispy and golden brown.

PUMPKIN HAMBURGERS

To 1 lb. ground beef, add ¼ cup pumpkin filling.
Make burgers as usual.
Tiny burgers can be fried in an electric skillet.

SOFT PUMPKIN ICE CREAM

Ingredients: 2 quarts vanilla ice cream
4 cups pumpkin filling

4 teaspoons cinnamon

1 teaspoon each of nutmeg, ginger, salt

Mix ice cream, pumpkin, and spices together. Spoon into dessert dishes.

National Popcorn Week

Popcorn Recipes. National Popcorn Week is usually celebrated the week before Halloween, and the two go together well. (Did you know that to dial for the time of day in San Francisco, you dial POP CORN?) Popcorn is a good snack because it is low in calories. Some dentists say that popcorn helps clean the teeth and massage the gums. Here are two popcorn recipes that could be used for your Halloween party:

POPCORN BALLS

2 cups sugar

1 cup lt. corn syrup

1 cup water

3 tablespoons butter

Combine ingredients and bring to a boil. Mix with a wooden spoon. Pour over 2 quarts of salted popcorn. Mix thoroughly and wait until mixture has cooled, then mold into balls.

CAUTION: Be extremely careful not to burn hands with hot syrup.

TIP: Have the children use oven mitts when forming the balls. Let cool on wax paper.

POPCORN TREAT

Pop the corn and serve with cream and sugar. This was a favorite meal of the early settlers and Indians. It was used as a corn cereal. Popcorn originated in Mexico. The Indians grew it!

Halloween

The Haunted Easel. At the easel, have only black, orange, and yellow paint. On the shape of a ghost, print instructions to children to "Paint a Scary Picture." The easel could even be enclosed inside of a huge box or placed behind a long curtain. This area can be called the *haunted house.*

Room Decorations. If you are planning to have a party, make sure that you have some extra brown grocery bags available so that all children will have a costume. To make a mask, person, animal, or creature from the large bag, put it over the child's head and then determine where the openings should go for eyes, nose, mouth. Remove bag and teacher can cut the shapes that the child would like. Child can decorate the bag using crayon, paint, felt markers, or materials.

Secure a large pumpkin for the room, and have children vote for a happy or sad jack-o'lantern. Make a tally. Everyone can be made to feel satisfied by having the "happies" draw their face on one side, and the "saddies" draw their faces on the other side. Teacher can carve out both sides. When you insert the flashlight to let the lantern glow, the children can sit on the side that they voted for. Place the pumpkin where both sides can be seen.

Festive Tablecloth. Place a giant sheet of brown butcher paper over the table that will be used for serving. Put orange and black crayons (or markers) and white chalk there. Have children go to the area, three at a time, and draw just one item on the tablecloth (pumpkin, ghost, bat, goblin, cat, witch, skeleton, etc.). They can place the item wherever they choose on the paper. This "tablecloth" adds a festive touch for party time!

Halloween Photos. Halloween is the time for picture taking. Perhaps a parent will volunteer to take party pictures, if the teacher does not have access to a camera. Later, the pictures can be placed in sequential order, and children can write captions for them.

Safety Rules. Children can draw a "color photo" of the witch and her baby, and also draw a "photo" showing the witch cat and her baby. This is a busy time for both of these mothers, as they train their children to follow in their footsteps for a Halloween career. Make two separate charts: one for the witch and one for the cat. Here are some headline and starter suggestions for each. These should help motivate the children to come up with many other suggestions.

SAFE HALLOWEEN PRACTICES (mother, witch, and baby)
Baby will have to learn the following:
- Wear masks that have big eye holes so you can see.
- Be careful not to wear too long a costume, or you could trip.
- Be sure to hold on tightly to broom handle when riding.
- Take deep breaths before letting out witch screams.
- Knock politely on doors for trick or treat time.
- Beware of stray cats and dogs.
- Take home treats for mother's approval before eating.
- Take mother's hand when mounting and dismounting from broom.
- Cast the proper spells at the proper time (make them up).
- Etc.

TIPS FOR THE WITCH CAT (mother cat and baby)
To be an excellent assistant, baby will learn:
- To arch its back.

- To bare its teeth.
- To stick its tail straight up in the air with the hair puffed up on all sides.
- To bare its front claws.
- To jump onto the shoulder of the witch and not fall off.
- To "meow" in a heart-stopping manner.
- To purr sweetly in order to distract you just before the witch is ready to cast a spell.
- Etc.

Discuss the safe Halloween tips, and how they apply to the children. Perhaps they can think of several more.

Discuss the witch cat tips, and see how many children can "act out." Perhaps they can think of several more. (See Activity Pages.)

Getting Ready for Winter

Trees. At this time of year, the trees are changing color in most parts of the country. We say they are getting ready for winter. People get ready for winter, too. Have a discussion of the changes that are taking place in your area during October (leaves are turning beautiful colors, leaves are falling, days are shorter, skies are more cloudy and gray, days and nights are colder, etc.). How is all of this affecting YOU? Do you wear different clothing during this season?

Animals. Animals are undergoing changes during this season. Squirrels are busy scurrying around and gathering nuts, birds are flying south, animals are growing another warm coat of fur. What else is happening in the animal world? (Get information books from the library about the seasons and focus attention upon autumn.)

A Bulletin Board. Children can make a huge brown construction paper tree (trunk and limbs) for the bulletin board. Label it: "Autumn is..." Have each child individually complete that phrase for you, print it, and post it on the bulletin board with their name by it. Then, using small sponges and red, orange and green tempera paint, have the children make the bulletin board tree "come alive" with colorful leaves on the branches, in the air, on the ground. Make it a lovely autumn "feast for the eyes." Turn it into the kind of tree that we would travel all the way to New England just to see! And to think...here it is, right in our own room! It's beautiful!

THE JACK-O'LANTERNS

In each row, color the TWO jack-o'lanterns that are alike. Put an X on the one that is different.

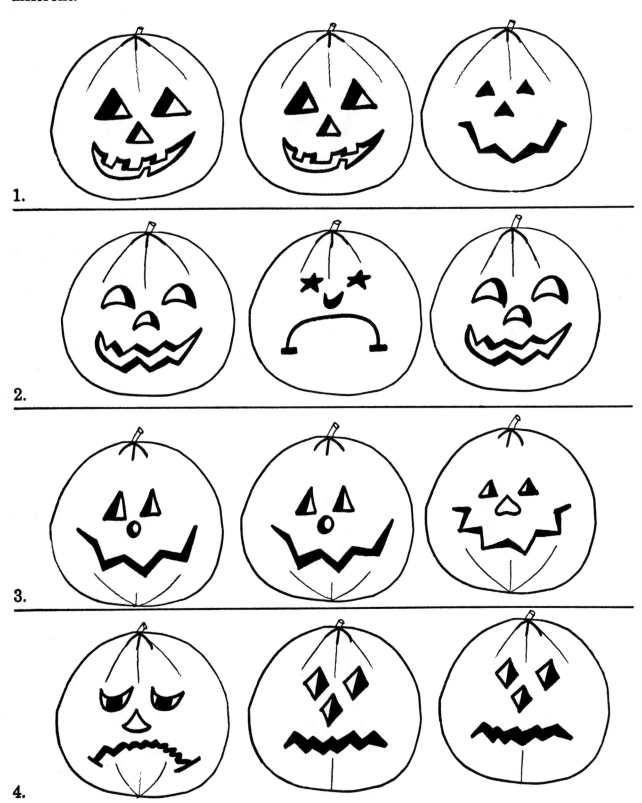

1.

2.

3.

4.

FIVE PUMPKINS

Color the pumpkins a bright orange. Then cut them out. On another piece of paper, draw a fence. Put the pumpkins on the fence with the biggest one on the left and the smallest one on the right. Paste them down so that they don't fall off.

YOU LOOK LIKE YOU'VE SEEN A GHOST!

Color the biggest ghost yellow.
Color the medium-size ghost red.
Color the three smallest ghosts orange.

Then, make a big pumpkin for the big ghost.
Make a medium-size pumpkin for the medium-size ghost.
Make three little pumpkins for the three little ghosts.

Name _____

POP! POP! POP!

We were lucky! All of our popcorn seeds popped! Match up the seeds in each pan with the same number of puffy pieces of popcorn. Popcorn is a nutritious snack.

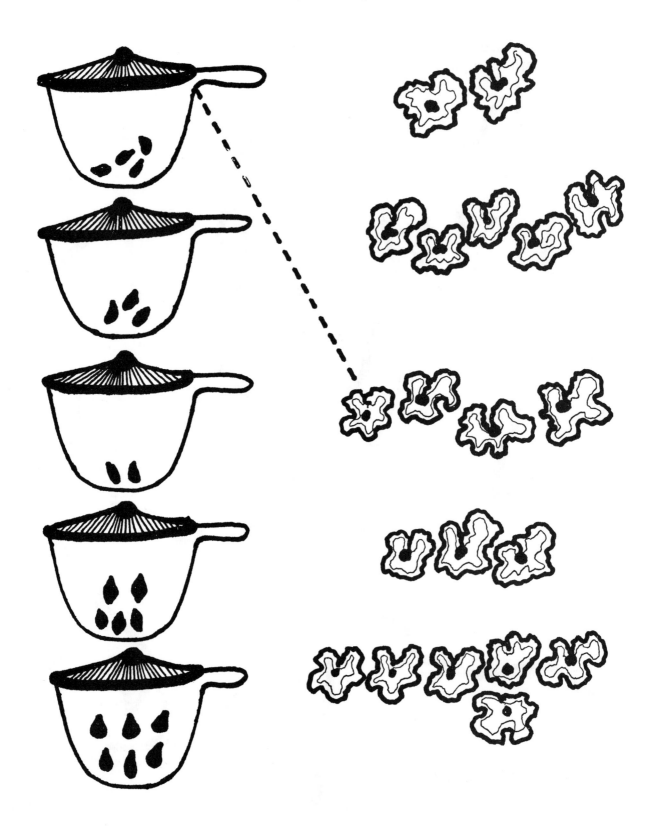

Name _____

WINNERS OF "HAVE A SAFE HALLOWEEN" CONTEST

This picture was taken of a Halloween witch and her little witch who are out campaigning for a safe Halloween.

They decided to wear low-heeled shoes so they wouldn't trip, and masks with big eye holes so they could see.

On the back, draw a picture of the little witch carrying out a safety practice for Halloween.

Now, using your crayons, show us what these two witches look like in their fancy costumes!

Name _____

WINNERS OF "HALLOWEEN CAT PHOTO" CONTEST

This picture was taken of a Halloween cat and her little kitten who is training to be a Halloween cat.

Halloween cats have to arch their backs, jump real high, and screech!

On the back, draw a picture of the little kitten practicing one of her Halloween duties.

Now, using your crayons, show us what these two fancy cats look like for Halloween!

FREDDIE THE FIREFIGHTER

Officer Freddie the Firefighter reminds us that October is Fire Safety Month.

He wants you to use his fire hydrant to list fire safety rules or to show the pattern of your fire escape route from your classroom.

On the back of this paper, draw your fire escape route at home!

Name _____

THE LANGUAGE OF COLORS

Colors can help us to describe things. If we say, "As RED as an apple," or "As GREEN as the grass," other people will understand what we mean. Try using the colors of the rainbow, one by one, to describe things. Start with RED, then ORANGE, YELLOW, GREEN, BLUE, and VIOLET.

In the squares below, draw and color one item to go with each color. Print in the name of the item, too. The first one is done for you.

As red as an _apple_	As orange as _____	As yellow as _____
As green as _____	As blue as _____	As violet as _____

FIRE HATS AND BOOTS

Draw a line from each capital letter in a fire hat to the matching lowercase letter in the fire boot. Color the hats and boots.

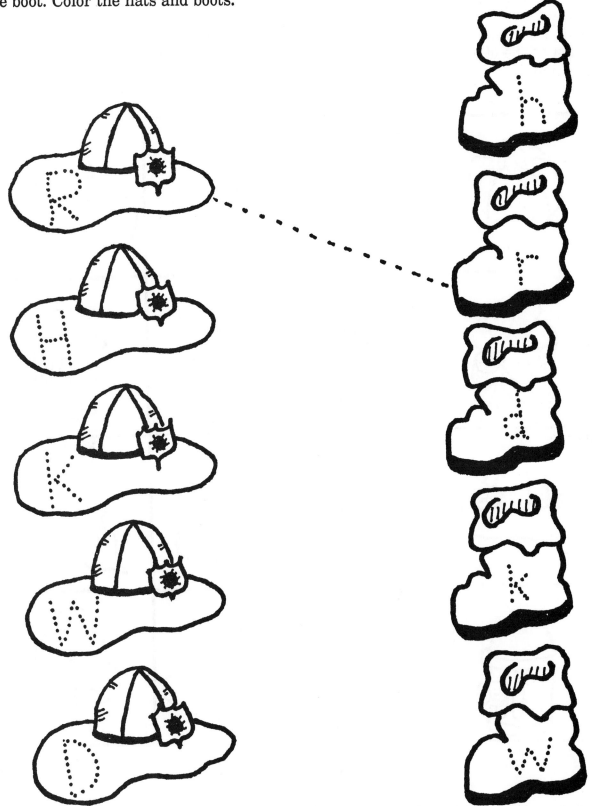

Name _____

AN OCTOBER CONCENTRATION GAME

Each of the boxes below contains an October picture. Color each picture and cut the boxes apart on the lines. To play the October memory game, lay the cards face down and turn over two cards at a time. If the cards match, you may keep them. If the cards don't match, turn them back over. Your turn is over. Try to remember where each picture is hidden as the other players take their turns. The person with the most matches wins the game.

HAPPY JACK-O'LANTERNS

Look at the seeds in each happy jack-o'lantern's smile. Count them. Write the numeral on the pumpkin's stem. Then complete the faces, using different shapes for eyes, nose, and ears so that they do not all look the same. Color them a happy orange or yellow. The first one is done for you to get you started.

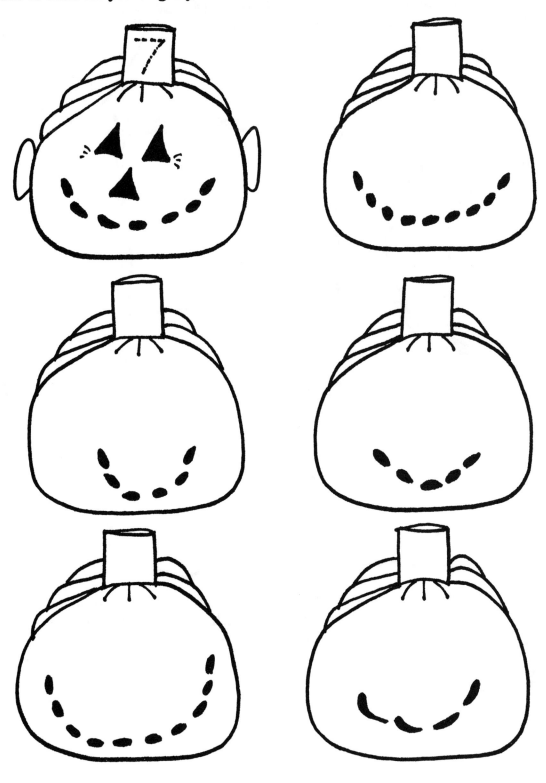

Name _____

POLLY WANTS A CRACKER WITH JAM

Pretend your crayons are the jam, and color these
crackers for Polly:

Polly wants red strawberry jam on the circle.
Polly wants purple plum jam on the square.
Polly wants orange marmalade on the rectangle.
Polly wants blueberry jam on the oval.

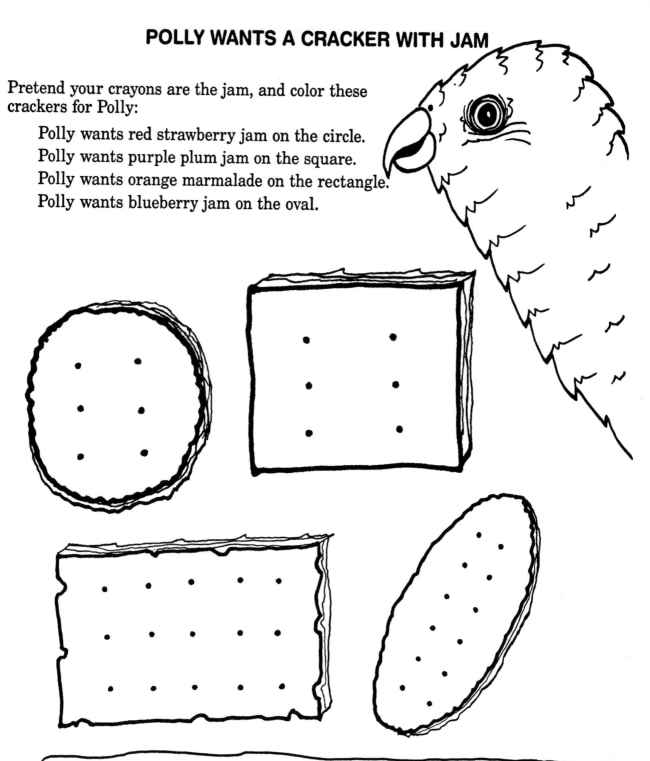

Polly says, "Thank you! Please color me with pretty colors too! I love green."

COLOR YOUR WORLD

Read the labels on the paint jars below. Use your crayons to show what colors they are. These three colors are called PRIMARY colors.

What happens when we mix colors using paint? Try it and find out. Color in all of the jars below, including the color answer. These are called SECONDARY colors.

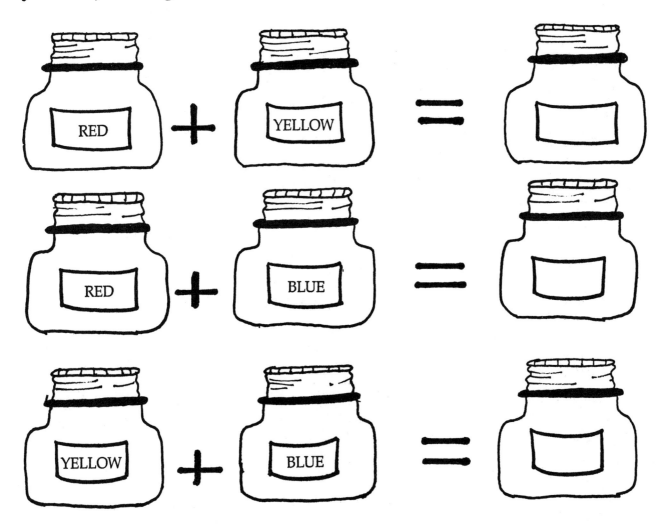

NOVEMBER

A Harvest of Good Ideas

73

November has a busy hum-m-m to it. For this month, we present a "harvest of good ideas" through the reading, math, and other special activities. You can sample or take a big heaping helping of ideas that relate to Children's Book Week, Veterans Day, bird migration, vegetables, and Pilgrims and Indians. These ideas can contribute to a plentiful harvest of learning that you can count among your Thanksgiving blessings!

Recommended Children's Books for November

Anno's Counting Book by Mitsumasa Anno (New York: Thomas Y. Crowell Co., 1975). This picture book remains with a single scene throughout four seasons, and 12 months of the year, but the colors give the mood and tone of time passing. The book begins with ZERO, showing a stark winter day. ONE shows the same snowy scene with one house, one snowman, etc. This process is repeated through number 12. An additional educational value of this book is the column of blocks along the border that enables the reader to keep a number tally. Children are attracted to this one, and it is an excellent teaching book.

A Farmer's Alphabet by Mary Azarian (Boston: David R. Godine Publisher, 1981). The setting is rural Vermont, and the illustrations are done with woodcuts. Letters and pictures are large and uncomplicated. The book is appropriate for this time of year when we give thanks for plentiful crops. Good ABC reinforcement.

Stone Soup by Marcia Brown (New York: Scribner, 1947). This tale is in the "magic pot" category. Can soup be made from water and a stone? Yes, if everyone will contribute something to the pot. The theme is one of cooperation and group effort. This is a good story to role play for Thanksgiving.

Petunia by Roger Duvoisin (New York: Pinwheel Books, Knopf/Pantheon, 1973). This is a delightful tale about a silly goose named Petunia who finds a book and tucks it under her wing. All of her barnyard friends think that now she must have knowledge and they ask her all sorts of questions. Since she can't read, she makes up the answers. Finally, things get out of control, there's an explosion, and Petunia discovers that the book has pages and "real print." She decides to learn how to read. Good book for young children who can't read and who need to learn the value of reading. (One of a series of Petunia books.)

My Cat Has Eyes of Sapphire Blue by Aileen Fisher (New York: Thomas Y. Crowell Company, 1973). A collection of short, delightful poems about cats by an author who obviously made a study of cat watching. This book also has beautiful illustrations by Marie Angel. This selection would be an asset to your read-aloud books during Cat Week.

Angus and the Cat by Marjorie Flack (New York: Doubleday & Co., Inc., A Zephyr Book, 1931). Children will delight in this easy-to-read short story about Angus, a Scottie dog, who finds a cat in his home environment.

He is forever chasing the cat but is frustrated in his attempts to catch it. Eventually, Angus chases the cat away and then misses it because he is all alone. Look for a happy ending. Children will be able to retell this story from the pictures.

Rosie's Walk by Pat Hutchins (New York: Collier Books, 1968). A short, easy-to-read book about a hen who goes for a walk followed by a hungry fox. The illustrations are delightful and portray concepts such as over, under, through, and around. Rosie outsmarts the fox and gets home safely. Children will be able to retell the story from picture clues.

Leo the Late Bloomer by Robert Kraus, illustrations by Jose Aruego (New York: Windmill Books, Inc. and E. P. Dutton, 1972). A fantasy tale about a young tiger, Leo, who is obviously a "late bloomer"—or one who is trailing behind the others. His father is very anxious but his mother is supportive. When Leo finally blooms, the colorful blossoms take up the whole page! This is a reassuring book for the late bloomers in your class.

Frederick by Leo Lionni (New York: Pantheon, 1967). This favorite tale is about a group of mice who are storing up food for winter—all but Frederick who is storing up the smells, sights, and sounds of autumn. The message is that everyone has something to contribute.

Arrow to the Sun by Gerald McDermott (New York: Puffin Books, 1978). An adaptation of a Pueblo Indian tale about a boy who is seeking his father and is transformed into an arrow. As an arrow, he is sent to the sun where he must successfully complete four tasks. The beautiful strong colors and bold angular forms help to convey the message. A Caldecott Award winner.

Reading Skills Activities

Language Development

Experience Chart. Take a brisk November walk. Note the sights, smells, and sounds . Take bags along for collecting items to bring back to the classroom (twigs, leaves, acorns, seedpods, etc.). Back in the classroom, do an experience story with the entire group. Gather the children together after they have had a chance to look through the items. Talk about your walk. The first sentence, then, may be "We just returned from our November walk," or "We were hunting for signs of autumn today." Then ask children to recall two or three things that they saw or did during the walk. Incorporate them into the story. Sum up the story with one sentence such as, "We came back and had delicious, hot cocoa," or "Br-r-r it's cold outside," or "We plan to make a great big collage with our autumn collection." Have the children illustrate the story.

Indian Sign Language Messages. Cut up large brown bags from the grocery store so that each student has his or her own 8″ × 10″ piece of brown "bark." Using felt pens, children can print a message using the Indian symbols found in the activity pages at the end of this chapter. The Indian sign language messages look very creative when displayed in the hallway. You may want to hang a copy of the Indian symbols, also, so that older children can decipher the "messages" from the younger Indians.

VARIATION: Sit in a circle around a pretend campfire (a wastebasket). Give each child a piece of 8½″ × 11″ gray construction paper. Show the children how to tear the paper gently around the edges to form "birchbark." The scraps can be tossed into the fire (wastebasket). Or, use the wastebasket to collect all of the scraps for the beavers who will come during the night to gather them up for their nest.

ANOTHER VARIATION: For writing instruments use a pounded stalk of cattail or a sturdy twig, just as the Indians may have used. They can be dipped into tempera paint (red, green, yellow, blue) to form the Indian symbols. When using these implements, it will be easier to work with small groups of three or four children.

Indian Names. Children can take on special names during Thanksgiving week. It was common for Indians to name their children after things in nature or events that happened on their day of birth. List some possible names and have children select one or create their own. Some suggestions for names are:

PRINCE—Running Deer, Snapping Twig, Singing Bird, Big Oak, Tiger Paw

PRINCESS—Bubbling Brook, Gentle Rain, Thunder Cloud, Maple Leaf

Print the names on a headband that the children can decorate, or print them on name tags. Also, make a large chart of the names and learn them. Call the children by their Indian names all during the week. Also, don't forget that the teacher should take an Indian name too, such as "Pretty Plum" or "Moose Horns."

A Thank-You Chart. Create a large chart in the shape of a turkey, pilgrim hat, or the Mayflower. Section it off so that there are enough spaces for everyone. Print each child's name in a space. Have them draw a picture of something they are thankful for at home, at school, or in the world. They can dictate a word or sentence to be printed in the space also.

VARIATION: Create a "Give Thanks" Book. Each child can draw a picture of what he/she is thankful for and dictate a sentence to go along with the picture. The booklet can be fastened together with bulky yarn. Present the booklet to the school library.

Expressive Leaf Words. Introduce the word "flutter." Explain that leaves flutter to the ground. Demonstrate a graceful fluttering motion with raised arm and hand, and then have children practice. Then, use two arms for flutter motion. Stand tall and straight (tree-trunk style) and "sway" arms and shoulders in a make-believe breeze. Then, "sway" and "flutter" at the same time, making sure to keep feet and legs still, since they represent the tree trunk. Other things "flutter" besides leaves; let's think of some and list them on the board. Make simple rebus shapes beside the words.

Bring in a big bushel basket, so that when children bring in leaf samples daily, they can deposit them in the basket. It will fill up fast. Each child can pick two leaves out of the basket—one for each hand. They stand tall pretending to be the tree, with arms outstretched for branches. Teacher reads the following verse. When children hear the word "fluttered" or "fluttering" they gently release the leaf and watch it make a path (flutter) to the floor. Stand still, and don't make a sound so that the fluttering leaves can be heard.

VERSE: I saw a leaf

A pretty little leaf

And it *fluttered* to the ground. (PAUSE)

I looked up high

Up to the sky

And I didn't hear a sound.

But I saw pretty leaves,

They were beautiful leaves,

They were *fluttering* all around. (PAUSE)

Pick up leaves and repeat.

VARIATION: Have children make the "fl" sound: (1) Place front upper teeth on bottom lip; (2) Place tip of tongue on roof of mouth in back of ridge; (3) Air is expelled as tongue slides forward until it is sticking out between teeth. Repeat the "fl" sound six times as follows:

"Fl, fl, fl, fl, fl, fl flutter" (let go of one leaf)

"Fl, fl, fl, fl, fl, fl flutter" (let go of second leaf)

Pick them up, and say:

"Fl, fl, fl, fl, fl, fl flutter" (release leaf in LEFT hand)

"Fl, fl, fl, fl, fl, fl flutter" (release leaf in RIGHT hand)

Repeat.

The Acorn. The acorn is the fruit of the oak tree. (Have a sample or a large picture.) The nut has a thick wall, set in a woody cup.  The acorn squash is a vegetable. (Have a sample.) It has a shape similar to the acorn nut.

Compare the acorn nut and the acorn squash in the following ways:

size (bigger than, smaller than, tiny, large, little, big)

color (brown, green, light brown, dark green, two-toned brown, green and yellow)

exterior (*shell:* tough, hard, smooth; *skin:* bumpy, ridges, hard)

weight (have a scale available for weighing)

Do other nuts share their name with items as the acorn does?

Butternut – Butternut Squash (compare)

Almond   – "Almond eyes" (shape)

Peanut   – Peanut butter, peanut brittle, peanut butter ice cream (all by-products of the peanut)

Chestnut – "Chestnut brown hair" (description)

Any others?

Do any children share a first name? Do they share a last name? We know that family members share a last name.

Name Sharing. This can be introduced in the following way. Teacher can take a tissue and blow her nose. Do this dramatically. Then, by either asking or telling the children, you should all reach the point where it is agreed that the teacher BLEW her nose. Print "blew" on the chalkboard. Tell children that "blew" shares its sound with another word, and that the word is a color word. Let's check our colors around the room for it, "...red, orange, yellow, green, BLUE...there it is!" Print "blue" on the chalkboard. Compare "blew" and "blue"—which letters are the same and which are different. The main idea is that they sound alike, but they don't mean the same thing. Use each one in a sentence. (For example, "I just blew my nose," and "The sky is blue.") Words that share the same-sounding name are called *homonyms*.

Depending upon the developmental level of the group, the teacher may be able to teach homonym lessons to the entire class or to small groups. Some other homonyms to use include: pear, pair; sent, cent, two (2), too (also); meat, meet; herd, heard; buy, by.

As Busy as a Beaver. Explain that words like to be used again and again. Some words even lend out, or share, their combination of sounds to help explain something. The color words are especially helpful to us. Have children create their own similes with these open-ended sentences (or phrases).

Red as a _____

Orange as a_____

Yellow as a _____

Green as a _____

Blue as a _____

Purple as a_____

Like the color words, there are other words that loan, or share, their title to help explain something to us, such as:

fox—sly as a fox

bird—free as a bird

beaver—busy as a beaver

ocean—deep as the ocean

Try creating similes with these words:

horse—"as ...... as a horse."

monkey—"as ..... as a monkey."

elephant—"as .... as an elephant."

USE similes for directions: "Let's be as quiet as mice as we take our seats!"

Sing a Song to the Squirrel. Place five or six different types of nuts in a little basket with a handle. Teacher, or children, can reach into the basket, get a nut for the squirrel, identify the nut, and then to the tune of "Happy Birthday" inform the squirrel that you have a present for it. Hold up the nut for all to see, and sing:

"Here's an ACORN for you

A big ACORN for you

You'll be happy, gray squirrel,

With this ACORN for you."

Reach into the basket again, find another nut, identify it, and sing:

"Here's a WALNUT for you..."

"Here's a PECAN for you..."

"Here's a PEANUT for you..."

"Here's a CHESTNUT for you..."

By singing a familiar song, the children have only one new word to learn. As children sing about squirrels and nuts they are learning to identify a wide variety of nuts.

VARIATION: Have children close their eyes while one reaches into the basket, picks out a nut and identifies it. Children open their eyes and verify it. Then, to the tune of "Found a Peanut" all children can sing:

"Found a peanut

Found a peanut

Found a peanut

For a squirrel

Just now I found a peanut,

Found a peanut for a squirrel."

Repeat:

"Found a walnut..."

"Found a pecan..."

"Found an acorn..."

"Found an almond..."

All About "A/An." One day, after singing the familiar "Found a Peanut" song, present this information as though you are letting the children in on some kind of a secret. In a loud whisper, with a note of mystery in your voice, tell the children that in our song we change *a* to *an* when we use it before words that begin with the letter "a." We say, "a walnut," but we say "an acorn" and "an almond." Is this true of a/an before all words that begin with the "a" sound? Let's think of some and see if it is so. (Have big magazine pictures available of the objects you will name.)

an apple	an arm	an afternoon
an airplane	an actor	an alley cat
an arrow	an athlete	an ankle
an astronaut	an ace	an apron

Encourage children to be "on the lookout" for this a/an switch. Maybe we're onto something here. Lead the children to what it is they are supposed to "discover" by having them be on the alert for the a/an switch, as you are working with vowels and consonants. An informal or a formal approach could be used.

Upper- and Lowercase Letters

Special Letter Days (N, P, T, F). Choose one day of the week for this activity so that children can anticipate it. (For example: every Tuesday or Wednesday). Select N (November), P (Pilgrim), T (Turkey), and F (Feast). On the Special Letter Day Celebration, have children bring in items that begin with that sound. (Letters sent home to parents in advance may help to make this successful.) The teacher can prepare the picnic basket by having five items already inside. Give hints and have children guess the items one by one. Then they can see the item, touch it, say the word, and listen to the beginning sound. Some item suggestions for the basket:

N—nuts, nickel, napkin, noodles, nachos, nectarine

P—pineapple, paper, pencil, paper clip, pillow, pear

T—tablecloth, teapot, towel, tissue, toothbrush

F—flowers, fork, feather, frame, felt, football, fry pan

Math Skills Activities

Number Words

Put the Feathers on the Turkey. You need cardboard, scissors, markers, and clothespins. Cut a large circle from cardboard and make a slit in the center.

Cut out a neck and head shape for a turkey and insert it into the slit. (Fold and tape neck on reverse side.) Using the felt-tip pen, divide the circle into pie shapes. Put number words and dots in each pie shape. Next, put corresponding numerals on clothespins with felt-tip pen. Children can match the numeral with the number word and dots by clipping the "clothespin feather" onto the turkey.

Measurement

Dry Measure. Materials needed: Large plastic tub placed inside of a large cardboard box; white sand (or rice or grain); measuring spoons; plastic measuring cups; bowls; bottles; containers; funnel; dust pan and brush broom.

Allow two children at a time to sift, measure, fill, and empty the containers. Children are gaining much information as they master these pouring tasks. They are working with concepts such as: more than, less than, full, empty, half full, teaspoon, tablespoon, cup, pint, quart, etc. The exploration experience will serve them well later when they meet the concepts formally. *Important:* Introduce the area with only a few items at first (sand, measuring spoons, containers, dust pan and brush broom). Add new items one or two at a time.

It will depend upon the group as to whether it is possible to use glass or plastic bottles. Glass has the advantage of allowing the children to clearly see levels of rice or sand. If using glass containers, they can be kept in boxes with cardboard separators (such as juice boxes from the grocery store, or art supply boxes). With masking tape, label each container and each space in the box, so they can be easily returned. The rules are as follows:

- Only two containers may be removed from the box at one time.
- Glass never touches glass.

Try to find glass bottles that are interesting and that have varied shapes and sizes. After a time of initial exploration, the children can begin to make comparisons such as:

__A__ is more than __D__		
_____ is more than _____		
_____ is less than _____		
_____ is less than _____		

This "More Than/Less Than" information can eventually be printed on a chart and placed by the sand/measuring area. Children can fill it in with pencil. Other children can verify the accuracy of the statement.

Measuring Three Items. After the sand or small grain exploration, the dry measure can be changed to include three items: lima beans, navy beans, and lentils. Children can count to see how many of each are contained in half a cup or in a cup. They can begin to estimate how many of each it would take to fill a specified container, keeping in mind that the larger the item the less it will take to fill the volume.

A Pound Is a Pound. Is a pound a pound? Bring in a one-pound bag of large beans and a one-pound bag of small peas. Weigh them. (To establish the concept of one pound, weigh the fruits and vegetables and items in the classroom. How close are they to the one-pound mark? Place an empty bag on the scale and fill it with nuts until you reach one pound. Try filling the bag with other items to make one pound.) Have the children estimate how many single beans or peas make up one pound. Open them up, count them (by ones, fives, ten). Check the estimations against the actual count. Get a half-pound container and ask children to estimate how many beans or peas it would take to fill the container. Fill the container, and check the actual count against the estimations. As children have more and more opportunities to estimate, count, and verify, those who are ready will begin to see relationships. For those who do not see it, the experience is not wasted. They are simply not ready to refine the information at this point, but they will benefit from pouring, weighing, counting, and learning the concepts of bigger than, greater than, less than. For some children, the basic concept of "big" and "little" will be reinforced.

Math Manipulatives

Objects from the Natural Environment. Natural items from the immediate environment can be collected and used for counting, sorting, and categorizing activities. Put such items as acorns, chestnuts, pumpkin seeds, seeds from a variety of fruits and vegetables, pinecones, pebbles, seashells, twigs, etc., in a shoebox. Children can categorize the items by placing them in the different compartments of a large cardboard box with separators. (Cover the outside of the box with wallpaper or prepasted paper for attractiveness.)

Objects from the Classroom. Items from the classroom environment can be collected and used for counting, sorting, and categorizing activities. In a container, collect the following items: pencil, crayon, paintbrush, eraser, scissors, chalk, felt pen, paper, sponge, soap, paper towel, assorted scraps of construction paper, book, triangle, circle and square shapes cut from construction paper, several beads, some blocks, a ruler, straw, milk container, etc. Make a grid from a huge piece of kraft paper that can be spread out on the floor. Working in groups of two or three, have children place the items that "belong together" on the floor grid. Ask children to explain their categories and their rationale. Record the information on a piece of paper (grid) if time permits. Replace all items. Then, have two or three different children categorize the items. The results may be very different from group to group. Ask for the rationale and accept it. Children will soon learn different ways of categorizing items from each other, or from the teacher, but the process should be gradual. (Some children may put the paper towel with the soap, and some may put all paper together. Both are acceptable.)

Picture Flashcards. Make picture flashcards of all of the items to be categorized. Have children match the flashcard with the actual item to practice the one-to-one correspondence. Working in pairs, have one child hold up a flashcard and the other child identify  and pick up the item. Also, reverse the process so that one child picks up the actual item and the other child has to locate the flashcard. It is helpful for children to be able to move from concrete items (real) to semi-concrete items (flashcards) AND to be able to reverse the process and move from semi-concrete items (flashcards) to concrete items (real). They need practice in moving back and forth with ease.

The Abstract Dimension. Collect items from the indoor or outdoor environment and place them in a plastic tub. Make sure that you have ONE of an item, TWO of another item, THREE of another item, FOUR of another item, and FIVE of another item. Make *two* groups of flashcards. One set should have the actual pictures of the items in the plastic tub (for example, a picture of two pencils, a picture of three rulers, etc.). The other set should have the numeral printed on it (1, 2, 3, 4, 5). Now we have a set of actual items (concrete), a flashcard set of the pictures (semi-concrete), and a flashcard set of the numerals (abstract). Select three children at a time to work with this kit. One child works with the real items, one child has a set of picture flashcards, and one child has a set of numeral flashcards. Children take turns being "in charge." If the child who has the picture flashcards is in charge and holds up a card showing two pinecones, the child who is working with the real items must hold up the two pinecones, and the child who has the numeral flashcards must hold up the numeral card that shows "2." All must agree. Each child can be in charge for *five* transactions. Then, another child must be in charge for *five* transactions, and then the third child is in charge for *five* transactions. THE POINT IS: children should be able to move back and forth and forth and back with ease through the concrete, semi-concrete, and abstract mathematical concepts.

VARIATION: When you have a group of children who are able to move back and forth with ease, they can do a variation of the above exercise. For example, suppose that Child A, B, and C are working together. Child A is "in charge" for *one* turn, THEN Child B for *one* turn, and then Child C for *one* turn. Repeat. For the more able child, this makes the exercise more challenging as the categories keep changing. Hopefully, all children should eventually be able to master this exercise.

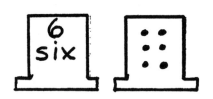

Pilgrim Hat Math. Make pilgrim hat shapes from 8½″ × 11″ construction paper. With felt pen, put the numeral

6

and number on one side (six) and the corresponding number of dots on the reverse side, such as (::::). Have children count out the nuts or seeds to the right of the pilgrim hat. For self-checking, they can turn the hat over to count the number of dots.

Color, Shape, Counting

Indian Beads. From colorful oaktag paper, cut out many triangle, circle, and rectangle shapes. With a paper punch, put a hole in the center of each one. String a sample bead pattern using the shapes. Knot the string, or yarn, at both ends. Children can *pattern* their beads by using the identical shapes and correct numbers of each. (For COLOR reinforcement all circles could be red, all triangles could be blue, etc. For SHAPE reinforcement, colors can be varied. For COUNTING reinforcement, children can count the total number of triangles, the total number of circles, the total number of rectangles, and then from left to right the total number of beads altogether.) When children complete the pattern correctly, the ends of the string can be tied together and this can be worn as beads.

The Big Chief. Have children sit in a circle. Big Chief Red Feather likes beads and is coming to inspect the tribe. As the chief calls out directions such as "Show Big Chief the red triangle," or "Big Chief wants to see a blue bead," or "Chief Red Feather wants to see TWO square beads," the children can reach down in front of them to the beads they are wearing, and lift them up for the Chief to see. This gives children more practice with color, shape, and number—and gives the teacher immediate feedback from the group.

Counting

Stars and Stripes Numbers. Use the classroom flag as a counting experience. Gather around the American flag and keep it in the holder. How many red stripes? (Seven). How many white stripes? (Six). How many stars? (Five rows of six, and four rows of five, a total of 50). What shape is the flag? Rectangle.

What shape is the blue field (union) in the upper left corner? What color is the top stripe? The bottom stripe? Are they the same or different? How many stripes are there altogether to the right of the blue field (union)? How many short stripes? How many long stripes? Are there more short stripes or more long stripes? When we say the Pledge of Allegiance we put our right hand over the left side of our chest. Practice.

A Flag Survey. Let's find out some information about the American flag in our school. For example: Where is the flag displayed *inside* of our school building? In the classrooms? Office? Auditorium? Where is the flag displayed  *outside* of our school building? Who is responsible for putting up (raising) and taking down (lowering) the flag each day? Do we have a school flag? If so, where is it? What colors does it have? What symbols are on it? What do they mean? Look at pictures of flags of other nations. Check with the library for resource books. (For more information about flag etiquette, see the material on Veterans Day in the November section. To make an American flag, see Activity Pages.)

Sorting

We're Nuts About Math. In November, squirrels are scampering for nuts. They bury them to eat later, and sometimes even forget where they are. Bring in a variety of nuts if they are plentiful in your area. Collect them on your autumn walk—acorns, buckeyes, horse chestnuts. Bags of the hard-shelled variety can be purchased at the grocery store (walnuts, pecans, almonds, etc.). Use egg cartons to sort the nuts from smallest to largest. Sort the nuts by light and dark colors. Categorize the nuts by type. Use the nuts for rote counting.

One-to-One Correspondence

Peanut Math. Bring in peanuts in the shells. Have them available in a colorful plastic bowl so that children can sift through them and count them repeatedly. From oaktag, make a nine-square grid. With felt-tip pen, print  numerals 1 to 9 in the squares. Also, make the corresponding number of peanut shapes in each square. Children can place the real peanuts directly on top of the peanut shapes to establish one-to-one correspondence.

Probability

Undercover Math. Under the outer cover of the shells you can find Spanish peanuts. Give each child five peanuts in shells. Have them line the nuts up in a straight row and count them aloud "1, 2, 3, 4, 5." Then, have them move the first one (on the far left) away from the others, but still in a straight line. Do we still have five? Yes. "One and four more make five." Next, move another nut to the left so that you have a set of two and three. Are there still five? Yes. Now, move all of the peanuts with shucks back together again. It has been established that no matter how we arrange them, there appear to be five nuts. BUT, things aren't always as they appear to be. If we shuck the nuts, how many should be inside? Five? Let's try it with JUST ONE. Have all children shuck one peanut. How many nuts are inside? (This can vary from two to one and even three). SO, under the peanut cover, we're not sure just how many nuts are inside. Let's shuck all of the nuts and line the inside peanuts in a row. Count them. Are they all the same? Does one squirrel have more? Does another have less? Select two or three of the busy squirrels to collect the shucks in a large paper bag. SAVE the shucks. Then, have a squirrel party and eat all of the peanuts that were shucked. Each squirrel will not have an *equal* amount of nuts.

Underground Math. Use an egg carton with the numerals 1 through 12 printed on the inside. Using only three nuts, place one nut in three different compartments. Cover over with a brown piece of construction paper (ground). A squirrel must try to guess which of the three compartments, from 1 through 12, are housing the hidden nuts. A typical guesstimate could be "1, 3, 9" or "6, 4, 12." An estimate of "1, 7, 2" or "5, 11, 12" would be more accurate if students tilted the container so that the nuts landed at the ends. Be sure to record the numbers that are given. Then "dig in" and uncover the carton and check the compartments. Record the numbers where the nuts were found. How many nuts did the squirrel find? How many numbers (or trees) away from the real nut was the squirrel? Repeat.

Other Skill Areas Activities

Autumn Harvest

Meet the Vegetables. Many children eat canned or frozen vegetables and may never have seen the "real thing." Prepare a table for your autumn harvest, and bring in the vegetables, one or two at a time, for exploration. Introduce the purple eggplant, waxy rutabaga, ruffly purple cabbage, bumpy squash, bright orange carrots, etc.

Outside: Examine texture—smooth, bumpy, shaggy, waxy

Examine color—bright, spotted, mixed

Examine hue—dull, shiny

Examine shape—round, oval, irregular

Ask: "Suppose you didn't know it was a vegetable. What could you use it for?"

Inside: Examine texture, color, hue, shape. Check sections under a magnifying glass or microscope for texture patterns. Draw it. Smell it. Taste it. (Carrots, celery, cauliflower could be tasted at snack time.)

Now that you have been introduced to the vegetables and they have been peeled, scraped, cut up, and torn apart, they are still useful in the following ways:

Creative Stories Tell stories from the point of view of the vegetable in the classroom. What did it see and learn today?

Dyes Cook onion skins to obtain yellow or gold color for dye. Dye white yarn and use it for weaving like the Indians did.

Printing Make vegetable prints on paper or cloth, using tempera paint. A cabbage wedge makes an interesting design. Make "designer" curtains, tablecloth, or pillow for the room.

Vegetable Soup Thoroughly wash, and cut up vegetables. Place in 3 qts. water and bring to a boil. Add beef broth cubes. For added interest, add pasta during the last ½ hour of cooking. Use as your Thanksgiving soup.

Seeds Wash and dry. Use for counters in math.

Leftovers For rabbits, gerbils, or other classroom pets. For zoo animals.

Thanksgiving

Thanksgiving Feast Ideas. One item on the menu could be vegetable soup, listed in the previous section. Act out the story of *Stone Soup* (see the recommended book section). Read the story aloud several times and rehearse it. Then on the day when the vegetables are cut up and ready, reread the story aloud and have the children act it out using real vegetable chunks. Serve a taste in styrofoam cups. Another popular Thanksgiving Feast idea in which children could be involved would be a "Pudding and Popcorn Feast." (Lots of opportunities for measuring and timing.)

Friendship Stew. Friendship Stew can be simmered overnight in a slow cooker. Each child brings in a vegetable from home (carrots, celery, corn, potato, green beans, tomato, onion). These are cleaned, cut up, and added to a bouillon broth. The Friendship Stew is served to the friendly Pilgrims and Indians the next day when they gather together to give thanks for good food, good health, and good friends.

Arts and Crafts

Turkey in the Straw. Materials needed: a potato for each child, assorted colored toothpicks, two sticks of plasticene, a bed of straw. Procedure: children can count out from 10 to 15 colored toothpicks, and then count them again as they insert the "pick feathers" in the potato, which will transform it into a turkey. At the other end, insert a pick for the neck. Place a ball of clay on the stick for a head. Place all turkeys on a bed of straw, and take them home later for a Thanksgiving centerpiece. This area can be used in a reading corner with a supply of picture books about Thanksgiving and turkeys.

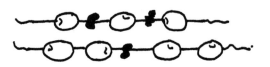

VARIATION: Place a whole cranberry on each toothpick. Or, place cranberries and raisins on each pick. Alternate the patterns. (This is good for math patterning.)

Creative Dramatics

Sail the Mayflower. Make a boat from a large cardboard box. With felt-tip pen, draw lines around the box to give it the appearance of a wooden boat. On two corners, tape yardsticks to the inside of the box. On each yardstick, tape a white paper sail. Since the Mayflower was crowded, allow three children to "sail" at a time. Make telescopes from paper towel cylinders. Children may be able to shuffle their feet and move the box until they land at Plymouth Rock (large brown bag stuffed with paper). Set the anchor, and get out. Have children tell two things they saw through the telescope (real or imaginary).

Children's Book Week

In November of 1731, Benjamin Franklin started the first circulating library. It seems appropriate, then, that Children's Book Week be in November.

A Picture Book. Have each child paint a picture at the easel. Put the pictures together to make a giant picture book.

Musical Fingerpaintings. Have children finger paint to music. Put together a large book of their fingerpaintings. Then let children wear headsets and listen to the music as they turn the pages and see the fingerpaintings that the same music inspired.

A Tree Book. To create a book about trees, staple five green shapes onto a brown rectangle. (Or use different colors to represent the tree foliage.) Children can draw the tree in four different seasons, or show different fruit trees in different seasons. Book title and author's name can go on the cover, and the pages flip over the top.

Paint a Squirrel. Have each child paint an easel picture of a squirrel gathering or eating some nuts. The paintings can be done with white and tones of gray. Allow the paintings to dry. Then, with a large easel brush have each child paint a splotch of glue onto the picture. Sprinkle peanut shucks onto this sticky surface for a two-dimensional appearance. (These were the shucks that you gathered up and saved from your math lesson.) Have each child dictate a story to go with this creative picture.

Favorite Books. Have the children draw or paint a picture from their favorite books. Print the titles, authors, and illustrators on the backs. Then read (or reread) some of the all-time favorite stories that the children vote for.

Veterans Day

Flag Etiquette. This day is set aside as a time to say "thank you" to the men and women who have spent time protecting you and me and our country from danger. They may have served in the Army, Navy, Air Force, Marines, Merchant Marines, Coast Guard, etc. When we are proud of our country, we say that we are *patriotic*. One way of showing that we are patriotic is by pledging allegiance to the flag. Did you know that there are rules and regulations for using the American flag properly? Some are as follows:

1. The flag should not be displayed outside on days when the weather is bad, unless it's an all-weather flag.
2. The American flag flies highest on the pole—no other flag (country, state) should be flown higher in the same immediate area.
3. The flag should not be flown upside down except to signal extreme danger.

How many other rules of flag "etiquette" do you observe in your classroom? (Stand when saying the Pledge of Allegiance, right hand over heart when saying the pledge.)

Besides the flag, another important symbol for our country is the Statue of Liberty (show picture). In 1985-86, the statue was repaired and cleaned. Among other things, it now has a new torch, new lighting, and a new elevator. The Statue of Liberty is located in Upper New York Bay between New Jersey and New York. Let's find it on the globe or map. How many have actually seen the statue? How many have seen pictures of the statue? Do we have statues right here in our city or town? What are they? Where are they? What do they mean? What shape are they? What writing is on them? Let's find out more about statues and monuments right here in our own community!

Cat Week

Cat Week begins with the first Sunday in November. Have a discussion about cats during circle time: Who has a cat? What's the color of the cat? What's the cat's name? Display picture books about cats. Other pets could also be discussed.

Cat Shots. Cats get "shots" just like people do. Theirs are for rabies, distemper, and leukemia. Discuss shots that are given by medical personnel and their useful purpose in helping to fight disease (measles, smallpox, polio, etc.).

Cats Can Calm You. Recent studies show that when people hold pets and stroke them gently, it reduces their blood pressure and they feel calm. Have a large, stuffed animal in class and allow children to hold it and pet it before, during, or after an upsetting time. Perhaps two or three animal "pets" could be available for this purpose. Maybe one could be placed on a little rug with a pillow.

Bird Migration

All About Migration. Introduce the term *migration*—moving from cold to warm climate for the winter. What birds migrate from/to your local area? Show pictures of them. Go outside and actually SEE birds, and identify them. What is your state bird? Does it migrate? Why don't *all* birds migrate?

The Canada Goose. When migrating geese fly in a V formation, you know they are Canada geese. When they fly in a straight line formation, they are snow geese. A group of geese together is called a "gaggle" of geese. During creative play period, pretend that you are geese. Migrate in a straight line to the playground. On the playground, have children (geese) line up in a V formation and move forward as a group. Then, line up in a straight line and move forward as a group. Slowly practice a group turn to the right, to the left. Scatter and play, but return to the classroom in a straight line formation.

Ducks. Most ducks live by water (marshes, ponds, streams, lakes, oceans). Some are divers, they go under water for their food, and some are surface eaters, they eat by dabbling in the water and tipping up and back, rather than by diving. Find a resource book of ducks from the library so that children can examine the pictures and note the  variety of colors, markings, and bird shapes. Find out where specific ducks spend the winter, and locate their migration route on the map or globe.

Mallard	Range:	From Great Lakes to Gulf of Mexico
Pintail	Range:	From Hudson Bay to Florida coast
Canvasback	Range:	From Minnesota to Gulf of Mexico

Eye-Hand Coordination

Lacing and Tying. Practice tying a bow, and lacing shoes. Make tying boards, so that children can practice from different angles. Materials needed: 4″ × 6″ pieces of heavy cardboard, fancy shoelaces, heavy-duty stapler. Each child can place the cardboard on the floor, put their foot in the center, and practice tying. Also, place the cardboard on a table top and tie a bow while facing the board. (Several sets could be made.)

VARIATION: Ask several parents to donate some old pairs of men's lace-up shoes. Spray paint them bright colors (red, green, orange). Several children at a time can slip into the "giant's shoes" and lace and tie them. Practice lacing and tying with old boots, ski boots, and athletic shoes too.

Small Motor Development

Snap, Zip, Buckle, Rip. Have a variety of old belts, sandals, purses, wallets, cosmetic bags, change purses, and clips stored together in a decorative container. Children can practice opening, closing, grasping, snapping, buckling, zipping, and opening and closing Velcro items. These activities strengthen small hand muscles and allow children repeated opportunities to gain control over movements of the hand and to gauge the pressure and strength needed for certain tasks.

VARIATION: Coordinate "Snap, Zip, Buckle, Rip" to music. Distribute to the children items from the container. Sing the following words to any tune, and have the children act it out with real items:

Oh, I have a little zipper that goes

    zip   zip   zip

I have a little snap that goes
        snap   snap   snap
I have a little clip that goes
        clip   clip   clip
AND, I have a little Velcro that goes
        rip   rip   rip.

Exchange items, repeat song. Children who are waiting for their turn to use the real items can sing along and use hand motions to simulate the action.

Name _____

CREATE A TURKEY

Read the color word on each turkey feather. Color the feathers. Create your own turkey body, head, and neck. Then, put on the feet ⅄⅄ ⅄⅄ , beak, ⪕ , eyes ●● , and wattle ◗

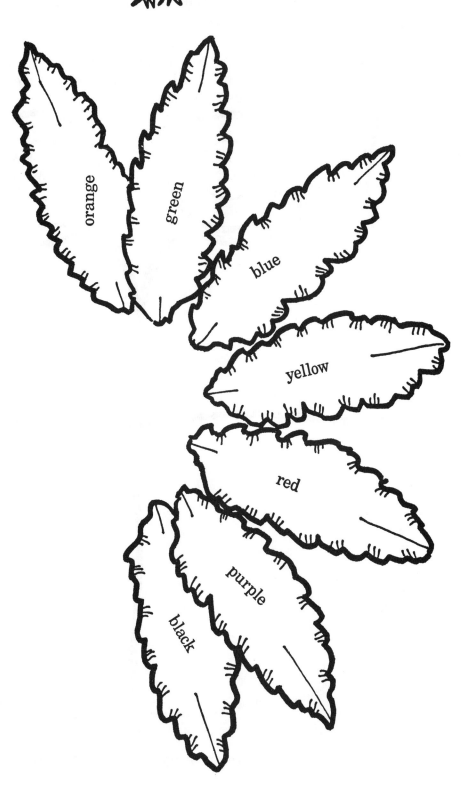

Name _____

AN AUTUMN LISTENING WALK

Owls hoot and screech during November nights. What do we hear during November DAYS? Go for a Listening Walk—listen for all the sounds of nature. Then, draw four things that made sounds.

LOOK UP

LOOK DOWN

1.

2.

3.

4.

On the back, draw something that you saw that did not make any sound at all!

PRACTICE THE LETTERS

Trace over the letters in the Thanksgiving shapes at the beginning of each row.
Practice the letters in the empty shapes.

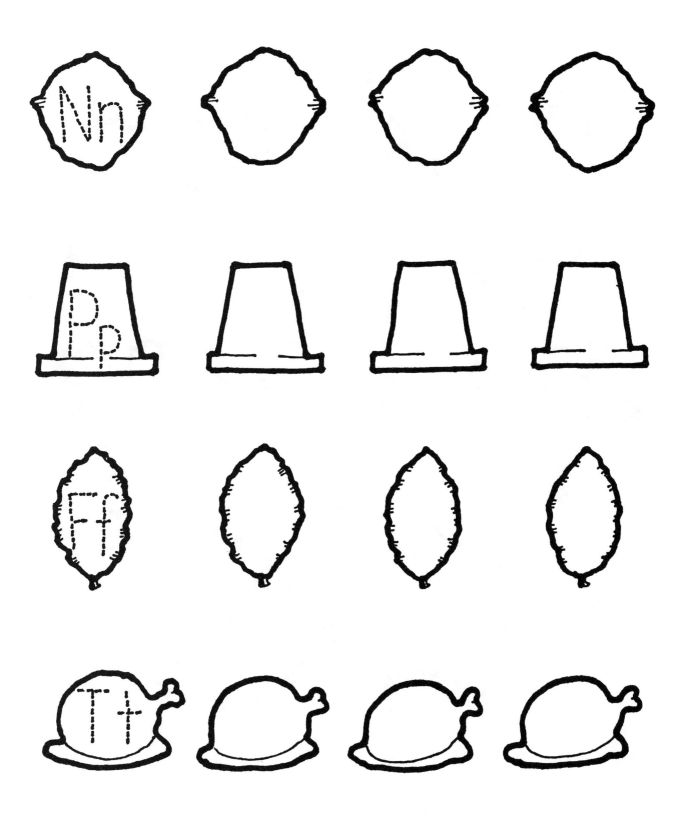

LEAF COLOR WORDS

These autumn leaves have fallen from a tree. Match the leaves by drawing a line from each capital letter leaf to the correct lowercase leaf. Color the leaves that are the same letter with the same color crayon.

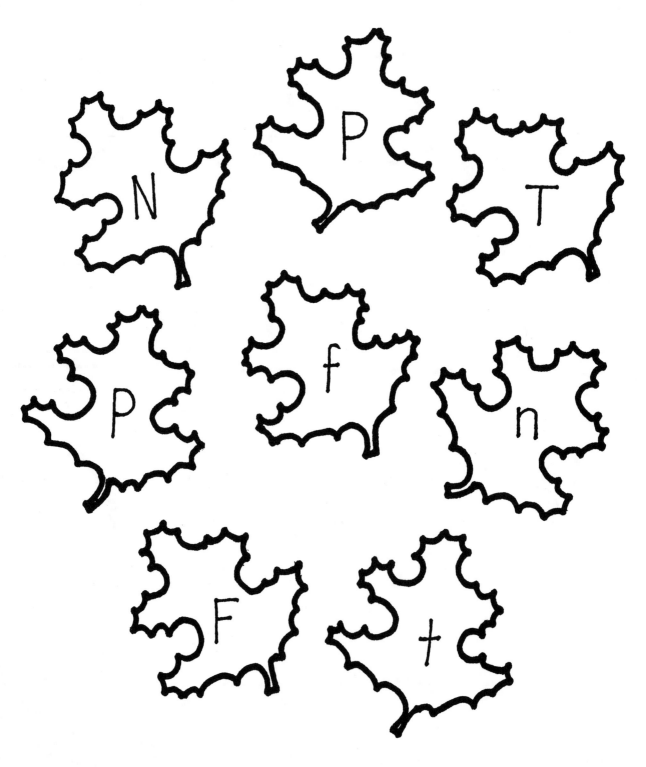

INDIAN SIGN LANGUAGE CHART

Write a rebus story using the Indian pictures to help you. Then, cut the squares and make a set of flashcards. Learn the words for a Thanksgiving treat!

greetings	peace	sun	sunrise
November	eat	to hunt	star
corn	happy	home	mountains
meet	sky	rain	fish

Name _____

NUTS IN A BASKET

These baskets have nuts in them that children found before the squirrels could hide them away. Count the number of nuts in each basket and write the correct numeral on the basket. Color the baskets fall colors. Color the nuts.

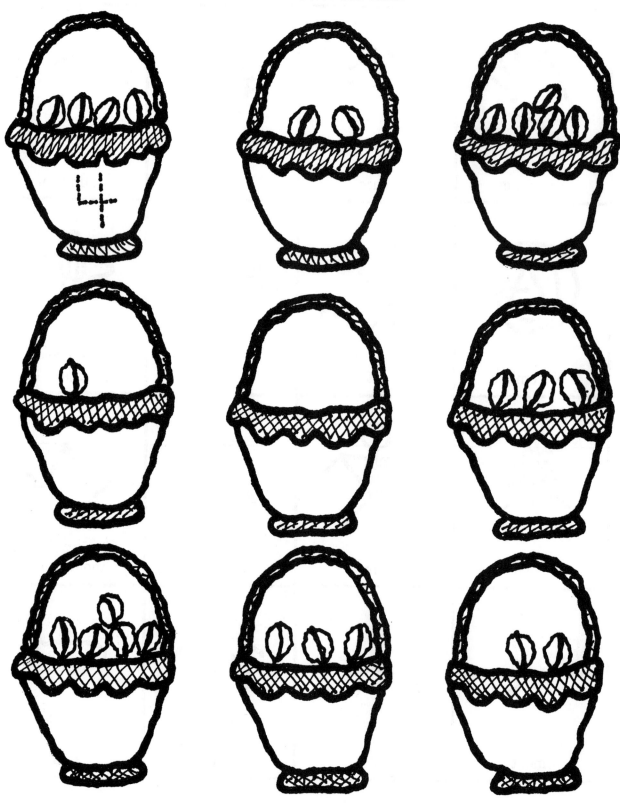

Name _____

PILGRIM HAT MATH

Count the number of dots on the first pilgrim hat. Match them up with the same number of items on the second hat.

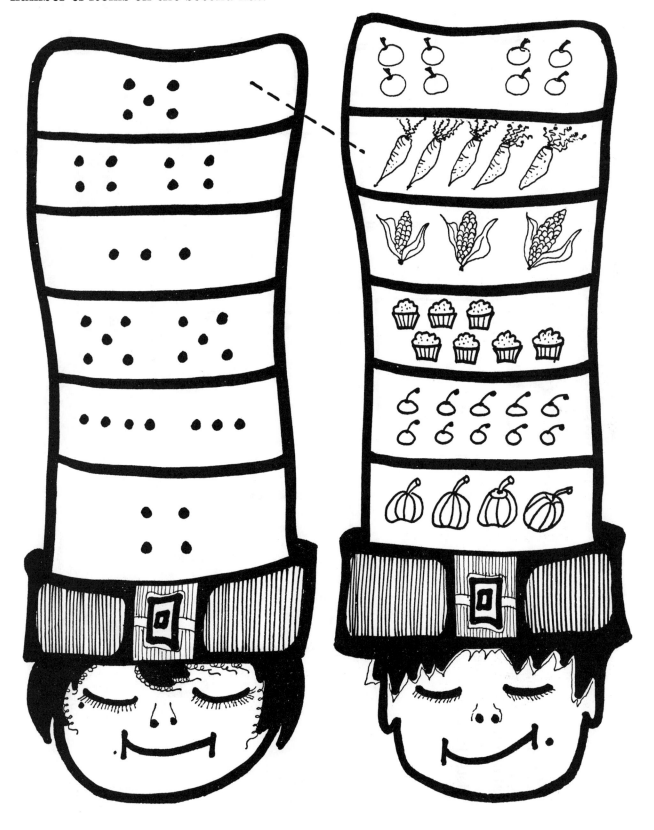

Name _____

GET READY TO SAIL

Cut off the numeral strip.
Cut into four squares.
Match the big numerals with
the correct number of
dots. Paste.

6 10 9 12

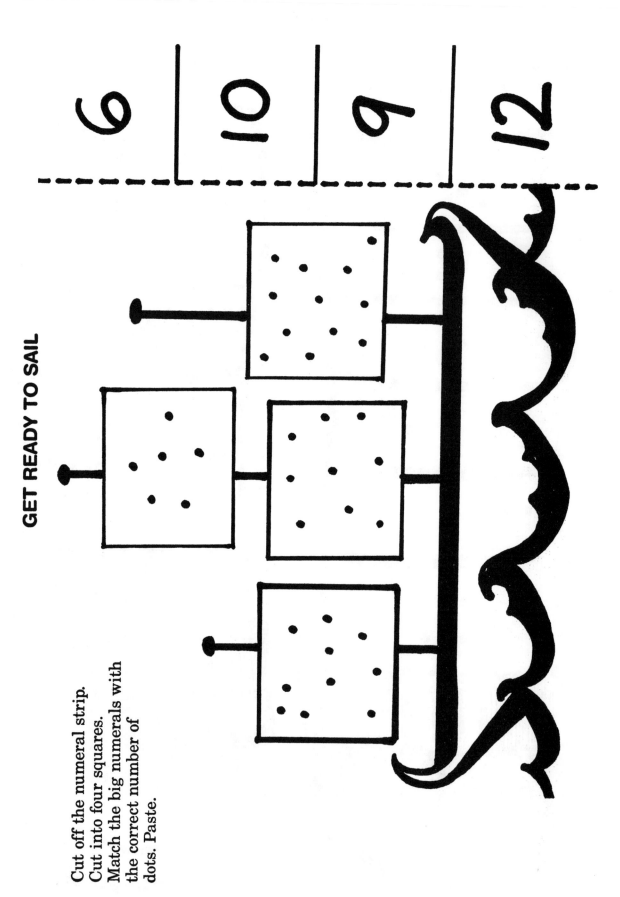

SQUIRRELS AND NUTS

Circle the two nuts in each row that are alike. Color the nuts.

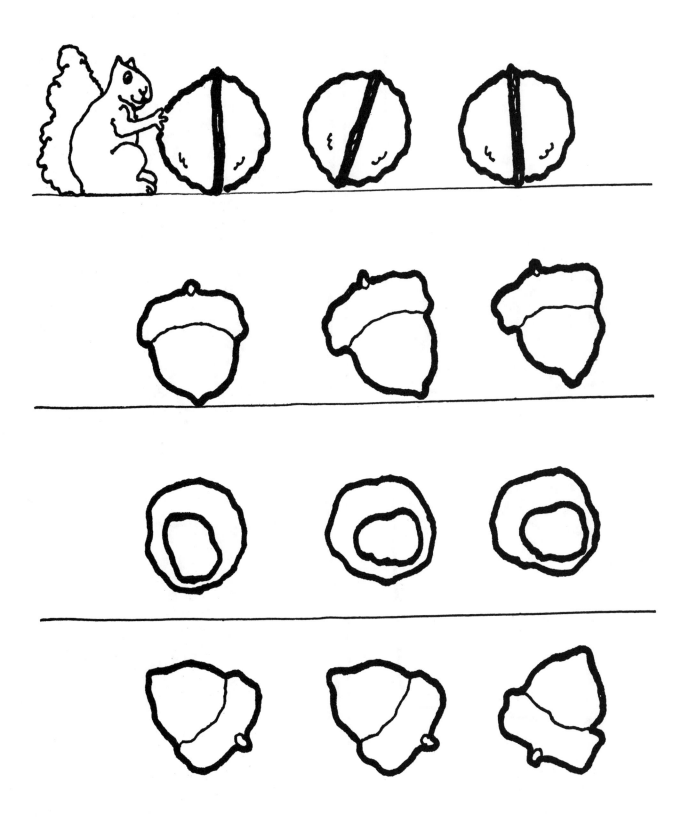

This bookmark belongs to:

_____

CHILDREN'S BOOK WEEK
November

This is my bookmark:

_____

CHILDREN'S BOOK WEEK
November

Name _____

THE CANADA GOOSE

Directions:

Cut out the neck and head shown here. Then cut out the body on the next sheet. Paste them together, or fasten with a paper fastener at the X.

The goose can be designed and colored as a decoy. ALSO, the goose can be used to aid in MIGRATION suggestions in teacher section.

CUT THIS GOOSE FACTS SHEET OUT AND PASTE ON THE BACK OF THE CANADA GOOSE:

CANADA GOOSE FACT SHEET
1. Canada geese fly in a "V" formation.
2. A group of geese is called a GAGGLE of geese.
3. Canada geese MIGRATE. That means they fly south for the winter.

THE CANADA GOOSE'S OTHER HALF

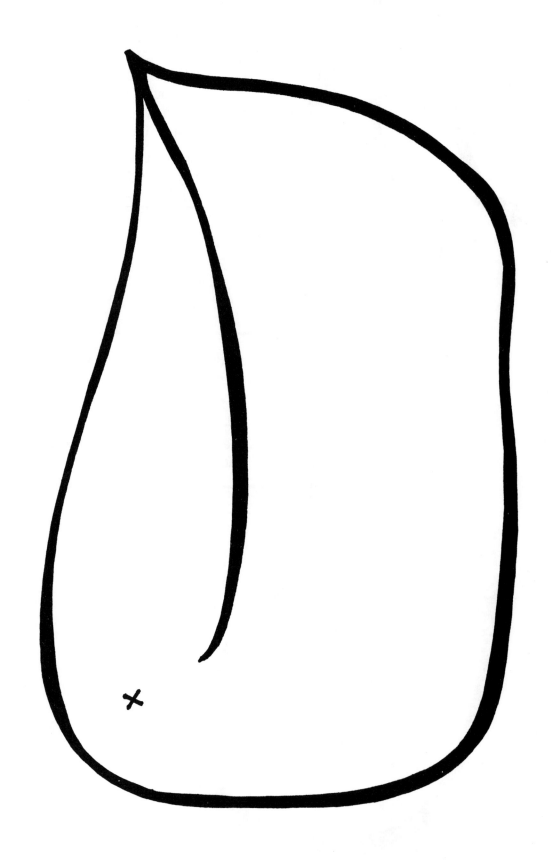

Name _____

STARS AND STRIPES

X	Red	X					
	Red	X					
X	Red	X					
	Red	X					
X	Red	X					
X	Red	X					
	Red	X					
	Red	X					

DECEMBER

A Festive Atmosphere

In kindergarten, the month of December is made even brighter by the sparkle and shine in the eyes of the children. It's the holiday season with its wonderful sights, sounds, smells, and tastes—and that calls for some classroom cooking! In this festive atmosphere, there are many new and exciting learning opportunities in the reading, math, and other skill area activities sections. We know that these ideas will help to make your holiday season a special time to remember—the children will keep coming back to tell you so!

Recommended Children's Books for December

Arthur's Christmas by Marc Brown (Boston: Little, Brown & Co., 1984). Another Arthur adventure. While all of the children are trying to figure out what they'll GET for Christmas, sensitive Arthur is fretting about finding just the right gift to GIVE to Santa. During shopping season, he keeps bumping into Santa Claus who is busy doing his own buying. From his observations, Arthur "puts together" a gift for Santa. D. W., Arthur's sister, learns a lesson in giving and saves the day.

Fourteen Rats and a Rat Catcher by James Cressy, illustrated by Tamasin Cole (Englewood Cliffs, NJ: Prentice-Hall, 1976). In a comfy, cozy cottage in the forest, there lived a nice old lady upstairs and a nice rat family downstairs. However, they did not get along. Even getting a big cat didn't solve the problem for the lady, so she called in a rat catcher, a creative problem-solver, and everyone lived happily ever after under the same roof. Lovely illustrations.

Babar and Father Christmas by Jean DeBrunhoff (New York: Random House, 1940). Zephir learns that a kind old gentleman with a large white beard, in a red suit, flies over the countryside on Christmas Eve and leaves toys for girls and boys. Babar decides to invite Father Christmas to Elephants' Country, and sets off on a trip that turns into a series of adventures before he tumbles into Santa's secret hideaway. Can Babar lure a tired, busy Santa away for Christmas? (One in a series of Babar books.)

Ed Emberly's A.B.C. by Ed Emberly (Boston: Little, Brown & Co., 1978). The emphasis in this alphabet book is upon the construction of the letters and upon a variety of items and things on each page that begin with the same letter and sound. Illustrations for each letter appear sequentially, each one showing a bit more of the letter until it is complete. For example, a big bear is patiently constructing the letter "b" with berries, a crow is constructing the letter "c" by eating his way through corn. The illustrations are bright, colorful, and whimsical—and children take delight in tracing the letter path. A good teaching book.

The Gorilla Did It by Barbara Shook Hazen, illustrated by Ray Cruz (New York: Atheneum, 1974). A little boy, alone in his room, is visited in his imagination by a gorilla and they have fun together but make a big mess in the process. When mother appears and asks who made the mess, of course "the gorilla did it." This pattern continues with the gorilla eventually promising to try to be good. Young children will identify with the imaginary companion.

Potato Pancakes All Around (A Hanukkah Tale) by Marilyn Hirsh (New York: Bonim Books, 1978). This delightful folk tale is in the "magic pot" category. A peddler appears at the door on the eve of Hanukkah with just the right recipe for potato pancakes—and he pulls only a crust of his bread from his pocket. He does, however, willingly take suggestions for adding a pinch of this and that, some eggs and grated potatoes, or latkes, and other ingredients. They turn out to be the very best potato pancakes! The book includes a recipe for the potato pancakes and a description of Hanukkah—the Festival of Lights.

Louie by Ezra Jack Keats (New York: Greenwillow Books, 1975). Louie, a young boy, never spoke aloud until he went to a puppet show. When he saw Gussie the puppet his face lit up and he answered. In fact, he was asked to sit down so the show could go on. Louie was so enthralled with the puppet that he hated to leave. Sadly, he went back home in silence. His friends, noting the change, do not let him down.

Odd One Out by Rodney Peppe (New York: Kestrel Books, 1974). In this bright colored picture book be on the alert for the item that does not belong. Peter has a busy day going from home, to school, to the zoo, to a toy shop, and to a variety of other places. Each event is portrayed on a two-page spread, but there is something odd in each scene, and the reader must discover what it is. An exercise in visual discrimination, and also in the concept of sets of like objects.

The Tiger Skin Rug by Gerald Rose (Englewood Cliffs, NJ: Prentice-Hall, 1979). An aging jungle tiger observes the warmth and comfort of the Rajah's palace and longs to join the family. One day, he sees a servant beating the dust from a line of rugs and spies an old tiger skin rug among them. He gets a bright idea, and drapes himself over the line in place of the other tiger skin. Thus, the tiger gets his wish and becomes a part of a loving family...and the fun begins.

On Mother's Lap **by Ann Herbert Scott, illustrated by Glo Coalson**

(New York: McGraw-Hill Book Co., 1972). Michael needs reassurance as he rocks back and forth on mother's lap. He finds that there's room for his boat and then for his puppy too. Then, the new baby cries and mother has to get up. She wants to bring baby to her lap but Michael says there's no room. Michael learns that mother's lap is special because it can make room for both him and the baby. Lovely Eskimo drawings for this universal tale.

Reading Skills Activities

Words and Colors

Holiday Symbols. December is a month filled with the exciting sights, smells, and tastes of wonderful holidays. The celebrations of both Hanukkah and Christmas offer many opportunities for activities that acquaint children with the traditional symbols of the season.

A Word Chart. With the children's help, write a list of holiday words on large sheets of chart paper. Illustrate each of the words with a simple rebus picture that will enable the students to readily identify the word. Go over the chart each day, spelling the words aloud. Some examples include:

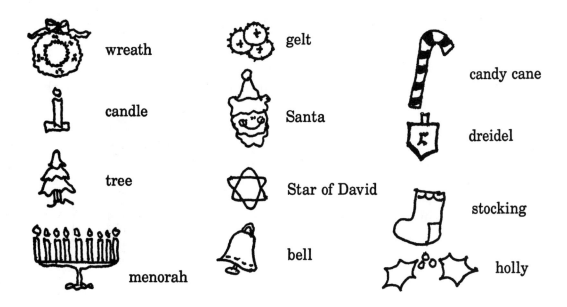

wreath

candle

tree

menorah

gelt

Santa

Star of David

bell

candy cane

dreidel

stocking

holly

Holiday Word Books. Students can make individual holiday books by writing a holiday word and drawing the symbol on each page. Covers for the books can be added by gluing wrapping paper to cardboard cut a little larger than the size of the pages. Staple the pages into the spine of the book.

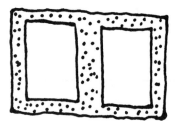 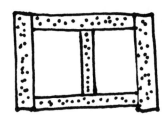 

A Holiday Matching Game. To make a holiday matching game, write each word and draw each holiday symbol on a separate 3″ × 5″ piece of oaktag. The game can be played during circle time by giving each child a card and asking him or her to find the child who holds the card that matches his/her own. The game can also be used in a learning center.

A Holiday Spelling Game. Make a holiday word spelling game by writing each word and drawing each holiday symbol on a separate 3″ × 5″ piece of oaktag. Keep each matching word and symbol in a separate envelope. Cut the word apart, letter by letter, and write the word on the front of the envelope. The students can look at the symbol and then reconstruct the word. Teach them to say the word aloud and then spell it aloud as they check the spelling with the front of the envelope.

Color Word Review. Since the holidays are so festive, it's a good time to look around the classroom and talk again about colors and the special color words that would describe the traditional symbols. Have the children think of all of the holiday things that are red, all of the holiday things that are green, all of the holiday things that are white, all of the holiday things that are yellow, and so on. Make lists of these items and have the boys and girls draw pictures to add to the charts. These lists could be used in special holiday books—the children could write the color word on a page and then draw holiday symbols that are that particular color.

A Circle Game. For a circle game, cover different-size boxes with various colors of kraft paper and tie with ribbons to resemble presents. On 3″ × 5″ cards, write the color words. Pass these out to the children in the circle and have the boys and girls come up and lay the correct color word on the matching present.

Letter Recognition

ABC Books. Read different alphabet books to the children and display them on a special table or bookcase in the classroom. Manipulative materials included in the display will reinforce the letter sequencing and identification skills. Suggested items might be alphabet blocks, foam letters, magnetic letters, and sandpaper letters. Cookie cutter letters and plasticene are also popular items.

Writing Alphabet Books. The children can make their own alphabet books by writing a capital and lower case letter on each page and then cutting pictures that begin with that letter and pasting them on the page. The pictures can be cut from magazines or drawn by the child. The books might be theme books—for instance, food alphabet books, animal alphabet books, the five senses alphabet books, holiday alphabet books, transportation alphabet books, farm alphabet books, or people alphabet books.

Class Alphabet Books. To make class alphabet books, write each child's name with a marker at the top of an 8½″ × 11″ sheet of white paper. Underline the first letter of the name. Ask the child to tell you something that begins with that letter and write at the bottom of the page, " (*letter*) is for (*child's word*)." The child can illustrate the word on the paper with crayons or markers. The pages can be punched and tied with yarn to make a class alphabet book. Not all letters will be represented.

A Sugar Cookie Alphabet. Prepare the following sugar cookie recipe and use tubes of icing to write the alphabet letters on the cookies:

Heat oven to 400°. Lightly grease baking sheet. Mix thoroughly: ½ cup soft shortening, 1 cup sugar, 1 teaspoon baking powder, ½ teaspoon salt, ½ teaspoon soda. Mix these dry ingredients into shortening mixture. Drop dough by rounded teaspoonfuls about 2 inches apart on baking sheet. Grease the bottom of a glass. To flatten each cookie, dip glass in sugar and press on dough.

Bake 8 to 10 minutes, or until a light golden brown.

Cool completely before icing.

Makes about 3 dozen cookies.

Special Letter Days (G, V, C, J, Z). It's time to bring out the picnic basket again but this time it can be a holiday basket. In the basket, arrange sets of holiday symbols with the letters attached: five ornaments with a letter attached to each; five dreidels with a letter attached to each; five gingerbread men with a letter attached to each; five pieces of gelt with a letter attached to each; five candles with a letter attached to each; five small wrapped presents with a letter attached to each.

Christmas Letters. Help the children make a Christmas list for each of the letters. Write the lists on large pieces of red or green kraft paper cut in the shape of a Christmas tree, a stocking, a bell, or any holiday symbol. The "G" list might include golf clubs, a geiger counter, a geyser, a go-cart, a gorilla, and a gumball machine. The "V" list might include a violin, violets, vines, vinegar, and a volcano. This lesson can serve as a language development time, as well.

Fill in What Is Missing. As the children become more familiar with the sequence of capital and lowercase letters and the sequence of numbers, begin leaving letters and numbers out of the sequence and ask that the students fill in what is missing. Write a series of letters or numerals on the chalkboard similar to the following: f _ hi _ k _ m _ o p, 3 _ 5 6 _ _ , r _ t _ v _ _ y _. Ask a child to come to the chalkboard and fill in the first missing letter or numeral. He/she can then be the "teacher" and choose another child to come up and fill in the next blank. The children also enjoy playing this game on small individual chalkboards with a friend. They can write their own series of letters and numerals, leaving blanks, and ask their partner to fill in the spaces.

Missing Letters in Words. Play the fill in what's missing game with color words, number words, and the children's names. For instance, on the chalkboard you might write: y_ L_ ow, re_ , bL _ k, or M_ry, Ja_on, Ji_m_. Ask children to tell you what belongs in the blanks or have them come up and fill in the blanks themselves.

Visual Discrimination

Visual discrimination is the ability to differentiate among visual patterns. It requires being able to see likenesses and differences in size, shape, and color. Because children at the readiness stage of development have difficulties distinguishing between letters that are similar (o and a, g and q, n and u, b and d), they need to be provided with opportunities to observe likenesses and differences among the things around them.

Patterns. Give the children a strip of wallpaper or wrapping paper that has an identifiable pattern and use a clothespin to clip it to a piece of white drawing paper. Ask the children to copy the pattern on the paper with their crayons. They can use the paper to wrap their gifts for their families and friends for the holidays.

Sorting. Ask the children to sort all farm animal pictures or figures into one box and all zoo animals into another. Give the children a box of old keys and ask them to sort the keys according to likenesses. Ask the children to use the separate compartments of an egg carton to sort buttons by color, size, shape, or number of holes.

Listening

When calling children to circle, to line up, or to special activities, use different questions or statements that will require them to listen and to think. The following are examples:

- If your name has an "a" in it, please line up.
- If you have the color yellow on, please come to circle.
- If your birthday is in March, please go to the art table.
- If you have a pet at home, please go to your seat.
- When I call your name, please tell me your favorite flavor of ice cream.
- If your daddy is bald, please come to circle.
- If you ride a bus to school, please walk to the door.
- When I call your name, please tell me your favorite book.

Math Skills Activities

Money

Holiday Shopping. Children love to look through catalogs, magazines, and newspapers at this time of year as they think about what they would like to buy for family members and what they hope that Santa will bring them for Christmas. It's a good time to talk about money—how much things cost and how the price of one thing compares to that of another. It's also an excellent opportunity for consumer education in a very simple way. Pick an item that is advertised in several places and cut out the ads. Glue them to a piece of construction paper. With real money, show the children how much money it would take to buy the item at the different stores. Ask them where they could buy the item and spend the *least* amount of money and where they could buy the item and spend the *most* money. Do this with several items. Talk about the advantages of comparison shopping and why some people would rather spend more for an item because of convenience.

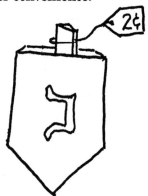

A Holiday Store. Turn the puppet theater or the playhouse into a holiday store and stock it with small Christmas and Hanukkah items—a little teddy bear, a box of potato latke mix, a dreidel, a holly wreath, a candy cane, a menorah, a stocking, a new box of crayons. Attach price tags to the objects, being sure to keep the prices within the understanding of the students—perhaps a few cents, nickels, and dimes. Use real or play money. The boys and girls can take turns being storekeepers and customers.

Graphing Sale Items. For practice with counting, have the children count the number of times a particular toy is advertised and graph the result. They might make a doll graph with different kinds of dolls represented and graph the number of times each of the dolls is advertised. (Consider a car graph, a truck graph, a train graph, a dollhouse graph, a pajama graph, etc.)

Numbers

Ordinal Numbers. Practice with understanding ordinal numbers can occur in a formal lesson or informally. As the children sit in circle, arrange a row of magnets, oaktag teddy bears with magnetic tape on the back, or oaktag pine trees and dreidels with magnetic tape on the back. Choose a child to go to the chalkboard and follow your directions. "Point to the fifth tree. Point to the first teddy bear. Point to the second magnet." It is important that this abstract concept be reinforced with concrete manipulatives. Picking which object is in a particular ordinal position involves the understanding of counting from left to right, so it is helpful to children to explain that we always begin counting at the left.

Practicing with Concrete Objects. To practice this skill at the semi-concrete level, give each child a piece of white drawing paper and a lima bean. Show them how to draw five simple stick chairs in a row across the paper. Tell them that the lima beans are pets and that they must follow your directions. "Put your pet lima bean *on* the first chair. Put your pet lima bean *under* the third chair. Put your pet lima bean *in front of* the fifth chair."

A Circle Game. The boys and girls can play the game with partners in the circle. Give each pair of children an envelope with five peppermints wrapped in cellophane. They can lay the candies in a row and then give each other directions similar to the ones given in the chalkboard game.

Ordinal Reinforcement. There are many informal times during the school day to give ordinal reinforcement. As the boys and girls line up on the playground, you can go down the row and say, "You are the first child, you are the second child, you are the third child," and so on. The same thing can be done in circle, as the class lines up for special activities, or as they come to the door to go home.

Shapes

It's a good idea to review shapes this time of year just to make sure that everyone has mastered the concept. The boys and girls will enjoy making a shape book to take home and share with their family. Provide them with shape patterns to trace on construction paper. They can cut out these shapes and paste them on pieces of 8½ × 11" white drawing paper to make pictures. A rectangle and two circles might be a wagon. A square and a triangle might be a house. Ask the children to sound out the word that represents their picture and write it at the bottom of the page. Put the pages together, add a cover, and staple the left side to make a book. The children can share these books in circle or in small groups.

Measuring and Following Directions

Festive Recipes. Cooking special recipes at school is such fun that children don't realize that they're actually learning to measure and follow directions. The following recipes are good ones to use this time of year:

POTATO LATKES

4 potatoes, grated

1 egg

1 small onion, grated

a dash of salt

1 tablespoon of flour

Mix all ingredients well, then drop by large rounded spoonfuls onto a hot skillet (greased generously with melted margarine). Fry on both sides until brown. Serve piping hot with sour cream or applesauce.

GINGERBREAD MEN

Simmer for 15 minutes: 1 cup molasses and 1 cup shortening

Cream together: 1 cup sugar, 1 egg, and 1 teaspoon vanilla

Dissolve: 2 teaspoons soda in ½ cup hot water

Add hot water and soda mixture to sugar and egg.

Sift together: 6 cups flour, ½ teaspoon cloves, 1 teaspoon cinnamon, 1 teaspoon salt, and ½ teaspoon ginger

Add to other mixtures and stir until flour is well mixed.

Roll thin and cut with a cookie cutter. Bake 10 minutes at 375°. Decorate. (This dough does not stick to the pan so a child can handle it.)

STAINED GLASS COOKIES

1 cup margarine	2 teaspoons vanilla
1 cup shortening	5 cups flour
1 cup sugar and ¼ cup honey	1 teaspoon baking soda
(or 2 cups sugar)	1 teaspoon salt
2 eggs	

Mix margarine, shortening, sugar, honey, eggs and vanilla. Add flour, soda, and salt. Add flour and then chill the dough overnight. On waxed paper, roll out the dough, and cut shapes with cookie cutters. Then cut out areas for "windows"—or roll the dough into "snakes." Shape the snakes into cookie shapes, leaving some spaces open. Place the cookies on a well-greased cookie sheet. Fill the openings with crushed hard candies or a whole breath mint. Bake at 350° for 7 to 8 minutes. Let cookies cool for five minutes before removing them from the cookie sheet.

RICE PUDDING

2 cups milk

3 tablespoons rice

3 tablespoons sugar

¼ teaspoon salt

½ teaspoon vanilla

⅛ teaspoon nutmeg

⅛ teaspoon cinnamon

¼ cup raisins

Mix and put in a one-quart casserole. Bake 2½ hours or until rice is cooked. Stir occasionally during baking.

HIDDEN JEWELS

Heat oven to 350°. Grease well an oblong pan, 13 × 9½ × 2 inches.

Beat in a bowl with a rotary egg beater: 4 egg yolks

Stir in: 2¼ cups brown sugar (packed), 1 tablespoon water, 1 teaspoon vanilla

Stir together in another bowl: 2 cups flour, 1 teaspoon baking powder, ½ teaspoon salt.

With kitchen scissors that have been dipped in water, finely cut up 1 cup multicolored gumdrops.

Mix the dry ingredients into egg mixture. Stir in gumdrops and ¾ cup walnuts. Beat in small bowl with rotary egg beater until stiff but not dry: 4 egg whites

Stir beaten egg whites into cookie dough. Spread in prepared pan.

Bake 30 to 35 minutes. Cool in pan 20 minutes; cut into bars.

Makes about 3 dozen bars.

Other Skill Areas Activities

Hanukkah

Hanukkah celebrates the great victory of the Jewish people over a cruel king. It is referred to as the "Festival of the Lights." Some of the customs associated with Hanukkah are: the lighting of a candle in the menorah each of the eight nights of Hanukkah; playing the dreidel game; making potato latkes and serving them with sour cream or applesauce; the giving of gifts.

Hanukkah

A Hanukkah Menorah. Make a large classroom menorah from kraft paper and glue it on a large piece of tagboard. Cut candles from construction paper and have the children put one on the menorah for each day of the holiday celebration.

Sharing Traditions. Ask any parents of Jewish children in the classroom to come and share some of their family holiday customs and traditions with the other boys and girls. Make a list of the customs on large chart paper.

The Dreidel Game. Have the children form a circle and ask two children to stand in the middle and pretend to be tops. They whirl and spin while music is being played. After they have had a turn, select two more children to take their places.

Hanukkah Books. Find books about Hanukkah in the library to read to the children. Then display the books in the classroom so that the children may look at them during the day.

Cooking Latkes. Celebrate Hanukkah by cooking potato latkes (see math section for recipe) and serving them with applesauce. The children can make special Hanukkah hats by taking a strip of yellow or purple paper that fits around their head, stapling it, and drawing a Star of David on the front of the headband.

Christmas

Christmas is a holiday celebrated around the world by Christian people. The Christmas season has many traditions including a visit from Santa Claus, Christmas trees, lights and candles, carols and songs, and the giving of gifts. In different countries, there are a variety of customs.

Holiday Traditions. Ask the children to share their family holiday traditions and write them on a large sheet of chart paper. For a holiday gift for families, combine this list with the Hanukkah list, type them and put them together in a booklet for each child to take home. The children can decorate the cover with their favorite holiday symbols.

Holiday Fingerpainting. Make red and green fingerpaintings and mount them on white cardboard to use as gifts or as wrapping paper.

Cookie Presents. Help the children bake cookies and wrap them for school helpers. School personnel love to receive these gifts.

Pine Cone Ornaments. Use the pine cones that the children collected for the fall counting activities and make tree ornaments. Hold the pine cones over a flat box lid and sprinkle it with glue. Then shake glitter over the pine cone to "dust" the edges with sparkle. Let the pine cones dry overnight. The next day, tie a piece of yarn or colorful string around the small end of the pine cone with a loop to hand over the tree branch.

A Rudolph Puppet. Make a Rudolph hand puppet by folding a 12″ × 18″ piece of brown construction paper in half lengthwise. Staple the long side shut, leaving the two ends open. Fold over the top third of the strip to form the head. Fold an 8½″ × 11″ piece of black paper in half. Have the children put  their hand on this sheet and trace around it with a yellow or white crayon and then cut it out, forming two antlers. Cut two blue round circle eyes and a big red oval nose. Paste the antlers at the top of the head and the eyes and nose on the folded part. Rudolph is ready to lead Santa's sleigh.

Winter

Winter Begins. Talk with the boys and girls about the winter season—what they wear in winter, what sports they play in winter, what happens to the weather in winter, what happens to plants and animals in winter, what foods we eat in winter, what special health problems might we have in winter. Just as people change the type of clothing that they wear in winter, so do animals. Their fur coats get thicker in cold weather to protect them from winter storms and chill. Smaller animals seek shelter in trees, in old  stumps, and underground. Larger animals hide in caves or thick forests where the trees can protect them from the cold wind. They huddle together so their bodies stay warmer.

A Winter Mural. Make a winter mural on blue kraft paper. Use white paint to add snow. Make trees from black construction paper with tiny bits of cotton glued to the tree branches for snow. Draw and cut out winter animals and people dressed for winter and add these to the mural. Have the children dictate a story about a winter day and display this with the picture.

A Winter List. Make a list of all of the clothes that could be worn in winter to protect adults and children from the bitter cold. Discuss the places in our country where it is warm all year round and people would not have to wear the clothes on the list.

Name _____

WARM UP WITH HOT CHOCOLATE

It's cold outside this month so come inside and warm up with a cup of hot chocolate with marshmallows. Before you can drink the chocolate, you must first get the marshmallows in the cups by drawing a line from the capital letter on each cup to the lowercase letter on the correct marshmallow. Trace over the letters. Color the pictures with warm colors.

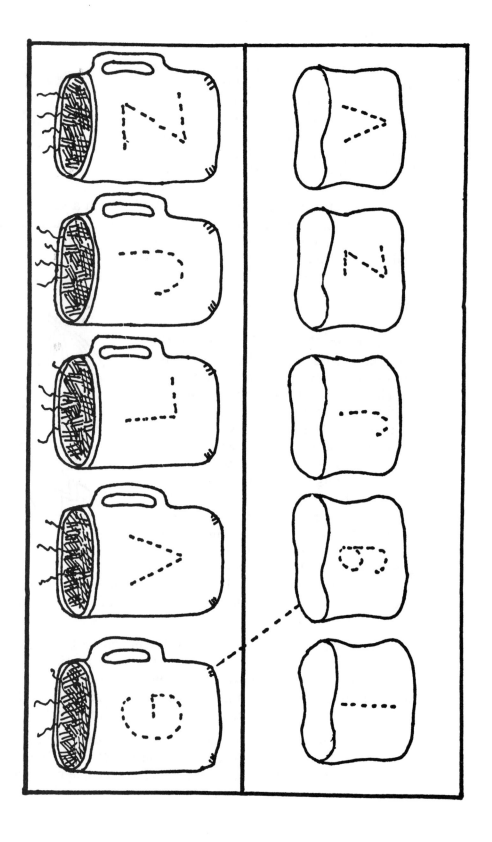

A DECEMBER CONCENTRATION GAME

Each of the boxes below contains a picture or word about December. Color each picture and cut the boxes apart on the lines. To play the memory game: Lay the cards face down and turn over two cards at a time. If the cards match, you may keep them. If the cards don't match, turn them back over. Your turn is over. Try to remember where each word or picture is hidden as the other players take their turns. The person with the most matches wins the game.

Name _____

A HOLIDAY COLOR BOOK

Ask an adult to help you read the directions for each page of the color book. The little drawing in the corner of each page will remind you what you are to draw. Draw the correct picture on each page and then cut the pages apart on the black lines. Put the pages in the correct order and staple the booklet at the left side.

1 MY HOLIDAY COLOR WORD BOOKLET Name _____	2 COLOR GREEN HOLLY
3 COLOR A RED STOCKING	4 COLOR A YELLOW PRESENT
5 COLOR A PURPLE CANDLE	6 COLOR A GREEN PINE TREE

Name

NUMBER STOCKINGS

These stockings are all hung by the chimney with care, waiting for Santa to arrive. They are hung in order but some of the numerals are missing. As you look at each row of stockings, trace over the numerals that are there and fill in the missing numerals. Check your work by counting.

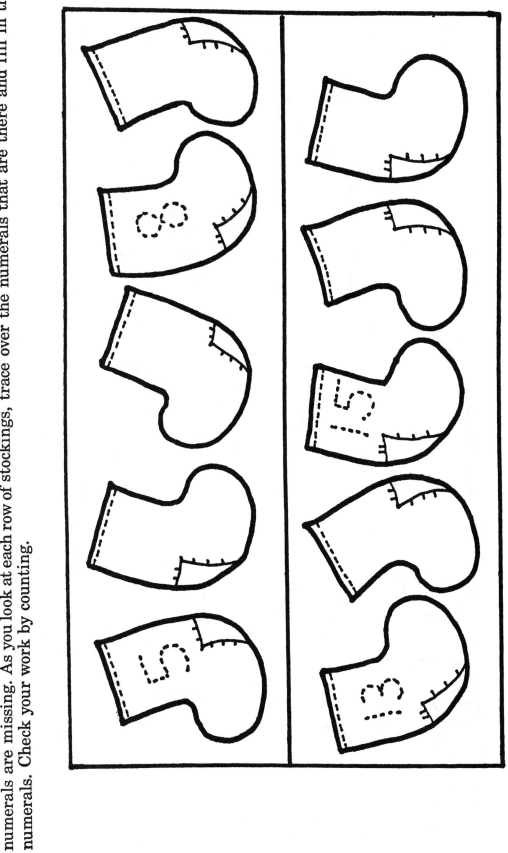

A HOLIDAY TEDDY

Color this holiday teddy. Make him look festive. Cut him out on the black lines. Attach his arms and legs with paper fasteners at the Xs.

A HANUKKAH BOOK

Hanukkah is a special time for the Jewish people. You can make a little booklet filled with Hanukkah things. Color the pictures and then cut the pages apart on the black lines. Put the pages in order. Staple the book on the left side.

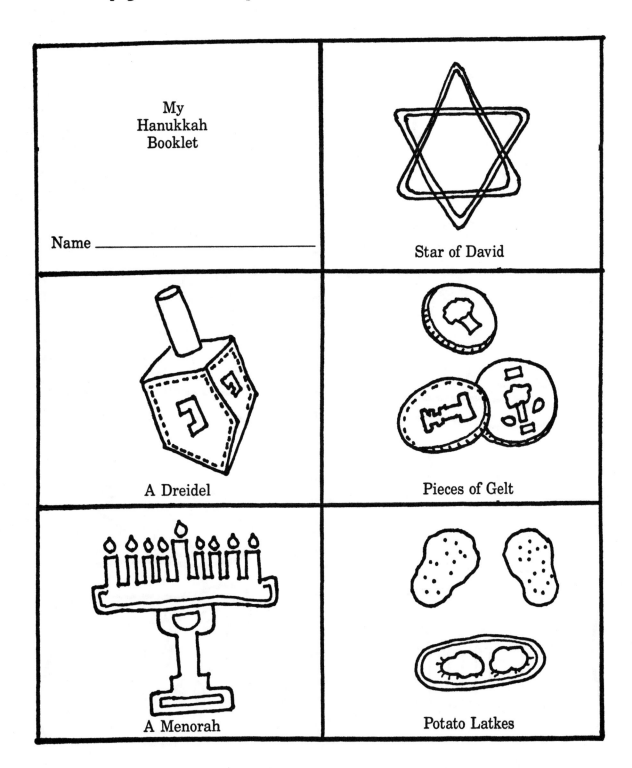

My
Hanukkah
Booklet

Name _____

Star of David

A Dreidel

Pieces of Gelt

A Menorah

Potato Latkes

HOW MANY HOLIDAY THINGS?

Count the number of holiday things in each of the boxes and then draw a line to the correct numeral. Color the pictures. Each box contains a set of objects. How many sets are on this page?

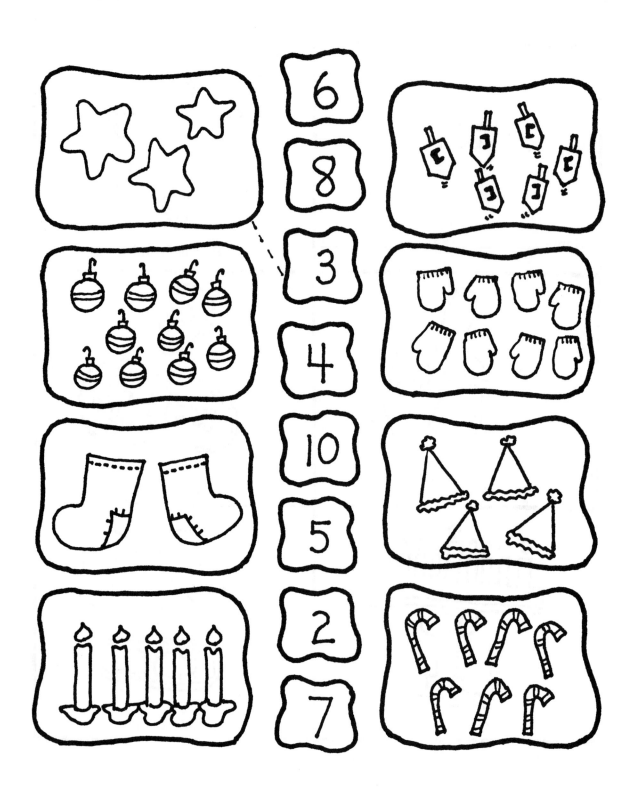

A HOLLY BERRY MAN

This holly berry man is a symbol of Christmas. Color him green with red berries. Cut him out on the black lines. Put him together with paper fasteners by attaching his arms and legs at the Xs.

FATHER CHRISTMAS LETTER FILL-IN

Father Christmas is here to wish you a happy holiday. Trace over the letters on his body and fill in the missing lowercase letters. Color Father Christmas in holiday colors.

A HANUKKAH DREIDEL

The dreidel game is a popular one during Hanukkah. The children play it with a dreidel top and gelt. Make this dreidel by coloring it and then cutting it out on the black lines. Cut slits on the dotted lines. Slip the two parts together. To play the game, spin the top to see which sign lands facing upward. The signs mean: NUN you get nothing; GIMEL you take all of the pot; HAI you take half the pot; SHIN you must put in 1 gelt.

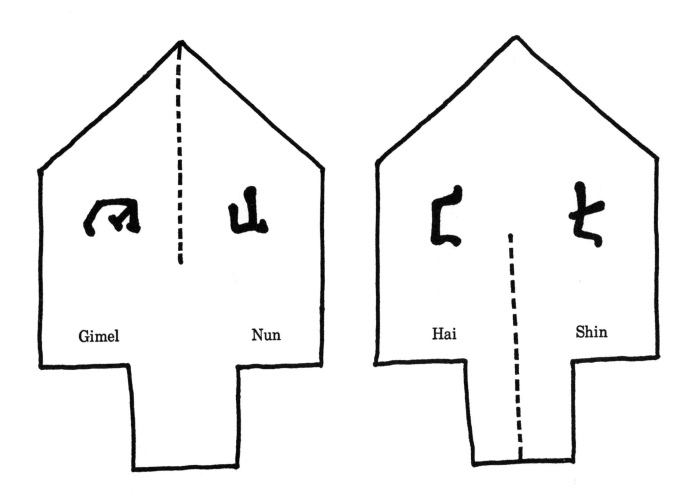

Gimel   Nun   Hai   Shin

Name _____

IT'S WINTER WEATHER

These sets of winter things are ready for counting. Count the number of winter objects in each set and then write the numeral that tells how many in the little box. Color the pictures.

Name _____

WINTER BIRDS

Some birds stay in cold climates during the winter and don't fly south. Several birds have stopped on this tree to nibble at tiny pinecones. Follow these directions:

Draw *three red*  .

Draw *four blue* .

Draw *two brown* .

Color the tree *green*.

MAKE A WINTER BIRD

What kind of birds stay around your house during the winter months? Color the bird below to look like the birds in your area. Cut the bird and wings out and then cut the two slits in the body. Fold the body on the dotted line and slip the wings through the slits. Punch a hole in the bird's back and tie a piece of yarn through so that the bird can hang.

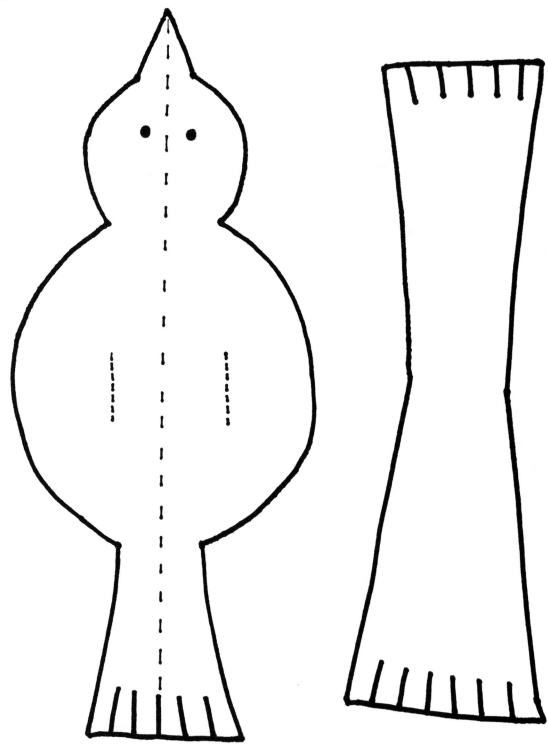

A JINGLE BELL NECKLACE

Santa's reindeer each wear jingle bell necklaces so that you can hear them coming. This necklace has nine jingle bells. Trace over the numeral on each bell and then draw a line from each bell to the correct number word. On the back of this paper, practice writing your numerals.

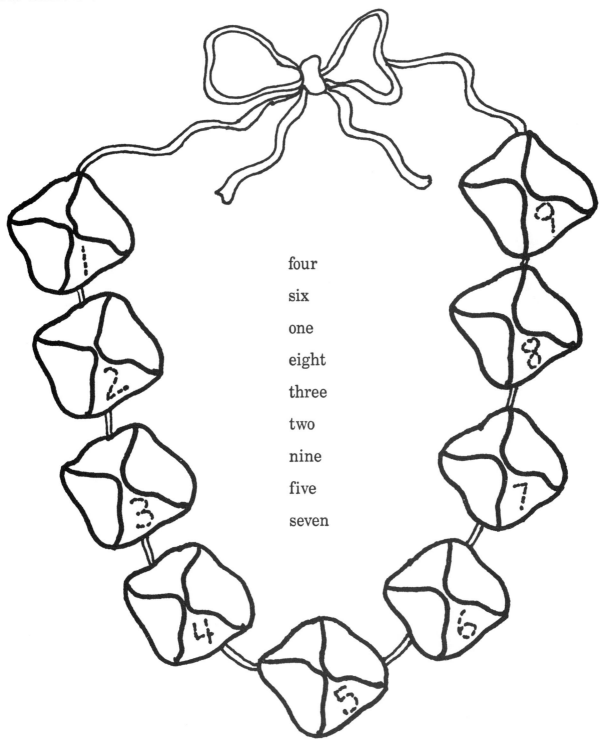

four

six

one

eight

three

two

nine

five

seven

JANUARY

A Blizzard of Winter Experiences

January is a good time to re-establish routines and to review and reinforce what has been learned so far. Those delightful Teddy Bears are "beary" happy to be back again to help. The reading, math, and other special areas offer a variety of review activities and also turn the spotlight on winter—with its snowflakes, sports, animal hibernation, and a general "blizzard" of winter-day experiences for the young learner.

Recommended Children's Books for January

What Is Black? by Bettye F. Baker, photographs by Willis Perry II (New York: Franklin Watts, Inc., 1969). This book helps children to identify in a positive way with the color black. The black and white photos of objects such as a black puppy that you can count on as a friend being held by a black child, a photo of a black tree trunk perfect for climbing, and black licorice sticks that you hope won't end, gives the reader an exploration into all aspects of the color black.

Little Bear's New Year's Party by Janice Brustlein, pictures by Mariana (New York: Lothrop, Lee & Shepard, Co., 1973). Little Bear is not invited to a New Year's party, but then neither is Mouse, Owl, Squirrel, or Sparrow. Owl knows all about New Year's parties, though, so the animals come up with a cooperative solution. Children get caught up in the excitement of party planning and sharing a celebration.

Loudmouth George and the Sixth Grade Bully by Nancy Carlson (Minneapolis: Carolrhoda Books, Inc., 1983). George, a young rabbit, is excited about going to school but Big Mike, a sixth grade bear, repeatedly bullies him into giving up his lunch. This practice continues until Harriet Bear, George's friend, learns of his dilemma and comes up with a creative solution to the problem.

We Read A to Z by Donald Crews (New York: Greenwillow Books, 1967). An excellent book that deals with math concepts and color, along with the ABCs. The bright, bold illustrations convey concepts such as shape, position, size, and quantity. It is a delightful teaching book that children can use repeatedly for the alphabet as well as for a variety of learnings.

What Do You See? by Janina Domanska (New York: Macmillan Publishing Co., 1974). What does the world look like to you? Ask a frog and it's wet, ask a fly and it's full of spiders. Ask someone else and you get their point of view. Maybe it's all of those things. Bright, fanciful illustrations.

The Pooh Cook Book by Virginia H. Ellison, illustrations by Ernest H. Shepard (New York: Dell Publishing Co., A Yearling Book, 1976). This little gem is filled with a variety of easy-to-make recipes for breakfast, smackerels, elevenses, teas, picnics, and special parties. There is also a variety of delicious honey sauces. This book will make cooking with children a delight! Another treat is the way illustrations and sayings from *Winnie the Pooh* and *The House on Pooh Corner* are interspersed among the recipes.

Why Couldn't I Be an Only Kid Like You, Wigger? by Barbara Shook Hazen, pictures by Leigh Grant (New York: Atheneum, 1975). A boy from a large family compares himself with Wigger, who is an only child. On the other hand, Wigger is getting a good look at life in a big family. This "grass is always greener on the other side of the fence" tale could be the start of a good class discussion on the subject.

Clocks and More Clocks by Pat Hutchins (New York: Macmillan Publishing Co., 1970). Mr. Higgins has many, many clocks in his home, but they all are minutes apart and so he brings in an expert clock repairman who inspects all of the clocks, and finds them all to be in good working condition. How can they ALL be correct?

The Snowy Day by Ezra Jack Keats (New York: Puffin Books, 1978). A small boy named Peter experiences the joy of the first snowfall. When he awakes in the morning, everything is covered with fresh snow. After breakfast, he dresses warmly and "experiences snow." The colorful illustrations enable the reader to experience the day's activities right along with Peter. (Caldecott Award Winner.)

One Way: A Trip with Traffic Signs by Leonard Shortall (Englewood Cliffs, NJ: Prentice-Hall, Inc., 1975). A family sets out on a vacation and sees many directional signs along the way. Each page is filled with traffic signs, store signs, billboards, and many rebus signs. The text is in verse. Children enjoy the visual excitement of this **trip** and the book can be used to sharpen awareness and to encourage reading. Everyone is bound to be able to "read" some of the signs.

Reading Skills Activities

Letter/Sound Review

The Mitten Match. If students have been exposed to the complete alphabet, this is a good time for review. If they have been exposed only to specific letters chosen for the Special Letter Days in each reading section so far, it is still an excellent time for review. Because of the holiday period, children have been away from formal instruction and will need to review the letter sounds and configurations again and again. MATERIALS NEEDED: A clothesline, clothespins, clothes basket, real mittens (possibly borrowed from the school Lost & Found box), or paper cutouts in the shape of mittens. PROCEDURE: Tape an uppercase letter and matching lowercase letter on each pair of mittens. It would be helpful to pin or paste a picture on each mitten to reinforce the beginning letter sound. String the clothesline just above eye level, and place all of the mittens in a clothes basket. Children can hang up all of the upper- and lowercase mittens for a complete mitten match.

VARIATION: Have one group of children hang up all of the mittens with uppercase letters, and then have another group hang the mittens with the matching lowercase letter to the right of the mitten (or on top of it).

VARIATION: Write a letter of the alphabet on each clothespin. Children can search not only for the matching mitten set, but also for the matching clothespin and use it for hanging mittens on the line.

VARIATION: Hang five mittens on the line. Children must find the letter that comes before and the letter that comes after it, and hang them on the line in correct order.

VARIATION: Bring in a variety of other real matching items for the clothes basket and pin letters to them, so they can be hung up. (For example, shirt, hat, pants, towel, washcloth, jacket, etc.)

Teddy Bear Reunion. It's a brand new year, and the teddy bears that visited in September can return during January for a reunion. This time, they are to bring something with them—an alphabet letter. If they don't bring it with them, they can make one at school. Have children select their "favorite letter" and be able to tell us one, two, or three items that begin with that sound. Can they think of a word that ENDS with that sound? Does their letter appear in the name of our month? Pin the letter on each teddy bear, and line them up all in a row, in ABC order. Are all of the letters represented? If not, let's make a paper teddy bear for each letter not represented, and make the letter for the bear to hold. Now we can practice writing all of the letters.

A Teddy Bear ABC Board. Make a cutout in the shape of a teddy bear for each letter of the alphabet, and print the uppercase letter on with a felt pen. Then, glue all of the bears in alphabetical order on a huge piece of oaktag. Next, make a matching set of bears for the lowercase letters. Children can match up the letters.

Pooh's Suitcase ABC Game. MATERIALS: Magazines, scissors, a real suitcase. PROCEDURE: First, have the children go through the magazines and find large pictures for each letter of the alphabet. Cut them out and paste them on cards. (Laminate them if possible.) Give a letter card to each child. Gather around the suitcase in the form of a big circle. Then say, "Pooh Bear is going on vacation and he's taking something with him that begins with the letter _____ and sounds like _____ (say a word). Who will put it in the suitcase?" Child with that card can come up, repeat the letter sound, tell what is on the card, and drop it into the suitcase. When everyone has had a turn, close the suitcase. Go back and forth through the ABCs and try to remember what Pooh is going to take.

VARIATION: "Pooh is going on a boat. Can you find a picture of something in the suitcase that begins with the sound of boat?" (Repeat for all letter sounds.)

VARIATION: "Pooh is now going to unpack his suitcase, but look, the letters got all jumbled up. Let's try to remember what Pooh packed in his suitcase." (Review and have the child who packed the item search for it with a friend.)

VARIATION: "Pooh is going to swim. What will he need that begins with the letter "s" and sounds like "sand"? (Find it.) "Pooh is going to visit a friend, what will he take that begins with the letter _____ and sounds like _____?" (Find it.) Do this for half of the letters, then look to see what is left and review them.

VARIATION: Use real items (honey, jacket, slippers, towel, book, etc.). Children can bring in the items they think a bear would take on a vacation.

VARIATION: After several formal sessions with the suitcase and the ABC review, make the suitcase available to children during play time as another option. This is excellent drill in the form of a game.

Hibernation Concentration. Hibernation is the long winter sleep of many animals. Make animal name cards (bear, squirrel, turtle, fox, beaver, mouse, etc.) and tie each end with string. Discuss the animals and how they spend the winter months. Put the tags around each child's neck. Then, have children follow instructions such as: "All foxes skip into the den," "All bears crawl into their cave," "All turtles dig into the pond mud," "All squirrels climb into your tree nest," "All mice scurry under the big rocks," etc. Now we are all resting during the long winter. Then, when the teacher (or a child leader) holds up a large picture of an animal group, they can get up and stretch, move, and go back to sleep. Repeat.

VARIATION: The teacher, or a child leader, can say "I'm thinking of an animal that begins with "s" and ends with "l" and you can come out now and sit in the circle." More hints include: "I'm thinking of an animal that begins with the same sound as "SSSix" and ends with the same sound as "biLLLL," and you can come out now."

VARIATION: To get everyone back into a circle, hold up a large picture of their hibernation location, i.e., cave (bear), tree (squirrel), etc.

Hibernation Booklets. Make hibernation booklets in the shape of one of the animals. The children can draw the different animals on each page, and print the animal's name at the bottom.

Letter Recognition

Special Letter Days (C, Q, Y, X, Z). Use the same basket that you have been using for the letter items, but use a colorful new cloth for the new year. As previously, work with one letter at a time on the special day of the week. Some suggested items for children to touch and talk about are:

C: Explain that "c" is rather special because it borrows its sounds from two other letters who are very good friends. First, work with the hard sound as in "k." Next, work with the soft sound as in "s." (This should be two separate lessons.)

C   (as in the sound of "k") comb, calendar, coins, carrot, cabbage
C   (as in the sound of "s") celery, one-cent piece, cereal, cement

C c   comb (k)   celery (s)

Q: Explain that the letter "q" rarely goes out without its good friend "u." As the items are lifted from the basket, print them on the board, so that children can see which the "qu" combination, that sounds like "kw."

Q   queen, question mark, quilt, quarter, quart container

Other "qu" words to elicit from children are: quick, quack-quack, quiver. Then, one day put in a box of "Q-tips" (brand name) to show that the "qu" rule does not always hold true. Every rule has an exception. (Children need to begin getting used to that concept as they develop pre-reading skills. Sometimes the phonetic rules just don't work for us, so we try another approach.)

Y   yellow yarn, yam, yucca, yo-yo

X: Explain that the letter "x" uses a different sound when it comes at the ending of a word than it does when it comes at the beginning of a word. At the ending, the "x" is a combination of two sounds—the letter "k" and the letter "s" as in "ks." Repeat it several times.

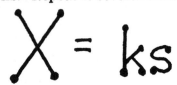

X (ending)   toy ax, flax, Max
Explain that when the letter "x" is at the beginning of a word, it SOME-TIMES uses its name ("eks").

X (beginning)   x-ray, Xmas

and it SOMETIMES borrows the "zzzz" sound from the letter "z" as in

X (beginning)   xylophone

Print the word "Xerox" on the board and pronounce it as "ZZZ ear oKS." In this brand name the "x" is really playing a game with us because it is using both sounds in the very same word. (Again, pre-readers need to at least be exposed to the inconsistencies in letter/sound relationships.)

Z   zero, zipper, (pictures of) zebra, zoo

Story Writing

Sponge Painting. MATERIALS: 12″ × 18″ navy blue construction paper, white paint, tiny sponges.

PROCEDURE: (1) Children can crayon a snowy day picture (snowman, winter sport, winter birds in the woods) and then dab white paint all over it with sponges to depict a snow squall, or (2) children can sponge paint (or brush paint) a snowman, tree, animal, with the glistening white paint (add a pinch of salt) on a dark contrasting background. Students can describe what is going on in their painting, and this can be dictated to an adult or older student, and printed on paper, and attached to the bottom of the painting. Young children can then trace the story letters. REMINDER: With children, we never ask what it is, but rather, say, "Tell me something about your painting," or "My! What a lot of action, tell me about it," or "How nice! I can't wait to see what you're going to have me write about this." The adult can call attention to the letters and words being printed as he/she goes along and ask the child to repeat them.

VARIATION: If you'd like to give the students a different painting experience, and if you want your classroom to smell fresh and clean, use soap flakes with water added instead of white tempera paint for this activity.

A Shape Book of Snowy Day Words. Make a "Shape Book of Snowy Day Words." Using the simple snowman with hat shape, cut out six shapes for each student, and staple together at the top of the hat. If using colored paper, use only white chalk dipped in water for illustrations and words. If using white paper, work with blue crayon or felt pen. Elicit "snowy day words" from the children, one per page, and illustrate and label them, for example, snowman, snow boots, snow sled, snow shovel, snowstorm, snowflakes, snow cones, snow tires, etc.

Story Sequencing

Let's Review. Each day immediately following story time, review the story. Ask what happened first, next, last. Review stories that are read daily for beginning, middle, and ending. Distribute strips of paper that have been folded into thirds. Have children draw or color beginning, middle, and ending scenes. Print the title very low on the chalkboard. Have children turn their paper over, come up to the chalkboard, place their paper strip under the story title, and copy the title onto their paper.

A Rebus Story. On large chart paper, print a rebus story about the Teddy Bear Reunion that students have dictated. Cut it into beginning, middle, and ending sections. Have children piece it together. OR, cut it into still smaller segments and have children piece it together. Type this story (primary typewriter), or print it, and make two ditto copies for each child. One can be the storyboard, and one can be cut up into smaller story sections, so that children can practice story sequencing at home.

Do "round robin" storytelling. Begin a story and have children add to it. Then have children retell the story sequentially.

Language Experience

Hurray for Winnie the Pooh. A. A. Milne's birthday on January 18, calls for a Teddy Bear Celebration. Since all teddy bears who attended school in September have been invited to return (each bringing a letter of the alphabet), this is a special event. Children will need to learn that A. A. Milne was the author of the Winnie the Pooh stories.

Happy New Year/Happy Birthday Cards. Make Happy New Year cards from Winnie the Pooh and send them to the principal, school librarian, secretary, nurse, and other staff members. If you have any extras, send one to the school superintendent and one to the mayor. You can also have the children make a large birthday card from Winnie the Pooh and send it to the bears at the local zoo, in care of the zoo director. The children can make birthday cards from Winnie the Pooh to all of the children in the school (or in the class) with January birthdays.

Teddy Bear Books. Make teddy bear books in the shape of a teddy bear. Illustrate the book by showing some of Pooh's very good friends (Tiger, Eeyore, and Owl, for example). On one page, of course, include a special recipe.

Reading to the Bears. Arrange to have a special storytime with the school librarian. Perhaps a story, record, or filmstrip could be included. Read stories about Winnie the Pooh to children. List his qualities. Then read picture books about other bears and make comparisons.

Party Recipes. To make "Pooh Snowballs," use an ice cream scoop for one dip of vanilla ice cream for each child. Roll the ice cream in white coconut. Insert each ball into a plastic bag and put each child's name on a bag. Freeze the filled bags. Later, serve the "snowballs" in cones or cups. To make "Pooh Tea," add lemonade and honey to a pot of hot water. Serve from the teapot with toast squares and jam.

Math Skills Activities

Graphing

Calendar Activities. On a huge bulletin board, make a giant grid for the January calendar. Each day, have the children print in the numeral and a symbol for the weather at that moment (for example, sun, umbrella, snowman, clouds, etc.). Every Monday, ask the students to recall what the weather was like on Saturday and Sunday, and have children add the symbols. (Outlining the symbols with black crayon makes them more readily visible from a distance.) At the end of each week, count the number of sunny days, cloudy days, wet days, etc. At the end of the month, count the number of different symbols that are represented. Count the number for each symbol and on a large sheet of chart paper, make a giant graph of January weather. Put your data collection sheet (calendar) and graph together so that students can "verify" the information. (Don't destroy this activity. Use it to hang up in the hall for Spring Open House as a sample of the mathematical procedures that you are having children experience, such as collecting and recording data, and representing information by way of graphs and charts.)

VARIATION: Numerals can be pre-cut, and students can sift through a container to find the correct numeral (identification) rather than writing it (recall), and tack it onto the board.

VARIATION: Use this giant calendar for counting the number of days in the month, and the number of days in each week. How many children's birthdays do we have in this month? (The children can color their birthday cakes in top left corner of these blocks.) How many special holidays this month? (A child can color a symbol in bottom left corner of that block.)

Use the calendar DAILY in a routine manner so that children will become accustomed to the idea that we keep records using numerals and that we are DOING MATH NOW!

One-to-One Correspondence

One-to-one correspondence, or simple enumeration, refers to the process of identifying the number of a set by matching the items or elements of the set with the number names expressed in order, such as "1, 2, 3, 4, 5" until each element has been named. Children can gain practice in the following ways:

- Make a set of cards from 1 to 10 using snowmen and hats. Print the numeral on the hat, and match it up with the correct number of buttons on the snowman.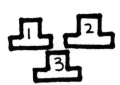

- Make a set of cards from 11 to 20 using bears and honey pots. Print the numeral on the honey pot, and match it up with the correct number of spots on the bear.

- Make a set of cards from 1 to 7, using snowballs and shovels. Print the numeral on the shovel, and match it up with the correct pile of snowballs.

- Make a large set of shovels (cardboard rectangle and handle), and print the numerals 8 to 15 on the shovel handles. Get a bag of cotton balls to represent "snowballs." Have children pile the correct number of snowballs on the shovel. (Cotton snowballs and shovels can be kept in a pail.)

- Ask all of the children to take off their shoes. Put all of the left shoes in a row, and all of the right shoes in a pile. Each child can take a shoe from the pile, and match it to the correct left shoe.

- Put numerals 1 to 25 (or more if there are more students in class) on tiny sheets of paper. Have each child select one and tell his number aloud so that it can be recorded after his name on a sign-up sheet. Then, at the easel, each child gets a chance to paint his HUGE numeral right in the middle of the page. Allow them to dry. Distribute the pages and children can make the appropriate number of items around the numeral (some children may need to work in pairs). Before children draw the items, talk about the way they could be grouped (by twos, fives, tens for easier counting) but if they prefer to make the items at random that, too, is acceptable. This could be turned into a giant number book for the month of January.

Sizes and Shapes

Big and Little. Match BIG/LITTLE using real items. Get two medium-size plastic tubs and label one "Big" and the other "Little." Have children reach into a paper bag, remove items, and sort the items into pairs. Place the items in the appropriate bin. Suggested items are: paintbrushes, baskets, pencils, erasers, crayons, teddy bears, books, candles, balls of yarn, plastic containers, cereal boxes, milk containers, styrofoam shapes, plastic balls, etc. Items can be checked by returning them in PAIRS to the paper bag.

Match BIG/LITTLE using semi-concrete items. Make a set of cards that has both a big and little picture of the same item. Children can match them. (For example: Match pictures of large house and small house.)

Shapes. Matching SHAPES using real items. Review the basic shapes of square, rectangle, circle. Using these three categories, have children reach into a container and sort the items. Suggested items are: various size blocks, jar lids, box tops, empty food boxes and tins, embroidery hoop, compass, clock, brick, floor tile, place mats, wreaths, styrofoam shapes, etc.

Match SHAPES using semi-concrete items. Make a set of cards that has five shapes—square, rectangle, circle, triangle, and oval. Cut out pictures of items that clearly represent these shapes, and make another card set by pasting these items on the cards. Children can match them. (Place basic shape cards in a row and put matching pictures above or below them. For example: Match picture of iron to triangle shape.)

Prediction

Explain that when we "predict" outcomes, we are using all of the information that we can possibly gather together first, and then try to "foretell" what will happen. Children will be able to identify with weather predictions—especially if sun was predicted for their picnic day and it rained instead. Sometimes stories are so obvious that the endings are predictable. (Encourage "prediction" as you read stories aloud to children.)

Snow Experiment. Use prediction in this snow experiment. If you live in a cold, snowy climate, have two children bundle up and go right outside your classroom window to collect some clean-looking, sparkling white snow in a pan (everyone can gather around to watch them). Bring it back into the room. Have each child look closely at the snow. When it melts, do they "predict" that this

white snow will leave clean water or dirty water? Why? Using two coffee cans for predictability containers, put black construction paper around one can and a "dirty" label, and white construction paper around the other can with a "clean" label. Give each of the children a small square of paper, and have them put their name on it. Then, they can drop it into the predictability container of their choice. Don't allow changes at this stage—remember, we predict with the knowledge that we have available at the time. Keep the pan on the window ledge or counter all during the day so that children can keep checking. Prediction changes can be made later in the day, but for sound reasoning and not just because a friend changed his/her mind. (Some children are absolutely amazed when they discover that the water is filled with dirt particles.)

This experiment can be duplicated two or three days later—see what the children "predict" AFTER they have had this experience. At this point, you may want to put yellow construction paper around a third container (yellow for caution) and place a big "?" label on it. The children can then predict "dirty," "clean," or "not sure."

Estimation

The "Feel" of Weight. One way to help children with this concept is by means of comparison. For this activity you will need a scale. Collect at least five items that weigh 2 lbs. each so that children can get the "feel" of 2 lbs. Then place several objects in a container by the scale. Children can pick them up and "estimate" whether they weigh more or less than 2 lbs. Check your estimation by weighing the item.

Begin to keep a tally sheet for estimation. Label it "ESTIMATION 2 Lbs." In rebus style, draw the items to be compared. Have child draw the same items in "more than" or "less than" columns. Check the results.

This can be done with 1 lb., 5 lbs., and ½ lb.

This can be varied by having children look for items in the room that they estimate to be more or less than the weight of a specified object, and then by checking the results with the scale.

Liquid Measure

MATERIALS: Plastic containers, juice cans, milk containers in a variety of sizes. PROCEDURE: First, demonstrate the expected behavior at this area. Then, let children work in pairs at the sink, or at a water table, with the containers and water and by filling and dumping the liquid, see what they discover on their own. (Through questioning, they can tell the group which holds "more than" and "less than.")

Some suggested learnings:

- The proper titles for "quart," "pint," "gallon," and "ounce"
- The number of pints in a quart
- The number of quarts in a gallon
- The number of ounces in a juice can
- The number of ounces in a soft drink can
- The number of ounces in the milk container at snack time
- Locate the weights on juice, milk, and cola containers
- Write the liquid measurement words

Other Skill Areas Activities

Art

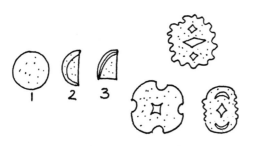

"Baloney" Snowflakes. Discuss real snowflakes (frozen particles of water vapor) that fall from the sky in winter. No two are exactly alike. They are individual, and they have six points. If you are on the playground during a snowy day, examine the snowflakes as they land on jackets and gloves to note the pretty designs. The "precipitation" in winter can change from rain to sleet to snow as the temperature drops. The freezing point on the thermometer (Fahrenheit) is 32 degrees.

For "baloney" snowflakes, distribute a circle of real bologna to each student after hands have been washed. Have them carefully fold the bologna in half, and then in half again. Now for the fun. Children can bite and nibble away at the bologna on the folds, along the edge, at the center point. Ready to open it up? Unfold it. Beautiful, aren't they? Hold them up for all to see. If any are especially pretty, have the nibbler describe his/her technique. Fold up again, and nibble some more if you want a more lacy snowflake bologna. Then, eat your snowflake and enjoy it!

Now, wash hands again. Get a circle of thin white paper and a pair of scissors. Fold paper in half, and in half again. This time let your scissors be your teeth, and cut out some jagged lines and swirly lines. Open up your circle that has been transformed into a snowflake! Spread on some glue, and dip snowflake in a big tin of colored sparklers. Hang from ceiling with white string.

Mashed Potato Snowmen. To help celebrate the season of snow, make a mashed potato snowman. You can use instant potatoes or peel, cut, cook, and mash real potatoes. Give each child a scoopful on a plate, along with a fork. Child can use the fork to "fashion" a snowman. Add peas for eyes, mouth, and buttons; a carrot slice for the hat; and a celery stalk for the broom. Children really enjoy being designer chefs. And, they enjoy eating this unique snowman.

Hibernation Art Mural. First discuss hibernation, the long winter sleep of certain animals, and then list the animals that hibernate and where they hibernate.

Next, tape up a long white or light blue sheet of kraft paper, for a woodland scene. Discuss what we would find in the woods (trees, a stream, hills, etc.). These should be sketched in with chalk about ⅓ of the way down from the top so that much area is left for the ground. Then, have the children imagine that we have an X-ray machine and can focus it upon the scene. Where would the animals be hibernating? (Bears in a cave in the side of a hill, a beaver dam on top of the water with their route visible underneath, frogs burrowed in the mud, a squirrel in a tree nest, etc.) These should all be sketched in with chalk. Using tempera paint, paint the X-ray scene of the woods in winter. NEXT, to add a little life to the mural, paint in some wildlife that we do see in the woods in the winter (spotted deer, white rabbit, a variety of birds, etc.). Put real cotton balls on mural for falling snow. Have class make up a title for it, and print it above.

Use the art mural as a focal point in the room for your further discussion of hibernation, and have children pretend they are walking through the woods and can hear the sounds (birds are chirping, twigs are snapping, etc.). Read a variety of picture books about animals as you are gathered around the mural. Each day you can read about one of the animals depicted on the mural, and proclaim it "Beaver Story Time," or "Squirrel Story Time." Children can write their own stories about the mural wildlife, and make their own mini-murals.

Holidays

New Year's Resolutions. Review and revise class rules for the new year. Then talk about new year's resolutions. People try to "turn over a new leaf" in the new year and do things in a different way. We all want to become better at what we do. Talk about the things that we do in the classroom and ways that we could do them more effectively. Children basically want to be helpful and like to please, so we need to set up a spirit of cooperation in establishing a new list of classroom procedures. Make up a chart labeled, "Let's all start the New Year right!" and list the "rules" that the children decide upon. Maybe you could put a big star in front of the really important ones.

Ask each child to think about an individual new year's resolution. Use the school "report form" as a way of approaching particular areas that may need some attention, if certain children seem to need a focus. Have each student discuss his resolution with the teacher and dictate the resolution (or write it themselves) on a great big white oak leaf shape. Then, turn over the leaf for them to print their name on the other side. Tack the leaves onto a bulletin board (silver gray background, light blue tree trunk) in the shape of a big tree that looks like it's covered with snow. Point out to the children that it takes "teamwork" for the leaves to make a tree, just like it takes teamwork to have a harmonious, pleasant learning/ working/playing environment. Work on the individual resolutions with the children and heap on the praise for desired behaviors wherever you find it! Maybe there is something "magic" about these leaves because they seem to ALL be working. (If the teacher keeps reminding and praising, using the "turning over a new leaf" idea as the vehicle, classroom behaviors can be noticeably changed.)

Martin Luther King, Jr., Day. January 20 is the day that has been set aside to honor Dr. Martin Luther King, Jr., the late black civil rights leader. Dr. King, a minister from Atlanta, Georgia, believed in equal rights for all people. He also believed in non-violence. He organized many marches, and many gatherings of underprivileged people so that they could make their point in a non-violent way. Often they would sing during their marches, and people could hear the echoes of the words "We Shall Overcome." This gained the attention of the press and they did make news headlines. Under Dr. King's leadership, progress for minorities, such as black men and women, was made especially in the areas of equal education and equal opportunity for jobs.

For this special occasion, make a friendship booklet. Have children place their hand on a sheet of orange paper, trace around it, and cut it out. That's the cover. Then trace around the hand again four more times on the colors brown, yellow, white, and red (to signify various skin colors). On each of the hands print one word, such as "friendship," "joy," "trust," "love," etc. Then cut out all of the hands and staple at the wrist for a flip-over book. On the orange cover print the title, "Hand in Hand," or "Martin Luther King, Jr." See reproducible activity pages.

Winter

Feeding Birds. Take a good look outdoors and see what birds are in the area. Some of the birds from the northern part of our country have gone south for the winter. We call this long journey *migration,* which means to move to another place. So, as you look outside of your window, if you live in the southern part of the country, you will be seeing many new birds who have made a long journey to stay in your area where they will be able to keep warm and find food. Make a list of the visiting birds, paint their picture, get bird books from the library to learn more about them, and watch their nest-building activity and habits.

If you live in the northern part of the country, many of the familiar birds are absent because they have "migrated." Make a list of the birds that you do see, and those that you no longer see. You can put a bird feeder right outside your window and feed the birds. They like stale bread, seeds, apple cores from your lunch, or any other seeds such as orange or grape seeds from your lunch. REMEMBER: Once you begin to feed the birds, you should continue to do so for the entire winter because they come to depend upon that food. Place suet (fat from meat) in an empty onion bag that has lots of holes in it, and hang it from a branch. Birds peck at it, the food keeps them warm, and it lasts for a long time.

The birds who stay behind in winter have strong beaks that can crack through tough seeds. The birds who migrate usually have beaks or bills that cannot penetrate through the seeds, and they eat softer foods such as fruits. Get some bird books from the library so that you can study certain bird features, such as: beaks, feet, feathers, nest-building, and nest shapes.

DELICIOUS BIRD FOOD RECIPE

> 1 tablespoon chunky peanut butter
> assorted bird seed
> nylon netting, wax paper
> string, aluminum pie plate

Roll the dry, chunky peanut butter into a ball on the wax paper. Then roll it around in an aluminum pie tin filled with bird seed until it is completely covered.

Next, carefully place it in the center of a square of nylon netting. Draw up the ends of the net and twist. Tie a string around twisted part and knot it. Hang these bird treats in a nearby tree. Go indoors and peek out of the window to watch the bird party.

Camouflage. Work with visual discrimination this month in connection with winter birds and animals in winter. Have children note the bird colors, size of beaks, and types of feet. Also, find picture books at the library that show animals who are "camouflaged" against the winter background and see if children can find them. Make a construction paper cutout of a white rabbit and place it on a black background, yellow background, white background. Children can gain practice working with various animal cutouts on a variety of background colors (brown bear on a white background, yellow background, brown background and green turtle on a brown background, red background, green background, etc.). Work from easy to more difficult contrasts so that children know what to be on the lookout for.

THE SING-ALONG SNOWMAN

To the tune of "Happy Birthday"
sing to the snowman as features
and items are added to make it
look "real."

Sample verses:

"Here's a big nose for you.
Here's a big nose for you.
It's a carrot, Mr. Snowman.
What a big nose for you!"

"Here are two eyes for you.
Here are two eyes for you.
They are blue eyes, Mr. Snowman.
Here are two eyes for you!"

"Here's a big smile for you.
Here's a big smile for you.
It's a red smile, Mr. Snowman.
Here's a big smile for you!"

"Here are buttons for you.
Here are buttons for you.
Six big buttons, Mr. Snowman.
Here are buttons for you!"

"Here's a new hat for you.
Here's a new hat for you.
It's a green hat, Mr. Snowman.
Here's a new hat for you!"

"Here are big boots for you.
Here are big boots for you.
Keep your feet dry, Mr. Snowman.
Here are big boots for you!"

Think of more verses using:

    arms
    hands
    mittens
    broom
    scarf

Can you think of anything else?

HELP SHOVEL THE SNOW

Count the number of snowballs in each square. Match the number of snowballs with the numeral on the shovel. Cut and paste the square with the correct number of snowballs on each shovel.

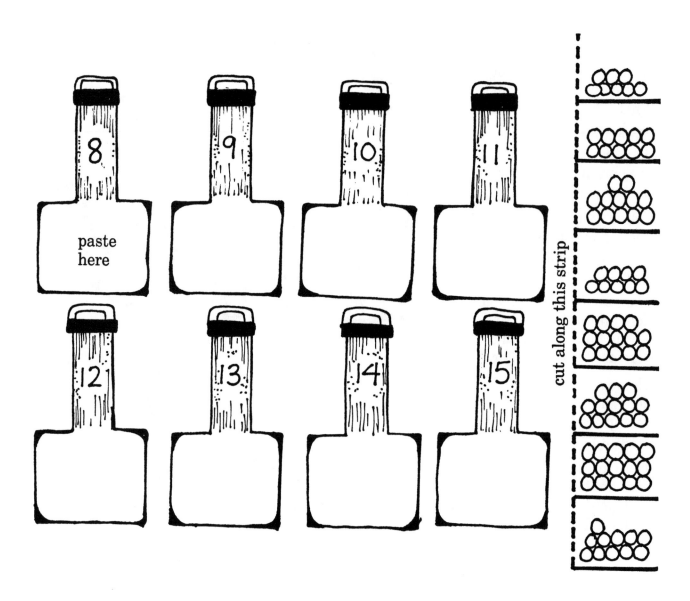

Name _____

A SNOWMAN IN WINTER

Cut out the four pictures. Put them in sequential order (first, second, third, fourth). Paste them on the snowman work-sheet provided. Learn to read the story.

A SNOWMAN IN WINTER WORKSHEET

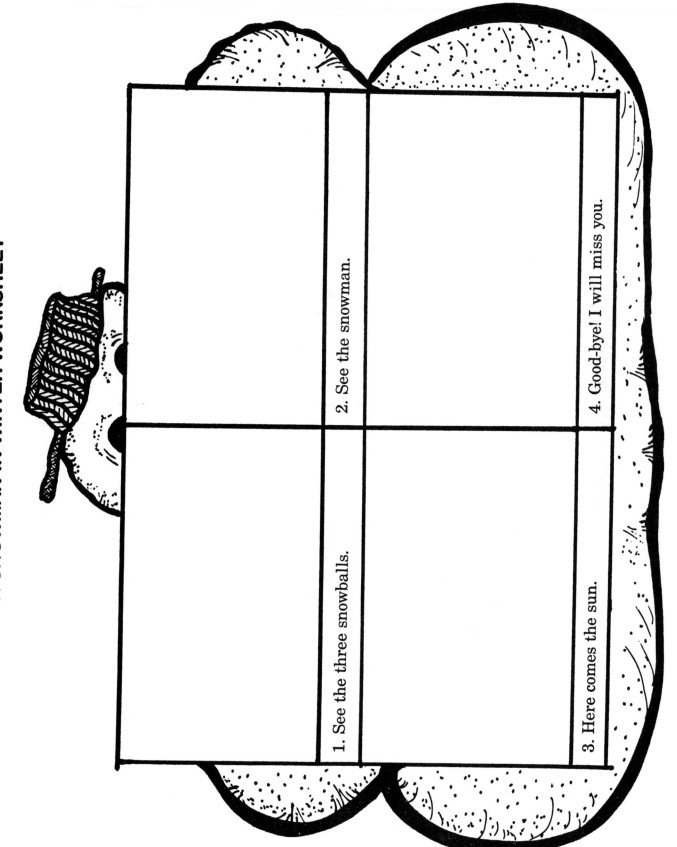

1. See the three snowballs.

2. See the snowman.

3. Here comes the sun.

4. Good-bye! I will miss you.

THE ABC HONEY BEAR

Here comes the ABC Honey Bear with his Alphabet Honey. He just stirred it. You can make sure that the CAPITAL letters get back in the right order.

Can you think of a word that begins with each letter?

Color this bear the color of honey.

THE ABC PICNIC BEAR

This bear is on his way to a Teddy Bear picnic. He must pack his basket with the small letters (lowercase) of the alphabet.

You can help!

When you finish printing the letters, use your crayons to show the color of the cloth for the basket. Also, use your crayons to show what the bear looks like.

THE TEDDY BEAR MEASURING CHART

When Teddy Bears get together, they like to make *comparisons*, so they measure each other. Then, they record the information. You can do it too! Using a piece of string and a yardstick, you and your classmates can help measure each other. First, measure the body part with the string. Hold on tight to the two ends of the string, and put it on the yardstick, at the zero end. What number does the string end closest to? Choose that number. Record it here. Make a class graph of the information so that you can see the *comparisons* in size.

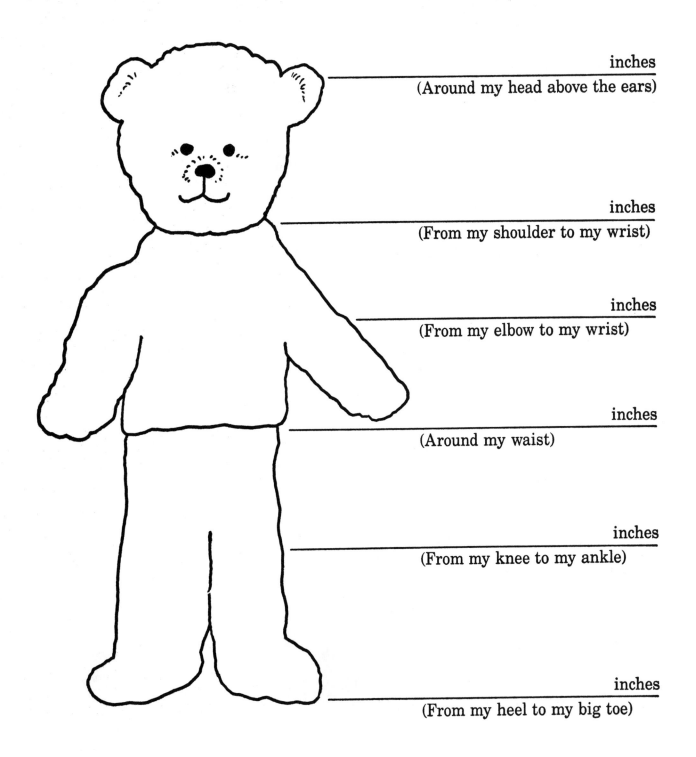

_____ inches
(Around my head above the ears)

_____ inches
(From my shoulder to my wrist)

_____ inches
(From my elbow to my wrist)

_____ inches
(Around my waist)

_____ inches
(From my knee to my ankle)

_____ inches
(From my heel to my big toe)

MATCHING BIG AND LITTLE

Draw a line from the big item to the little item that is EXACTLY THE SAME. The first one is done to help you.

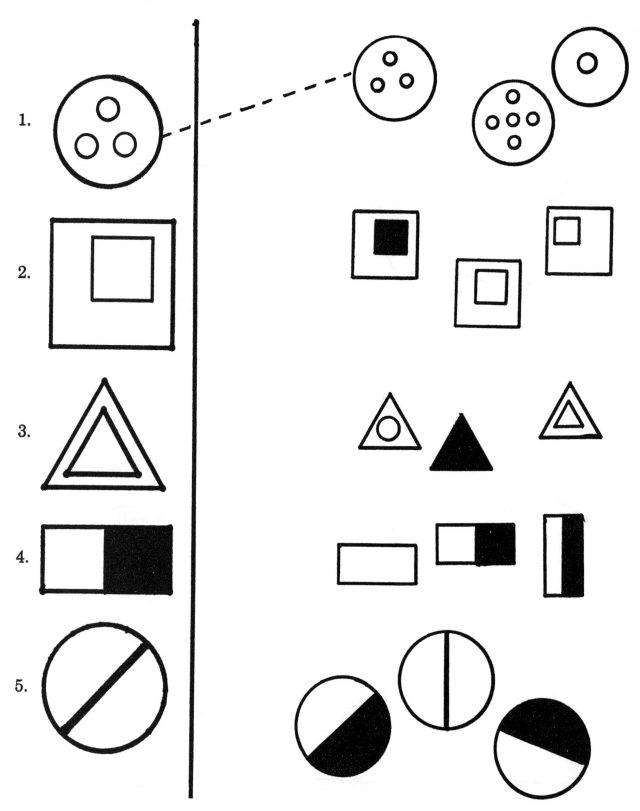

Name _____

LARGER AND SMALLER

With time or use, some things get larger and some things get smaller. Below are six pictures. Look at each one carefully. Will it get larger or will it get smaller?
Draw a red circle around each item that will get larger. Draw a blue circle around each item that will get smaller. Color the items.

tube of toothpaste

kitten

ice cream cone

hamburger

bar of soap

tree

MATCH THE MITTENS

These mittens are all mixed up in the lost and found box. Match the mittens by drawing a line from each capital letter mitten to the correct lowercase letter mitten. Trace the letters. Then, color the mittens that have the same letter with the same crayons.

Hand In Hand
with

Martin Luther King, Jr.

name

Directions: Make a Martin Luther King, Jr. "Brotherhood Book"

1. Have students trace their hand on different colored construction paper.
2. Cut out the hand prints.
3. Paste the hand prints on the appropriate square, *by color*.
4. Cut the book into squares. Arrange in any order, and staple.
5. Read the book.

WHITE is for friendship.

BROWN is for brotherhood.

YELLOW is for peace.

ORANGE is for _____ .

RED is for love.

BLUE is for loyalty.

GRAPH THE CLOTHING FOR THE SNOWMEN

The winter snowmen want to keep warm. You can help count their winter clothing.
Look at the items in the box. There are four different types. Count how many there are
of each type. Graph that number by coloring in the correct number of boxes above each
item of clothing below.

5				
4				
3				
2				
1				
	hat	glove	scarf	earmuffs

Name _____

Who's Hibernating?

Draw pictures that show "who's hibernating" in a cave, in a pond, in a tree. Print their name too.

_____ in a tree.

_____ in a cave.

_____ in a pond.

FEBRUARY

A Sweetheart of a Month

Valentine's Day

Patriotic People

Welcome to February, a sweetheart of a month! Our reading basket is packed with poetry, rhymes, and long vowel sounds. In math, we're ready for counting with bigger numbers and for number words. During this busy month, we also turn our attention to presidents, patriotic people, good nutrition, and good dental health habits to prepare for those new teeth. We can even begin the long countdown to Spring!

Recommended Children's Books for February

The Valentine Bears by Eve Bunting, pictures by Jan Brett (New York: Clarion Books, Houghton-Mifflin, 1983). Bears hibernate all winter and miss Valentine's Day, so Mrs. Bear decided to set her alarm clock early, for February 14, so that she and Mr. Bear can celebrate this special day. She awakens and happily makes many preparations but there is one problem—how to awaken the snoring, hibernating Mr. Bear. She's in for a pleasant surprise, and so is the reader.

Animal Alphabet by Bert Ketchen (New York: Dial Books, E. P. Dutton,

Inc., 1984). A large picture book with the alphabet letter taking up the entire page. Each illustration shows an animal interacting with the letter. For example, bats hang from the B, an elephant pushes an E, a frog perches on an F, etc. All of the animals are listed in the index for easy identification. Good ABC review.

My Friend Jacob by Lucille Clifton, illustrations by Thomas DiGrazia (New York: E. P. Dutton, 1980). Sam and Jacob live next door to one another. Sam, the younger of the two, likes it when Jacob helps him to do things. In turn, Sam helps the older boy with things like remembering that when the traffic light is red it means "stop," and green means "go," and you knock before entering someone else's house. This is a book that supports special friendships.

Push, Pull, Empty, Full by Tana Hoban (New York: Collier Books, 1972). This is a book that deals with the concept of "opposite." There are fifteen different concepts that are illustrated with photographs of people and animals and city scenes. It's also a good teaching tool for children who return to it on their own.

When I'm Sleepy by Jane R. Howard, illustrations by Lynne Cherry (New York: E. P. Dutton, 1985). A delightful picture book about a sleepy child who wishes, and through the appealing illustrations, imagines that she can curl up with a kitten, sleep in a swamp with turtles, crawl into a cozy bear cave and sleep all winter, sleep standing up with the giraffes, on a tree branch with an owl, and much more. This creative approach will touch the children's imagination.

Loose Tooth by Steven Kroll, illustrations by Tricia Tusa (New York: Holiday House, 1984). The twin bats, Flapper and Fangs, do everything together and are good friends, that is until one day when Fangs gets a loose tooth and Flapper does not. Losing your tooth can cause one twin to become the center of attention and one twin to feel neglected. When the tooth is finally out, Flapper decides to take things (the tooth) into his own hands. Oops!

The Hunt for Rabbit's Galosh by Ann Schweninger, illustrations by Kay Chorao (New York: Doubleday & Co., Inc., 1976). If children don't know what a galosh is, they will by the end of this humorous book. Rabbit has all of his valentines mailed but one, and he has to get it in the mail today except that it's raining very hard and he needs his galoshes to get to the mailbox. Everyone in the house is very helpful, especially Tiger, who keeps bringing forth items that partially fit the description. Look for a sweet ending. The use of the color red in the illustrations is particularly effective.

Truck Song by Diane Siebert, pictures by Byron Barton (New York: Thomas Y. Crowell, 1984). In this book we follow a trucker in his rig. The story is in rhyme, and illustrations take us on a visual journey through all kinds of weather in the city, country, and right in the middle of a rush hour traffic jam. We are introduced to a wide variety of trucks that are on the highways.

The Real Mother Goose illustrated by Blanche Fisher Wright (Chicago: Rand McNally & Co., 1916, 1973). This is a 128-page volume of Mother Goose with bright, colorful illustrations on every page. These poems and stories expose children to rhyming, counting, days of the week, the alphabet, repetitious verse that invites children to chime in (for example, the House That Jack Built), and a variety of names and places. Good for language development.

Albert's Toothache by Barbara Williams, illustrations by Kay Chorao (New York: E. P. Dutton, 1974). Albert, a young turtle, insists that he has a toothache and stays in bed all day. His family doesn't believe him and Albert is crushed to think he's not trusted. His mother tries to pacify him, but nothing will do until grandmother comes and saves the day.

Reading Skills Activities

Long Vowels

Long Vowel Words and Pictures. Vowels are found in every word and are responsible for many of the letter-sound relationships in our language. An introduction to vowels with kindergarten children should be simple and centered around skills that they already have, such as knowing that letters are symbols for sounds. Tell the children that the vowels are a, e, i, o, u, and sometimes y. These letters can represent many sounds, depending on where they are located in a word and what other letters are beside them. This month we are talking about long vowels. We recognize that a vowel has a long sound when we listen and hear the vowel say its own name. (Examples: a—ape; e—eagle; i—ice cream; o—boat; u—unicorn.) Make large construction paper cutouts of these objects and hang them in the classroom where the children can see them and identify the vowel sounds. Have magazines available in the art center and ask the children to cut out pictures of objects that have long vowel sounds.

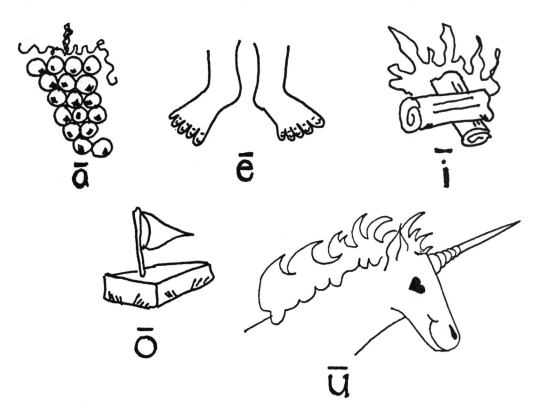

The Vowel Picnic Basket. For the picnic basket this month, use pictures of objects that have long vowel sounds. Ask the boys and girls to remove the pictures, one at a time, and name the vowel represented by the picture. If possible, find small objects that are representative of the vowel sounds and add those to the basket.

The Vowel Animal Game. Play the long vowel animal game. Choose a child and ask that person to pretend to be an animal and make a long vowel sound. The other class members are to guess what animal is being pantomimed and what vowel is evident in the animal sound. For instance, a child might crawl around on the floor and scamper quickly saying, "Eeeek!" The other children might ask questions that could be answered by the animal shaking its head yes or no. "Do you live in a house?" "Are you one of the colors of the rainbow?" "Do you like to eat cheese?" "Are you afraid of cats?" "Are you a mouse?" The student who guesses the riddle can be the next animal. Don't forget to identify the vowel.

Vowel Crowns. Make a crown out of construction paper for each vowel and write the letter on the front of each crown. You will have an A crown, an E crown, an O crown, an I crown, and a U crown. During circle time, give each of the crowns to a child and have them say, "I am the A queen (or king) and I like apes." Proceed with each of the vowels. As each person finishes his or her statement, they stand up and put the crown on someone else's head. That person must repeat the first object and then add another. "I am the A king (or queen) and I like apes and acorns." This is a wonderful game for reinforcing auditory memory skills as well as working on long vowel sounds.

Vowel Murals. Cut pictures from magazines and glue them onto large chart paper to make vowel murals. Have the children write words below the pictures, either by phonetically sounding them out, or having you dictate the spelling to them.

Vowels in Names. During the opening circle time, ask the children to think of their own names and figure out what vowels are in it. Have the vowels written on the chalkboard so that the boys and girls can see them. Choose children to go to the chalkboard and write their names and then pick a friend to come up and circle the vowels in the name. This child can write his or her name and proceed in the same way.

Stepping on Vowels. Cut pictures from magazines of objects, some with long vowel sounds and some without. Lay these out on the floor in the middle of the circle of children. Choose a child and ask him or her to step on only the pictures that have the sounds of long vowels. Say the words as the child steps on each picture so the boys and girls are really listening for the sounds.

Rhyming Words

Rhyming Objects. Try to find objects in the room that rhyme and collect them for circle time. A child might see a block in the block corner and a sock in the playhouse and bring those two things to circle. When you have many objects in the circle, mix them up, and then choose a child to come up and match the rhyming objects.

Mother Goose Rhymes. Mother Goose is a wonderful way to reinforce rhymes. Choose several Mother Goose books from the library so that the boys and girls can see the variation in the illustrations and sometimes even the words that are used in the rhymes. After you've read several of the rhymes, ask children to pantomime the actions in the rhymes and see if the others can guess what story is being acted out.

A Rhyming Word Game. In circle, play a rhyming word game. Tell the children that you will say two words. If the words rhyme, they are to put thumbs up. If they don't rhyme, they are to put thumbs down. No one can say a word out loud.

Poetry

Funny Poems. Once you have talked about rhyming words and Mother Goose, it's a good time to talk about poetry. Read poems to the children, being careful to provide a variety of poems as examples. The Shel Silverstein books, *Where the Sidewalk Ends* and *A Light in the Attic,* are good ones for beginning poetry. The poems are easy to remember and very funny. The children also love the crazy illustrations. They quickly choose their favorites. It's fun to act out these silly rhymes.

Writing Poems. Together, work on writing a class poem or several poems. Encourage the children to use rhyming words, although poetry doesn't necessarily have to rhyme. Be sure to read both kinds of poetry to the children. When you have finished writing the class poem, type it on a ditto and give each child a copy. Ask the students to illustrate the poem and hang the finished products in the hallway where the rest of the school can enjoy them.

Capital and Lower Case Letters

This is a good time to review upper- and lowercase letters. Most of the children should be very familiar with the letters by this time of the year. Find as many ways as possible to encourage the boys and girls to practice the letters. Since this is dental health month, cut out teeth shapes and have the children match capital and lowercase letters. Heart shapes could also be used. Have the children write the letters often emphasizing order and formation.

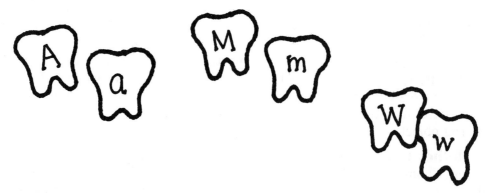

Sentences

Punctuation Marks. As the children begin to be aware of words and sentences, talk about the punctuation marks at the end of sentences. Keep the explanation simple. A period is at the end of a telling sentence, a group of words that tells someone something. A question mark is at the end of an asking sentence, a group of words that asks someone something. An exclamation point is at the end of a sentence that is said in a very excited way. Write several simple sentences on the board and read them to the boys and girls. Ask them to tell you what punctuation mark should go at the end of the sentence. A little trick to remember is that usually your voice goes up at the end of a question, so the children could listen to the inflection of their own voice to decide whether or not a group of words is a question.

Answering Questions. Children enjoy answering questions by writing "yes" or "no" at the end of very short rebus sentences at this time of year. Remember that a rebus sentence is a sentence made of little words that the students must memorize such as is, an, to, on, in, for, he, she, it, go, and, etc. and pictures. A rebus question might be, "Is it ☀ ?" "Is it ☁ ?" "Is the 🐱 on the 🪑 ?" Write a series of these sentences on the chalkboard or on a worksheet and have the children read them one at a time. They should decide whether the answer to the question is "yes" or "no" and write that word after the question mark. They very quickly learn to spell these two words and begin writing them whenever possible.

Math Skills Activities

More with Sets

Set Games. Make several set games to play during circle time. Cut teeth shapes, heart shapes, toothbrush shapes, flag shapes, coin shapes, and food shapes and put them in separate envelopes. Divide the children into several small groups as they sit in circle and give each group an envelope of shapes. Ask them to take turns making sets of objects and asking the other children in the group to identify how many are in each set. They can begin to informally make two sets and count the number first in one set, then in the other set, and then in both sets together. As they become more adept at this game, one of the people in each group can begin to write the number sentence for each combination of sets on a small chalkboard or a piece of paper. This part of the game should really be a reinforcement of the idea that the set of concrete objects has a number that represents how many there are of that particular object and that we can join sets of objects together to make a larger set. Ask people from each group to share what combinations they put together and how many they had in all. Write some of the number sentences on the chalkboard and ask all of the groups to duplicate the addition of the sets with their groups of objects and to copy the number sentence on their own chalkboard or paper.

Counting

The Long Countdown Until Spring. Although sometimes it seems as though the winter days will never come to an end, spring is most certainly on the way. If you live in a climate where winter is evidenced by cold and snow, or even if you live where the sun shines all year long, everyone enjoys the onset of spring. Find a calendar, or make one, that has the first day of spring marked in March and have the class count the number of days from today to the first day of spring. Practice counting that far forward several times and then counting backward from the high number to 1 again. On a long strip of paper (the tape from an adding machine works well), write the number of days until spring and then the numbers backwards from that number. (For example, 45   44   43   42   41   40   39   38   37   36   35   34   33   32   31   30   29 etc. Each day cross out another number in the countdown until spring. Be sure to count all of the numbers backwards from the day you have marked off. It is important for children to understand that the numbers always stay in the same order, no matter whether we are going forward or backward. Number sequence is exact and does not vary depending on order. The boys and girls will become excited as they near the first day of spring. It might be fun to have a special celebration on that day—wearing spring clothes, writing spring words, saying spring things ("Aren't the flowers lovely?" "Isn't it warm?" I just love to watch the birds come back from the south."), playing spring games such as baseball, soccer, jumping rope.

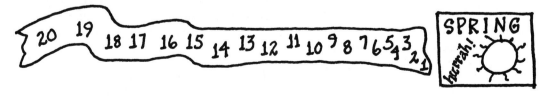

Number Series. Another way to practice number sequence at this time is to write a series of numerals on the chalkboard, omitting some of the numerals and asking children to fill in the blanks. It might look like this: _____ 24 25 26 _____ _____. In this way children begin to look carefully at numerals that come before and after other numerals. Be sure to go both forward and backward when reading the numerals.

Addition

Concrete Objects. Having introduced the concept of addition when working with sets, the students are familiar with the idea before you work with it in a more formal way. Again, it is a good idea to present the concept with manipulative objects before expecting the boys and girls to do any paper work that deals with addition. Have the children make sets from concrete objects in the room such as counting blocks, pattern blocks, marbles, bread tags, old keys, chips, shells, small stones, buttons, or any other small objects. Begin by telling the children to make a set of _____ objects and a set of _____ objects and then count to see how many objects there are in all. After much practice at this level, write a number sentence on the chalkboard and have the children duplicate it with concrete objects. As the class becomes more skilled, have them write their own number sentences on paper and duplicate it with objects.

"Goodies" Addition. To reinforce the skill, give each child a small bag of cereal, raisins, peanuts, and pretzels and have them make sets and number sentences using the "goodies" in their set bags. They love to eat their counting objects when they are finished.

Rainbow Books. Instead of having children write their number sentences on paper, have them do it in rainbow books. These books are made from small strips of colored paper in a variety of colors. The strips are ½″ × 3″ and can be cut on a paper cutter. Use pastel or light colors so that the children can use their pencils and still see the numbers. Staple the little booklets at the left end so that the boys and girls can flip each strip back as they write the number sentence. Remind the children that they have to work out the number sentence with manipulatives before they can write it on the strip.

Number Words

Number Word Games. Prepare number word games to be used at circle time. Some examples might include matching teeth with the number words written on them with toothbrushes with the numerals on them, matching hearts with the number words written on them with arrows that have numerals on them, or matching hatchets with the number words written on them with cherry trees with the numerals written on them.

Number Word Books. Make number word books by folding 8½″ × 11″ paper in half and stapling two or three sheets together. The children can write the number word at the bottom of the page and then draw the correct number of objects on the page. A good way to introduce this is to look at several number concept books and share with the children the idea that some number books don't have sentences in them but instead just have numbers or number words and pictures of objects. The children can share their books with one another or with another classroom.

Working with Numbers to 30

Writing Numerals. By this time of the year, many of the boys and girls will be familiar with the numerals to 30. Practice writing the numerals, both in and out of sequence. For those having trouble remembering the name of the numerals, make flash cards and have them play a game with a friend in which one of the pair holds up a numeral and the other has to identify it. Have the children count sets of objects to 30 and write the numeral on a small scrap of paper and lay it next to the set.

Assessing Number Knowledge. Be sure to reassess the children to determine who can recognize the numerals to 30 and who still needs to practice the skill. Keep a list of those numerals that are difficult for each child. If you have adult volunteers in the classroom or even older students who are capable of working with younger children, they can help those boys and girls who are still having difficulty with particular numbers.

Making Tallies

A Tooth Tally. During February, Dental Health Month, it's an appropriate time to tally the number of teeth lost by the children in the class. It's so exciting to lose a tooth, and kindergarten children seem to do that often. Have each child write down on a small slip of paper the number of teeth they have lost so far. Collect the slips of paper and then tally the number of teeth on the chalkboard. As you read each number, a child can make the appropriate number of tally marks on the chalkboard. Teach the boys and girls to make four marks and then a diagonal mark across for the fifth mark. (*HH*) When all of the teeth are tallied, the group can count by 5s to see how many teeth have been lost by the entire class.

Other Skill Areas Activities

Dental Health

Things to Talk About. February is Dental Health Month and a good opportunity to introduce children to healthy ways to care for the teeth and gums. Some important information to share with the children during this month is:

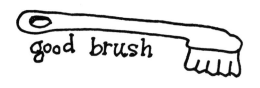

- Teeth need to be kept clean to prevent plaque and cavities from forming.
- Primary teeth save a space for permanent teeth.
- To keep our teeth clean, we need to brush and floss every day.
- If you can't brush, swish and swallow or eat something crispy, crunchy, or juicy such as an apple.
- Toothbrushes should be soft, but not "mushy" and bent.
- Dentists and hygienists help keep teeth clean and healthy and keep little problems from becoming big ones.
- Good gums are firm and light pink and hold the teeth in place.
- Teeth do different jobs—some are cutters, some are breakers, and some are grinders.

Tooth Necklaces. Make happy tooth necklaces. Have the children trace a tooth pattern on white tagboard and cut it out. They can use markers to make a happy face on the tooth. Punch a hole at the top of the tooth and string the tooth on a piece of yarn long enough to go over the child's head and form a necklace.

Food Collages. Cut very large teeth from white roll paper. Give the children magazines and ask them to cut pictures of food, some of which would be good for the teeth, such as vegetables, dairy products, and meat and some of which would be bad for the teeth, such as cake, candy, and soda pop. Use markers to make one of the teeth a happy tooth and the other tooth a sad tooth. On the back of the teeth, paste the pictures of the appropriate foods in collage fashion. Suspend the teeth from a light fixture or the ceiling so that the children can see both sides of the teeth.

VARIATION: Have each child trace a pattern and make teeth from 8½" × 11" paper. They can draw one tooth as happy and the other as sad. On the back of the teeth, they can draw foods that would make teeth healthy and foods that would not be good for teeth.

Tooth Puppets. Make happy tooth puppets. Use a white paper bag and add a crown to the top of the bag and roots to the bottom from white paper. Draw on eyes and a mouth so the puppet can talk. The students can use the puppets to speak from a tooth's viewpoint about smart snacks and taking care of your teeth. (If you cannot find white paper bags, use brown ones and cut the tooth from white paper to glue on the front of the bag.)

A Visit by a Dentist. Invite a dentist or a dental hygienist to visit the classroom and talk about caring for the teeth. Often these visitors will bring along complimentary toothbrushes for the children to practice brushing correctly.

Large Stuffed Teeth. Make large stuffed teeth. Cut teeth shapes from large sheets of white roll paper. Staple two teeth shapes together around the edges, leaving enough space to have the children stuff the teeth with newspaper. Staple the remaining opening shut. Use markers to make happy faces on the teeth. Hang them in the classroom or in the hallway. You might also want to make a large stuffed toothbrush and have the boys and girls practice brushing the large stuffed tooth. A large stuffed tooth fairy would complete the set!

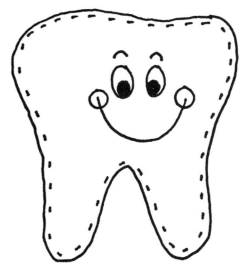

Losing Teeth. Talk with the children about why the primary teeth come out (to make room for the permanent ones) and about how many teeth they might lose during their kindergarten year. Remember that each child is different. Usually if children cut their teeth early, they will lose them early. A homework assignment might be to ask mom or dad when a child got his/her first tooth.

A Tooth Fairy Game. Play a tooth fairy game in opening circle. Ask each child to cut tooth shapes from white paper before they come to circle. Make sure they put their name on each tooth. They should cut the number of teeth they have already lost or the number they think they might lose during their kindergarten year. Remind them to think carefully and make their best guess. ("Could you possibly lose 100 teeth this year? Would you really lose 20 teeth this year?") The boys and girls should bring these teeth to circle and put them in a little pile behind their backs. You can dress up as the tooth fairy, wearing a paper crown, carrying a magic wand made from a ruler and a glittering construction paper star, and holding a bucket with a paper tooth on the side. As the children sit quietly in circle, go around and pick up the teeth and put them in the bucket. "I'm taking three teeth from Jeremy." "My goodness, Chris has lost four teeth.") Later, the children can use the teeth to practice sorting and classifying. They can wear the tooth fairy costume and put the teeth in piles according to the names on the teeth. They could graph the number of teeth lost by each child.

Nutrition

Things to Talk About. Since dental health is so closely tied to nutrition, February is a good time to talk about the four basic food groups and the importance of eating healthy foods. Some things to teach the children are:

- There are four main food groups and we need something from each group each day in order to stay healthy.
- The four food groups are the dairy group, the fruit and vegetables group, the meat and poultry group, and the bread and grains group.
- Some snacks are healthy and some are not. Healthy snacks should be crispy, crunchy, and juicy.
- Eating healthy food makes you feel better and have more energy.

Sorting Good Foods. Cut pictures of foods, some good for you and some not good for you, from magazines. Paste a happy tooth on one grocery bag and a sad tooth on another grocery bag. Have the children sort the foods into the correct bag, depending on whether or not the foods are ones that will keep you healthy.

"Snacko." Play "Snacko." This is like Bingo, but instead of numbers and letters on the game card, draw or paste pictures of smart snacks in each square. As the caller names a smart snack, the children mark their cards with a real smart snack, such as a piece of popcorn or a peanut. When the game is over, the boys and girls can eat their game card markers.

A Crunch Brunch. Send a note home with the children that says on a specific day there will be a "crunch brunch." The children are each to bring a smart snack to school that is crispy, crunchy, or juicy. The boys and girls can share with their classmates why their snack is a smart one, and why they like it. Graph the snacks as to food groups.

The Smart Snack Mystery Game. In circle, play the "Smart Snack Mystery Game." Put smart snacks in brown paper bags (pretzels, popcorn, dried fruit, grapes, etc.). The children should close their eyes as the bags are passed and they reach in and take out a smart snack to taste. They should use their five senses to guess each snack.

Valentine's Day

Valentine's Day is celebrated on February 14 and is a time when we tell others how much we care about them. We use heart shapes on Valentine's Day because love is a special feeling that comes from inside your "heart."

A Valentine Circle Game. Play a valentine game in circle. Make a valentine for half the number of children in the class. Cut each heart in half in a zig-zag fashion. Each child is given part of a heart and must find his/her partner by matching the valentine halves.

"Queen of Hearts" Tarts. Enjoy making and eating the following tarts: Cream together 1 cup flour and ⅓ cup plus 1 tablespoon shortening. Add 2 tablespoons water and a pinch of salt. Mix well. Shape the dough into small balls and press into small muffin tins. Bake 8 to 10 minutes at 350°. Cool and fill with your favorite cherry pie filling.

"Five Pretty Valentines" Game. Put five valentines in the center of a circle of children. Then teach the children the following:

Five pretty valentines waiting at the store.

_____ bought one and then there were four.
   (name)

Four pretty valentines shaped just like a "V"

_____ bought one and then there were three.
   (name)

Three pretty valentines said "I Love You!"

_____ bought one and then there were two.
   (name)

Two pretty valentines, this is so much fun!

_____ bought one and then there was one.
   (name)

One pretty valentine sitting on the shelf.
I felt so sorry that I bought it myself!

Patriotic People

Things to Talk About. President's Day is celebrated the third Monday of February and is a time when we recognize two famous presidents, George Washington and Abraham Lincoln. Some information to share with the children is:

- Not all countries are free.
- People helped to make this country a free place.
- Presidents Washington and Lincoln were two of our most important presidents.
- _____is our president right now.
- Our flag is a symbol of our country.
- Any natural-born citizen can grow up to become president—maybe even a child in this classroom.
- The Pledge of Allegiance is an important way to recognize our flag and our country.

Graham Cracker Log Cabins. Talk with the children about Abraham Lincoln. Tell them about his childhood in a log cabin and his love of books. Divide the children into small groups and give each group graham crackers and a small dish of peanut butter and ask them to decide how they might use these two things to build a miniature log cabin. Each group seems to go about the task in a different way. After the children have shared their cabins with the other groups, they may eat them.

The President's Job. Write an experience chart about what a president's job might be like or the qualities necessary to be a good president.

The Meaning of Freedom. Write an experience story about the meaning of freedom. Duplicate a copy of the story for each child to take home and share with his or her family. The families could write their own special thoughts about freedom and send them back to school to be shared with the class.

Red, White, and Blue Chains. Make red, white, and blue chains to decorate the classroom.

Honesty. Make a George Washington picture about honesty. Give each child an 18″ × 24″ piece of white construction paper. Ask them to draw a tree trunk with their crayons. With green paint, they can sponge paint the top part of the tree. They can use markers or crayons to draw cherries on the tree and George Washington standing beside the tree with a hatchet. They can write the word "honesty" at the top of the picture.

Money Rubbings. Make penny or quarter rubbings by putting a coin under a sheet of thin newsprint. Hold the coin steady as you rub over it with the side of a crayon. You will begin to see the head of a president as the crayon markings get darker. Be sure to rub both sides of the coins.

A PATRIOTIC BOOK

February is a patriotic month because George Washington and Abraham Lincoln have birthdays during this month. You can make a patriotic book. Color the pictures, cut the pages apart on the black lines and staple the book together.

MY

PATRIOTIC

BOOK

Name_____

A Stovepipe Hat

A Hatchet and Cherries

The American Flag

A Log Cabin

A Three-Cornered Hat

Tell a story about each of the pictures.

THE TOOTH FAIRY DREAMS ABOUT TEETH

When the tooth fairy sleeps, she dreams about teeth. Look at each of her dream clouds, read the number word, and draw the correct number of teeth.

Name _____

LONG VOWEL FLASH CARDS

Now that you know about vowels and their special sounds, it's time to practice. Each of the pictures below represents a vowel. Color the pictures and then cut the little cards apart on the black lines. You should have ten cards—five picture cards and five letter cards. Mix the cards up and then match each vowel to its special picture. Have a friend hold up the picture cards and you say the name of the vowel.

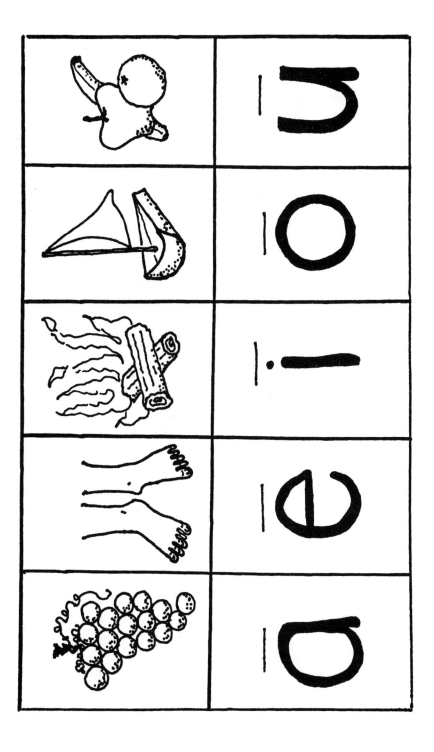

ADDING HEARTS

Count the number of hearts in each set. Add the hearts together and write the correct numeral under the box. The first one is done for you. Color the hearts.

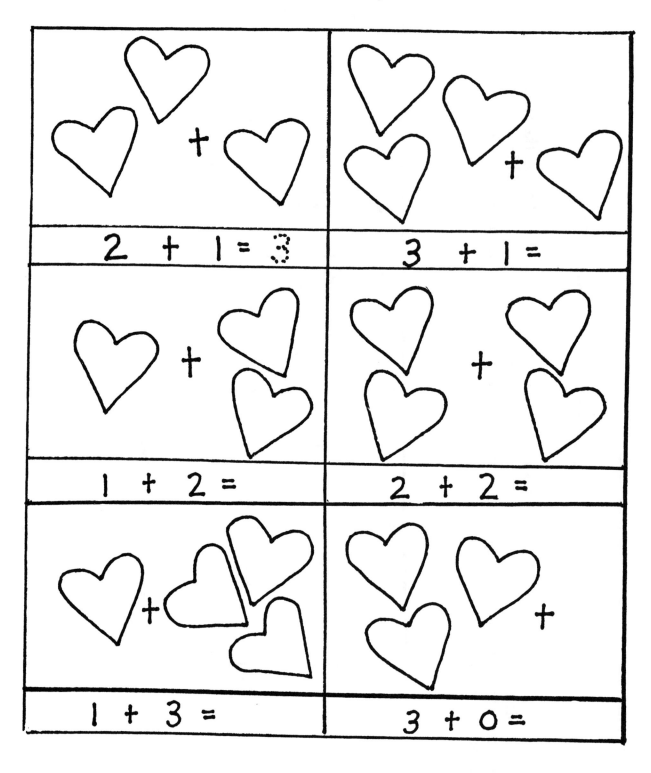

$2 + 1 = 3$

$3 + 1 =$

$1 + 2 =$

$2 + 2 =$

$1 + 3 =$

$3 + 0 =$

HEART OUTLINE PAGE

Color the heart pieces on the HEART PUZZLE PAGE. Cut the pieces apart on the black line. Lay the pieces on the heart outline on this page, making sure that the parts all fit together. Glue the pieces to the heart.

Name _____

HEART PUZZLE PAGE

Name _____

BRUSH THE NUMBER WORDS

Use this page with the Teeth for "Brush the Number Words" page. Color the toothbrushes. Cut them out on the black lines. Look at the numeral on each toothbrush and then find the tooth with the matching number word. Lay the toothbrush on the correct tooth. Keep the toothbrushes in an envelope with your name on the front.

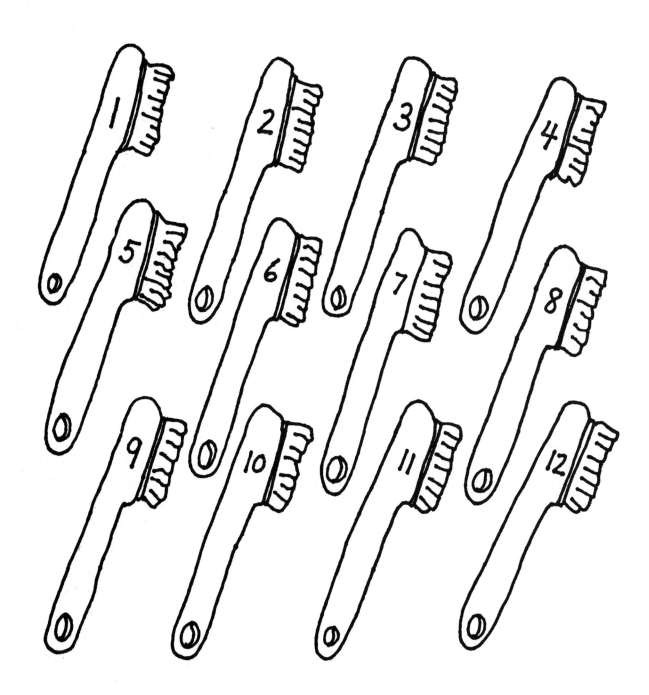

TEETH FOR "BRUSH THE NUMBER WORDS"

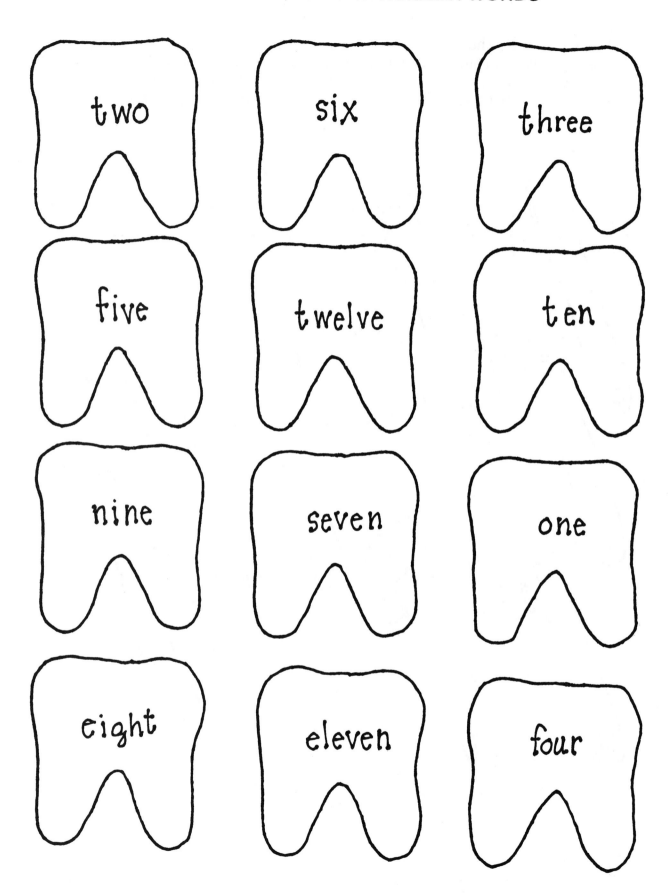

THE GROUNDHOG AND ITS SHADOW

Will the groundhog see its shadow? Color this groundhog and cut it out on the black line. Lay the groundhog on a sheet of black paper and trace around it. Cut out the black "shadow." Use a paper fastener to attach the shadow to the groundhog between its feet. You can make the groundhog see its shadow.

THE TOOTH FAIRY

The tooth fairy has been here and left some teeth and some magic wands. Draw a line from the lowercase letter on each tooth to the matching capital letter on each magic wand. Make a wish for each one you get right.

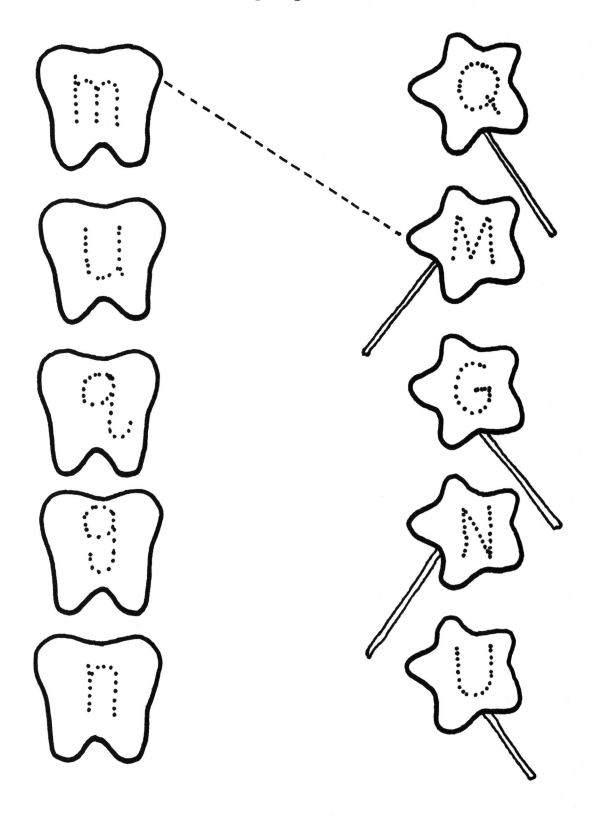

I LOVE VOWELS

Trace over the lowercase vowel in each heart and write the matching capital letter on the line. Color the hearts.

Name _____

THE FOUR BASIC FOOD GROUPS

FRUITS AND VEGETABLES

Draw fruits and vegetables in this box.

BREAD AND GRAINS

Draw bread and cereal in this box.

DAIRY PRODUCTS

Draw dairy products in this box.

MEATS

Draw meats in this box.

A FEBRUARY CONCENTRATION GAME

Each of the boxes below contains a picture or word about February. Color each picture and cut the boxes apart on the lines. To play the memory game: Lay the cards face down and turn over two cards at a time. If the cards match, you may keep them. If the cards don't match, turn them back over. Your turn is over. Try to remember where each word or picture is hidden as the other players take their turns. The person with the most matches wins the game.

A FRUIT AND VEGETABLE GRAPH

Look at the food in the box. Which of these are fruits and which are vegetables? Color the fruits and vegetables.

Ask five of your friends which of these fruits or vegetables is their favorite. Graph that choice by coloring in the box above the food. Which had the most? Which had the least?

Name _____

COUNTING VALENTINES

These valentines are all in order, waiting to be delivered. Some of the numbers are missing. As you look at each row of valentines, trace over the numerals that are there and fill in the missing numerals. Check your work by counting.

MARCH

Lions, Lambs, and Learning

Kindergarten children often experience growth spurts in learning at this stage in their development. Many concepts that you have been working on all year long suddenly seem to "click" in the springtime. Welcome to the new season, where we have provided many opportunities for learning. For reading we can explore short vowel sounds, fairy tales, and fantasy. In math, we can focus upon weighing, subtraction, and even predictions. The lions, lambs, and leprechauns help to make this spring a time for growth!

Recommended Children's Books for March

Wanda's Circus by Amy Aitken (New York: Bradbury Press, 1985). Wanda decides to have a circus and all the kids are willing to sign up but Wanda says it's only for the "big kids." So, all of the "little kids" who are in the way, decide to leave. But wait, the circus is ready to begin and there's something missing—the audience. Now the "little kids" who are the audience have the upper hand and have to be wooed back again. Great fun!

Arthur's Eyes by Marc Brown (Boston: Little, Brown & Company, 1979). Another Arthur adventure. This time, Arthur is in need of eyeglasses and eventually does get them but is too embarrassed to wear them to school. He does everything to try to get rid of them, but they keep turning up. Finally, Arthur's eyes, minus the glasses, really cause bizarre behavior and he has a private talk with his teacher...who wears reading glasses.

Encouraged by this, Arthur faithfully wears his glasses and his grades improve. What effect does this have upon his classmate, Francine?

St. Patrick's Day in the Morning by Eve Bunting, illustrations by Jan Brett (New York: Clarion Books, Houghton-Mifflin, 1980). Jamie awakens early on St. Patrick's Day, March 17, goes quietly downstairs and spies all of the green sashes to be worn by the family members in the big parade—all but him because's he's too small. Determined to make the march, Jamie dresses and travels the route. When he returns the town is just waking up. An amused big brother finds Jamie asleep in the kitchen chair. Beautiful illustrations highlight green colors.

The Hungry Leprechaun by Mary Calhoun, illustrations by Roger Duvoisin (New York: William Morrow & Co., 1962). Young Patrick O'Michael O'Sullivan O'Callahan was so poor he had only dandelion soup for food. He believed that if he could just catch a leprechaun the magic could make his life better. Alas, he catches a poor, hungry leprechaun who has used up his magic—almost.

If I Were a Bird by Gladys Conklin, pictures by Arthur Markovia (New York: Holiday House, 1965). This helpful book introduces twenty-seven different birds, in color, to children. The pictures show birds in their natural habitat with their typical nest and type of eggs. Also, bird calls are given, and in some cases the musical notes accompany the text.

Freight Train by Donald Crews (New York: Greenwillow Books, 1976). The freight train passes by with a good review of colors and a variety of railroad cars. Also, the concepts of moving, going through, going by, crossing over, and the freight train traveling both day and night are illustrated with bold pictures. (Caldecott Honor Book.)

What Kind of Bird Is That? by Mirra Ginsburg, pictures by Giulio Maestro (New York: Crown Publishers, 1973). This is a picture book about envy. A goose, dissatisfied with his looks, trades his neck with a swan, his beak with a pelican, his tail with a peacock, and on and on until he is no longer recognizable and is awkward. He realizes what he has done and knows what he must do to be happy—be himself. This familiar theme in children's books is a reassuring message.

The Island of the Skog by Steven Kellogg (New York: The Dial Press, 1973). On National Rodent Day, a group of mice decide they are tired of living and hiding in holes, so they set out to sea in a sailing ship. They land on an island and declare themselves to be free. The isle has one other inhabitant—the skog! The mice mastermind a plan to catch this huge monster and are in for a big surprise.

Harriet Goes to the Circus by Betsy and Giulio Maestro (New York: Crown Publishers, 1977). Harriet, an elephant, wants to be FIRST in line for the circus. She counts her friends as they line up to see who is SECOND and THIRD, etc., until the TENTH patron is in line. But the door opens at the other end, and now the tenth one has become first, and so on. Inside, however, they sit in a big circle where there is no first and last. Good for use of number cards.

An Edward Lear Alphabet, **illustrated by Carol Newsome (New York: Lothrop, Lee & Shepard Books, 1983).** This is an ABC book that has playful nonsense rhyming words that make children giggle. While it is not a basic beginning ABC book, the illustrations are geared toward young children. Those who are already familiar with the alphabet will especially enjoy it, but all will enjoy finding the little mouse who romps playfully through the letters.

Reading Skills Activities

Short Vowel Sounds

Paper Cutouts. Phonics is a method of teaching/learning the sound of letters and letter groups. A phoneme–grapheme correspondence means a letter–sound relationship. One challenge in teaching children to read is teaching them to deal with forty-five phonemes (sounds) with only twenty-six graphemes (letters). That means that many letters do "double duty." The vowels certainly qualify as double-duty, triple-duty, and even quadruple-duty letters. An exposure to the "short vowel" sound is in order here. Many children use rote-memory to repeatedly voice the sounds, and that will serve them well later on as they gain practice with word-attack skills.

Some appropriate words that begin with short vowel sounds and, thus, can be used to help teach short vowel sounds are: A–apple, E–elephant, I–indian, O–octopus, U–umbrella. Make large construction paper cutouts of these items, or have large magazine illustrations. Have children listen for the short vowel sound, and say the short vowel sound. A class that employs the use of phonics will have much groaning as "ah," "eh," "ih," "aah," and "uh," are sounded by the children.

Picnic Basket of Vowels. For the picnic basket this month, prepare the children to be very bright little animals in the park who only speak "short vowel language." Reinforcement and praise from the teacher is essential, such as "Let me hear that "Iiiiindian sound," or "That's a good "ehhhlephant" sound!" Some items for the basket are:

SHORT A: mAgazine, hAt, fAn, bAg, rAg;

SHORT E: bEd, rEd, hEn, tEn, jEt;

SHORT I: fIg, pIg, hIp, lIp, dIll pIckle;

SHORT O: pOd, rOd, mOp, tOp, bOx;

SHORT U: cUb, sUb, jUg, mUg, rUg.

Simple Sentences. Print simple sentences on the chalkboard or a chart, such as: "Nan ran with a fan" or "Kim and Jim saw Tim." Have the children practice the sentences.

Word Families. Work with such word families as -at, -in, -up. These can be placed on house shapes, and children can talk about the word family that lives in the house.

A Floor Game. Make a floor game for short vowels. Print five vowels and four other letters on a 9-square grid. Say a word that has the short vowel sound "in the middle" of it, and have the children jump to the letter that is doing the talking.

Cozy Corner Reading Area

Set up an area in the room that looks "cozy." For a start, the teacher can send a letter home asking for certain items such as a comfortable chair, throw pillows, rug, table or TV tray, and lamp. Encourage children to bring in used magazines from home for this area. And, have an abundance of good picture books and some stuffed, cuddly animals. Children can go to the area, turn on the lamp, and settle down comfortably with a good book. This area may become so popular that a sign-up sheet will be necessary.

Rebus Stories

Explain that we can also use "picture writing" for our stories. Some sample rebus shapes are:

sun	bird	dog
cloud	boy	girl
happy	sad	bike
flower	house	tree

Some words that can be used repetitively to make lots of sentences are: in, and, to, out, at, the, she, he, it, on, no, a, of, I, so, see, for, etc.

Make a set of word cards and a set of picture cards. Store them in an envelope. Children can make sentences from them. Also, a set of word cards and picture cards could be reproduced for each student, cut apart, stored in envelopes, and used for making sentences. Children can then begin to print their sentences. By making two or three sentences, they are making a "story," and can gain practice with writing by printing that.

Counting and Colors

"Signs of Spring" Booklets. This can be correlated with counting and with colors. Pages can be stapled together or folded. Children can cut out or draw the items, and print the labels. Some suggestions are: 1 yellow sun, 2 blue birds, 3 green leaves, 4 brown bugs, 5 orange flowers, 6 red balloons, 7 purple kites, 8 black ants, 9 white clouds, and 10 pink raindrops.

Fairy Tales and Fantasy

Focus upon fairy tales and fantasy. Children never seem to tire of fairy tales and like to listen to them, retell them using cutouts or puppets, and role play the stories. Read *Jack and the Beanstalk, Snow White and the Seven Dwarfs, The Three Little Pigs, Red Riding Hood, The Three Billy Goats Gruff,* etc.

Children, as they listen again, can be listening for some of the elements of fairy tales such as: the number 3, magic spells, wishes, witches, kings, queens, and animals that talk.

Easy-to-Make Puppets. Here are four puppet suggestions:

- Make Jack and the Beanstalk Picture Sequence Story Strips.
- Use white cotton garden gloves for re-telling of *The Three Bears*. Attach Velcro or a felt circle to the glove fingers with glue. Make cloth cutouts of Goldilocks and the Three Bears.
- For *The Three Little Pigs*, make stick puppets: three pigs, one wolf.
- For *Red Riding Hood*, make a fold-up basket. Inside put a paper checkered napkin, paper chocolate chip cookies, and a tea bag for Grannie. (Children can make a set of this to take home.)

The Magic Pot. From construction paper, make a large pot shape, adding shiny gold circles for coins. Have the children make up a class story to be printed on the pot shape. This class story can be reproduced and sent home for more reading.

The Leprechaun Look. What does a leprechaun look like? With the children, list characteristics. Have the children draw a picture to incorporate all of the listed characteristics.

Look Closely! Paint leprechauns with light green paint on dark green paper. Since no one knows for sure exactly what leprechauns look like, everyone is successful!

Catch a Leprechaun. Make a leprechaun using green gelatin in a flat aluminum pan. Decorate the large face using olive eyes, carrot slice nose, raisin mouth, whip cream hair and beard. Cut into slices and enjoy for a snack. Now we all have some of the "magic" inside of us. Can we feel it tingling in our fingertips and toes? Have children wiggle their fingers and rapidly tap their toes on the floor for a warm up exercise.

Then, to the tune of "Mary Had a Little Lamb," teach the children to do (line by line and with motions) the following leprechaun song and dance:

We just ate a leprechaun, leprechaun, leprechaun

We just ate a leprechaun, at it likes to dance.

See my fingers touch my HEAD, touch my WAIST, touch my TOES
See my fingers wiggle, wiggle. They land on my NOSE.

Hear my toes go tap, tap, tap, tap, tap, tap, tap, tap, tap.
Hear my toes go tap, tap, tap, tap (silent) tap (silent) tap!

Now it's time to count to eight, count to eight, count to eight
1 - 2 - 3 - 4 - 5 - 6 - 7 - 8 (hold up fingers)
We "ate" (open mouth wide for a big bite) a leprechaun!

A leprechaun will make you smile, make you smile, make you smile
That will make you feel worthwhile! Let's see that GREAT BIG GRIN!
(Have children laugh and hold the big grin for 30 seconds).

Math Skills Activities

Working with Coins

Pot of Gold Math. Put gold foil around a wooden bowl. Place real coins in the gold pot and have children identify them: pennies, nickels, dimes, quarters. Later, foreign coins could be added for interest and to show the difference in the coins. Examine the real coins with a magnifying glass. Whose picture is on the coin? What are the buildings? Symbols? Letters and numbers? Look for the date. What does "E Pluribus Unum" mean? (One nation made up of many.) Here are other Pot of Gold activities:

- Have two students reach into the pot of gold for six coins each. How many match? The one with the most coins that match wins the draw. Put them back. Repeat.
- Put a gold cloth over the gold pot. Have children reach under (no peeking) and remove a penny, a quarter, a nickel, etc. They will gain experience in being able to identify coins by feeling the different sizes.
- Make a coin card set. Reach into the pot for the coins, and match up the real coin with the coin picture.
- Make great big construction paper coins. Cut them in half. Scramble them, and then match them.

Weighing Items

Bring in a kitchen scale for weighing items. Have a bag of items available that weigh different amounts. Children can bring in items to be weighed also:

- Paint two lunch bags a gold color. Put rocks in each. See which bag weighs the most. Mix them up. Lift them and see if students can estimate which bag weighs the most. Weigh them for verification.

- Buy a 10 lb. bag of potatoes, and divide it into smaller bags of "St. Patrick's Potatoes" for the hungry leprechaun. (Read THE HUNGRY LEPRECHAUN listed in recommended books.) Put a green cutout of a large shamrock on a paper bag and fill it with potatoes until it weighs 1 lb. Have children do this for 2 lbs., 3 lbs., 4 lbs., and 5 lbs. These can be emptied and refilled repeatedly.

- When bags are filled, have children lift the bags and estimate the weight in pounds from 1 to 5.

- On March 17, St. Patrick's Day, tie a green yarn ribbon around each potato and have children take one home as a gift from the leprechaun.

- Bring in a bathroom scale. Have children weigh themselves. Record the weight. Hold a class pet (rabbit, gerbil) and step on the scale again. Now how much does it register? Record the weight. What is the difference? The difference is the weight of the pet. So that's one way that we can weigh a moving, wiggly, squiggly animal that won't stay still on the kitchen scale.

- Weigh marbles in a basket. Keep adding more and taking away (subtracting) marbles for weight change.

- Spray a large pair of men's old workboots a bright green, and while still wet sprinkle gold dust on them. Have children step inside the shoes and weigh themselves. (Someday the leprechaun might put a small, but heavy, rock way up in the toe to try to play a joke on us.)

Subtraction

Concrete Items. Introduce the concept of "taking away" by using concrete objects. You can start with a GROUP or BUNCH of something, and then remove some of the items. For example:

    take away magnets from a group of magnets on the chalkboard

    take some of the crayons out of a box of crayons

    take a drinking straw out of a glass

    take three coins from a purse

    take a handful of potatoes out of a big bag of potatoes

    take two children from a group of children

Work on the chalkboard, using magnets. Call attention to the TOTAL number (count them together), TAKE AWAY a specified number (either the teacher or a student can remove specified amount), and then count HOW MANY ARE LEFT.

Use this three-step process repeatedly so that we are working with: total number, number removed, number remaining.

After working with the concrete items on the board, some children are ready for the recording of the items. Count the total number of magnets and with chalk, write that numeral on the board. When children remove items, record that numeral underneath (or to the right) of the total number. Count the remaining items that are on the chalkboard and record that numeral on the chalkboard. (Teach the subtraction sign [−] and the equal sign [=] for horizontal recording, and teach the subtraction sign [−] and the straight line [___] drawn underneath the second numeral for vertical recording.)

Move from the magnets (concrete items) to drawing circles on the board (semi-concrete). Put an "X" on the ones that are being taken away. How many are left? Record on the chalkboard.

Silly Subtraction Stories. Make up "Silly Subtraction Stories" and have children figure them out. Children like it when you talk about familiar people, for example:

"Mr. _____, the principal, ordered french fries for lunch.

There were 10 in the bag. He ate 3, how many are left?"

"Our music teacher was so hungry that she ordered 5 hamburgers!

She ate 3, now how many does she have left?"

Subtraction Food Bags. For each child prepare a bag that has cereal chunks, raisins, and tiny cheese crackers inside. Do not count them; all children will receive different amounts of each, but in general will have similar bulk. Have students take out all of the cereal chunks. How many do they have? Eat three. Now how many are left? They will have different amounts. Now, have them all eat two cereal chunks. How many left? Some will have five, some will have four, etc. Ask, "Why is it different if you all ate two?" The answer: The number that you started out with is very important in determining how many you have left. Repeat this process using the raisins, and then the tiny cheese crackers.

Weather Charting and Predicting

This is good review again from January, because the weather is different. The weather in March is usually changeable, or "unpredictable," which means that we can't always count on it!

Lion and Lamb Days. Introduce children to the saying, "March comes in like a lion and goes out like a lamb." Explain the meaning. Use lion/lamb weather statements, such as "This is a lion day," or "This is a lamb day." Make lion and lamb sticker-size shapes and have children paste them on the calendar each morning. At the end of the month see how many days belonged to the lion and how many belonged to the lamb. Which one had more?

When teacher asks, "What kind of a day is this today?" children can respond with a ROAR (g-r-r-r-r) for lion, and by BLEATING (ba-a-a-a-a) for lamb. If you predict that tomorrow will be a lion day, respond appropriately. If you predict that tomorrow will be a lamb day, respond appropriately.

Unpredictable Weather. We said that March weather is "unpredictable" but let's try to "predict" or guess what the weather will be tomorrow. How many lion days have we had this week? How many lamb days? If the weather is "changeable" how many think tomorrow will be a lion day (record number), how many think it will be a lamb day (record number).

Tens and Ones

Kite Tails. Use two real kites with a rope tail on each. For ten days, "ceremoniously" add a ribbon or tie to the tail of only one kite and rote-count (1,2,3,4, etc.) until you are "at the end of your rope." (Make sure that the tenth tie is the end of the rope.) "What will we do?" Take off all of the ties, and replace them with one great big green tie that will "stand for" or represent 10. That green tie can fly on the rope tail of the other kite that has the great big "10" on it. Now, let's start over again on the first kite with a tail a day until we get ten more ties. Can anyone "predict" what we'll do when we get to the end of our rope again? (Some children may be ready for the 10 ties on the "tens kite" and may be able to work with a supply of ribbons or ties at their own pace. Then the third kite, or "100" could be introduced...very ceremoniously! Maybe that one could be taken outdoors on a breezy day for a ride.

Story Problems and Keeping a Tally

Make up simple story problems, and keep a tally as the story is told. Example:

"Two little leprechauns went to find the pot of gold at the end of the rainbow (/ /).

Two more joined them. (/ /).

How many are there all together?" (/ / / / or 1-2-3-4 = FOUR.)

OR   "A leprechaun was walking and spied a pot of gold by a tree (/).

Then he spied two more under a bush (/ /).

How many pots of gold are there?" (/ / / or 1-2-3 = THREE.)

OR   Have the children make up simple leprechaun stories and have *them* keep a tally on the board.

WHEN children are familiar with this process, just put the tally marks up on the board and see if they can make up a simple story to go with them. (For example: / and / /, / / and / /, and / and / / /.)

Other Skill Areas Activities

St. Patrick's Day

Children do have fun joining in the celebration of this special day. Is anyone Irish? Ireland (locate it on a map or globe) is the home of the potato, and as mentioned in the math section, the potatoes that have been used for weighing can be taken home with a green ribbon tied around them as a gift from the leprechaun. Perhaps a baked potato recipe topping could be attached.

The Color Green. Green is the color of Ireland, and children can be encouraged to wear green for this day. "March 17 is a great day for the wearin' of the green." For color review, name all of the green things in the room.

Green Riddles. (Examples: "I'm thinking of something that is green and comes in bunches [grapes]; "I'm thinking of something that is green and you mow it in the summer" [grass]; "I'm thinking of something that is green and it's in a tossed salad," [olives, lettuce, spinach, or pepper.] Let children make up their own riddles. This is a good language development exercise as well as an opportunity for creative thinking.

O'Irish. Many Irish names begin with "O". Cut out name tags in the form of shamrocks, and print students' first and last names on them so that when they come in to school they must locate their name tag. Instead of Sally Jones, it will say "Sally O'Jones" and instead of Peter Westlake it will say "Peter O'Westlake." That leprechaun did it! That means there must be one hiding someplace in the room. But since their large pointed ears can't take loud noises, we can have a quiet day and be on the lookout for the leprechaun who will come out if we're so quiet he thinks no one is here! We can also pause for 30 seconds and "listen for a leprechaun." What sounds did we hear? Let's list all of the sounds that we did hear. What made the sounds? Were any of them GREEN?

"End of the Rainbow" Salad. The following recipe makes approximately thirty-six servings:

1 pint sour cream
five 3-ounce packages of gelatin (raspberry, orange, lemon, lime, and cherry)
boiling water and cold water
bowls and wooden spoons
8″ × 8″ glass pan

To one package of gelatin, add 1 cup boiling water. Divide in half, put ½ cup in one bowl and ½ cup in second bowl. To one of the bowls add ¼ cup cold water. To the other bowl add about ⅓ cup sour cream. Mix. Begin layering with clear half first. Allow to cool. Gently pour the second bowl mixture that has become cloudy with the sour cream. (The first layer takes a little longer to set than the rest.) Mix up another flavor, and add the two layers. When third package is mixed with water and sour cream, put sour cream layer in first. (First and last layers will end up clear layers.) You can see the rainbow effect "building" as you look through the sides of the glass pan. When set, cut into tiny squares. Enjoy!

A Special Song. To the Tune of "London Bridge is Falling Down" make up nonsense rhyming verses. Some suggestions are:

"All the cats wear big green hats, big green hats, big green hats

All the cats wear big green hats, on St. Patrick's Day!"

"All the turtles wear big green girdles, big green girdles, big green girdles,

All the turtles wear big green girdles, on St. Patrick's Day!"

"All the pigs wear big green wigs, big green wigs, big green wigs,

All the pigs wear big green wigs, on St. Patrick's Day!"

"All the bears wear big green hairs, big green hairs, big green hairs,

All the bears wear big green hairs, on St. Patrick's Day!"

"All the goats wear big green coats, big green coats, big green coats,

All the goats wear big green coats, on St. Patrick's Day!"

"All the ewes wear big green shoes, big green shoes, big green shoes,

All the ewes wear big green shoes, on St. Patrick's Day!"

"All the girls wear big green pearls, big green pearls, big green pearls,

All the girls wear big green pearls, on St. Patrick's Day!"

"All the guys wear big green ties, big green ties, big green ties,

All the guys wear big green ties, on St. Patrick's Day!"

Children will come up with many, many nonsense rhymes for the song, and will be singing it (and learning rhyming words) for days.

Spring Green Frosting. You need sugar cookies, confectioners sugar, water, and green food coloring. Add water to the confectioners sugar to make it of a spreading consistency. Add one drop of green food coloring and have the children observe the change in color. Add another drop and observe the color change. Have the children decide when the green color is "just right" to spread on the sugar cookies. Each child can use a plastic knife to spread the frosting on the cookie. Serve with limeade for a green treat!

Spring

Lion and Lamb Mobiles. Make lion/lamb mobiles using white and brown construction paper. Cut off corners, and fringe (cut in 1″ all around) and curl the edges. Add lion features on one, lamb features on the other, and glue them back to back. Features include eyes, nose, mouth, whiskers for lion. Use cotton balls for fuzzy lamb. Attach string, and hang from ceiling. Also, these can be made from paper plates in less time, and glued back to back so that everyone has his own lion/lamb. (See math section for keeping track of lion/lamb weather days in March.)

Birds

A Nesting Station. Make a nesting station for the birds! Get a large mesh potato or onion bag. Have children bring in materials for the birds to help them build their nest, and stick it into the bag. Some suggested items are tissue, cotton, string, fiberfill, fluff from dryers, straw, etc. Hang up the nesting station where it can be seen from the window. Watch the birds pull and tug at it and carry items off to their nest. (In olden days when people cut their hair in the spring, they spread it out in the yard so birds could use it for a soft lining for their nests.)

Migration Review. A renewed interest in birds takes place at this time of year as many birds are migrating and building nests and having families. Encourage bird watching, and secure many picture books about birds. Caution children that spring is NOT the time to hunt for bird's nests.

Picture Sequence. Students can make a sequential picture strip: nesting station hanging in a tree, birds at the station, birds building a nest, bird sitting on a nest with eggs in it, eggs hatching, etc. This can be made shorter or longer, depending upon the students.

Bird Blindfolds. Make a bird blindfold with side holes in it. Have children sit down, and put it on. From this sitting position, children can "see" what it is like to be able to only see what is on either side of their head. They must cock their head to see straight in front of them, as a bird would do. Have several items placed in front of the student(s) wearing a bird blindfold. Identify them. LOOK and pick one up with your hand. LOOK, then LOOK AWAY and pick one up with your hand. (Imagine the skill it takes for a bird to see a worm in front of it, then twist its head and with its beak get the worm that it can't see. Some children may be able to get this concept.) The owl is one bird that has two eyes in the front of its head and can see straight forward, and rotate its neck.

Kites

Make a simple kite for flying. See the math section on kites for flying them outdoors on a breezy day.

IT'S YOUR LUCKY DAY!

A shamrock is a clover that grows in Ireland. If you find one, you're sure to be lucky!
You'll also be lucky if you know all of the vowels. Trace over the capital letter vowel in
each shamrock and then write the lowercase vowel beside it. Color the shamrocks.

Name _____

HAVE YOU SEEN THE FLOWERS?

In March, we begin to see signs that spring is coming soon. Look for flowers that may be peeping out of the ground. Read the number word in each box and then circle the correct number of flowers. Color the flowers with cheery colors.

three

two

four

six

one

five

zero

Name _____

SHORT VOWEL FLASH CARDS

Now that you know about vowels and their special sounds, it's time to practice. Each of the pictures below represents a vowel. Color the pictures and then cut the little cards apart on the black lines. You should have ten cards—five picture cards and five letter cards. Mix the cards up and then match each vowel to its special picture. Have a friend hold up the picture cards and you say the name of the vowel.

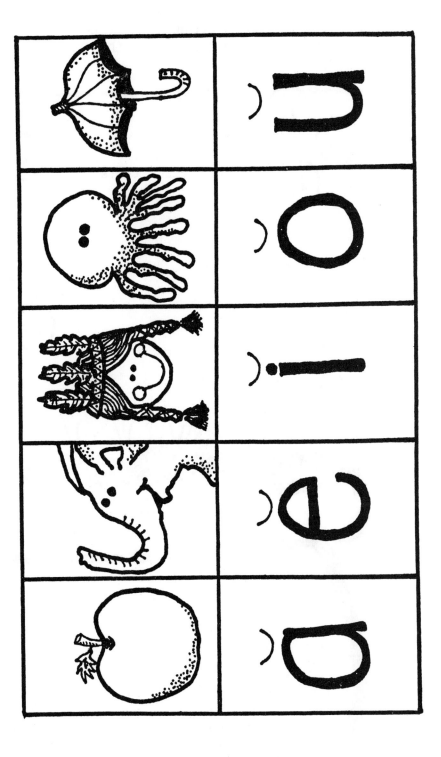

Name _____

A POT OF GOLD

You have just found a pot of gold. Before you can keep the money, you must count the number of pennies in each set and write the correct numeral on the line. Each penny is worth one cent. How many cents are on this page?

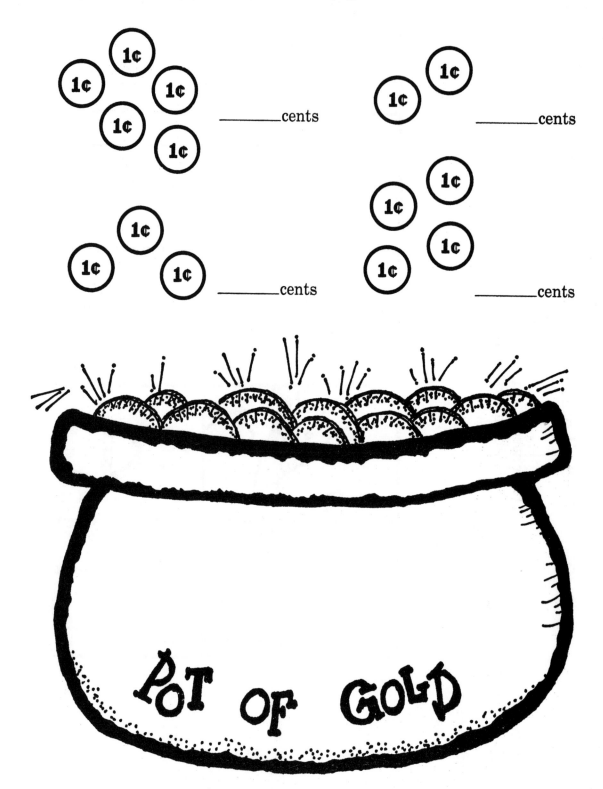

Name _____

OVER THE RAINBOW

We often see rainbows after a rainstorm. Some people say that they bring good luck and that if you find the end of a rainbow, there will be a pot of gold there. Read the color words and color the rainbow.

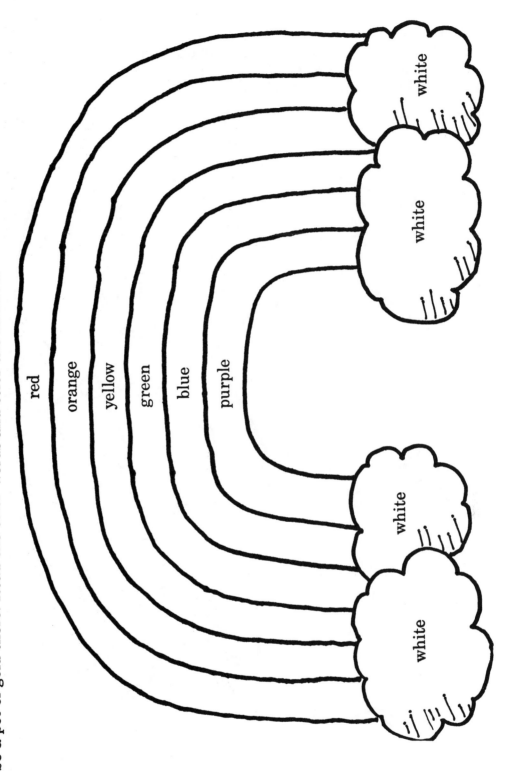

red

orange

yellow

green

blue

purple

white

white

white

white

LET'S GO FLY A KITE!

You can make these kites soar high in the March sky. They won't fly, however, unless you add the ties to the kite tails. Look at each kite carefully. Trace the numeral on each kite and then add the correct number of ties to the tail. The first one is done for you. Color the kites with bright colors.

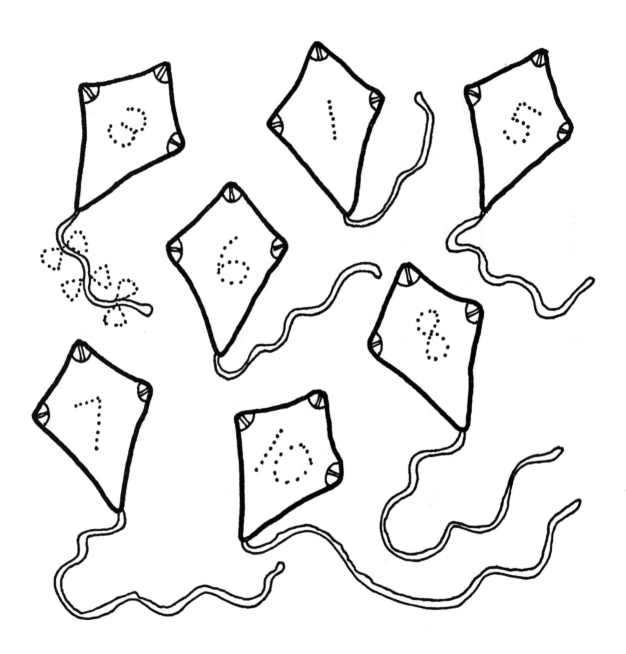

A MARCH CONCENTRATION GAME

Each of the boxes below contains a picture or word about March. Color each picture and cut the boxes apart on the lines. To play the March memory game: Lay the cards face down and turn over two cards at a time. If the cards match, you may keep them. If the cards don't match, turn them back over. Your turn is over. Try to remember where each March word or picture is hidden as the other players take their turns. The person with the most matches wins the game.

(kite)	(lamb face)	March	(pinwheel)
windy	(cloud)	Pot of Gold	(lamb face)
(pinwheel)	(lamb)	(kite)	(cloud)
Pot of Gold	March	(lamb)	windy

Name _____

SPRING THINGS

These boxes are filled with things that you might see in March. Look at each box and count the number of objects in it. Then find the matching number word and draw a line to it. The first one is done for you. Color the spring things.

REBUS PICTURES

Color the pictures below and then cut them apart on the black lines. Use them with the rebus words to make up sentences. Read the sentences to a friend. Read them to the teacher. Read them to your family. Aren't you proud that you can read! Keep the rebus picture and word cards in an envelope with your name on the front.

REBUS WORDS

Rebus sentences contain both pictures and words. The words below are little ones that you can read and remember. Practice reading the words, then cut them apart on the black lines. You can use the words and the pictures from the rebus picture page to make sentences. Arrange the picture and word cards in a row on the floor to make a sentence that you can read. Don't forget the period or question mark at the end of the sentence. First, write sentences that make sense. Then make up silly sentences.

and	with	go	to
will	he	she	it
is	on	in	a
the	I	.	?

LIONS AND LAMBS

You can practice subtracting with lions and lambs. Each box has a number sentence written beneath it. The first numeral in the sentence tells how many animals are in the box. The second numeral tells you how many lions or lambs to cross out. You write the numeral that tells how many animals are left. Color the lions and lambs.

$2 - 1 =$

$3 - 1 =$

$4 - 2 =$

$3 - 2 =$

$1 - 0 =$

$5 - 3 =$

Name _____

MARCH COMES IN LIKE A AND GOES OUT LIKE A

March weather is always changing. Below there are symbols to show four different kinds of weather to expect in March. Count how many there are of each kind. Graph that number by coloring in the correct number of boxes above each one.

5				
4				
3				
2				
1				
	snow	rain	cloudy	sunny

THE LEPRECHAUN LOOK

Nobody knows for sure what a leprechaun looks like. Some people claim to have seen one. In picture books, leprechauns usually wear a pointed hat ✎ . They have pointed ears ⟩⟩ , a mustache ∽ , and a long beard 🦷 . Their shoes have pointed toes 👞👞 . And they usually wear the color green. What do you think a leprechaun looks like? Finish the picture below.

Shhh! Work quietly. Leprechauns like quiet places. If it's quiet, maybe one will come out of hiding and you can get a good look at it, and it will help your picture!

Name _____

WHO WILL MOVE IN?

Some birds make their home from a dried gourd that has been hollowed out and hung over a tree branch. The birds are "house shopping" today.

   Color two red birds on the branch.

   Color one black bird on the right side of the gourd.

   Color two blue birds on the gourd.

   Color the gourd a bright yellow.

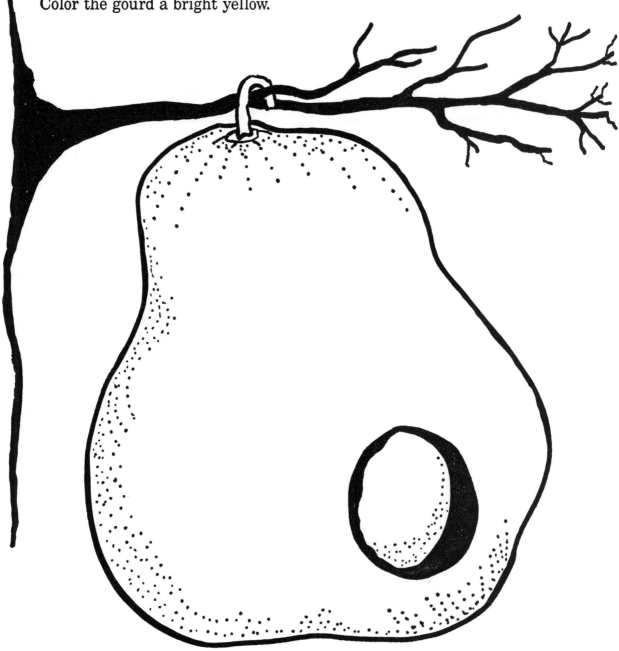

Who moved into the gourd? Make a picture of the bird in the hole that has been carved in the gourd. What is the name of the bird? What color is it? Find pictures of different kinds of bird nests. Draw one on the back of this page.

WORKING WITH WEIGHT

We have a scale in our room and can weigh many things. Today we are working with 2 pounds (2 lbs.). The cookies weigh 2 pounds.

Find two items that weigh MORE THAN 2 pounds and draw them in the spaces. Find two items that weigh LESS THAN 2 pounds and draw them in the spaces.

Cookies
2 lbs.

2 pounds can be written like this _2 lbs._

This weighs MORE THAN 2 lbs.
It weighs ____ lbs.

This weighs MORE THAN 2 lbs.
It weighs ____ lbs.

This weighs LESS THAN 2 lbs.
It weighs ____ lbs.

This weighs LESS THAN 2 lbs.
It weighs ____ lbs.

Can you find something that weighs 1 lb.? 3 lbs.? ½ lb.?

APRIL

A Cloudburst of Classroom Creativity

It's April, and there's a cloudburst of creative ideas in the air. This month in reading, we're emphasizing sentences, and focusing upon children's literature with related activities. For rainy-day math, there is graphing, problem-solving, and estimation. The Easter Rabbit comes to call this month with many learning opportunities. Even though teachers work on self-esteem all year, we renew the effort this spring. A warm, supportive, understanding teacher makes the sun shine indoors—even on rainy days!

Recommended Children's Books for April

The Easter Egg Artists by Adrienne Adams (New York: Charles Scribner's Sons, 1976). The Abbot family earns their living decorating Easter eggs. Orson, the youngest Abbot rabbit, enjoys painting so much that he paints designs on things other than eggs. He designs a special egg with a face that becomes such a hit that the family can hardly keep up with the demand for them. This book is good for the budding artist.

Benjamin's 365 Birthdays by Judi Barrett, illustrated by Ron Barrett (New York: Atheneum, 1974). Benjamin, a thoughtful, sensitive dog, has a birthday on April 9. He gives a wonderful luncheon party for his guests and receives many nice presents. It makes him a bit sad to think that birthdays only come once a year, so he thinks up a solution for celebrating his birthday every day of the year.

Easter Treat by Roger Duvoisin (New York: Alfred A. Knopf, 1954). Santa Claus is eager to get away from the icy wind and snow and take an Easter vacation. Mrs. Santa reminds him that he can't be seen in his red suit, so he disguises himself as a tourist and heads for a big city. With that long white beard, those twinkling eyes and the red nose, can Santa really remain incognito for long? ("Incognito" is a vocabulary term that is introduced and explained in the book—language development.)

The Easter Bunny That Overslept by Priscilla and Otto Friedrich, illustrated by Adrienne Adams (New York: Lothrop, Lee & Shepard Co., 1957). A friendly tale about the Easter Bunny who is prepared for Easter but is sound asleep in his burrow when the big day comes. In fact, he oversleeps for one month! He tries to fit into several other holidays including the Fourth of July, Halloween, and Christmas but it just doesn't work. Finally, Santa presents him with the perfect gift for his job.

The Wonderful Tree, A Story of Seasons by Adelaide Hall, paintings by Gyorgy Lehoczky (New York: Golden Press, 1974). Young Christopher goes through the seasons of the year, as his kindly grandfather adds his recollections as well as his wisdom about the ways of nature. Beautiful illustrations. The story is told in a way that will help children to gain an understanding of nature's calendar.

Shapes and Things by Tana Hoban (New York: Macmillan Publishing Co., Inc., 1970). This book of common items found in the home, school, office is an exciting visual experience. It's a startling black and white representation of objects that children will be able to identify by the outlines and solid shapes. Very good for visual discrimination.

I Unpacked My Grandmother's Trunk by Susan Ramsey Hoguet (New York: E. P. Dutton, 1983). This familiar alphabet game has been put into book form. The first child reaches into grandmother's trunk and takes out an acrobat. The second child turns the page and finds an acrobat and a bear. The third child turns the page and finds an acrobat, a bear, and a cloud. By the time we get to Z the pages are crowded with wonderful illustrations. The value of this book is that it appeals to two learning styles, visual as well as verbal, to help children with memorization.

Will It Rain? by Holly Keller (New York: Greenwillow Books, 1984). As the robin is pulling on a fat worm he feels a change in the air. The reader is taken through a storm via pictures of animals experiencing dark skies, loud winds, lightning streaks. They all run for cover and when it's all over, the fresh, sunny day is a treat.

Inch by Inch by Leo Lionni (New York: Astor-Honor, Inc., 1960). A picture book that could help children begin to develop an interest in measurement. An inchworm measures animals, tails, beaks, and legs and even is able to get himself out of potential trouble by slowly moving along inch by inch.

The April Fool by Alice Schertle, illustrated by Emily Arnold McCully (New York: Lothrop, Lee &

Shepard Co., 1981). In this "once upon a time" tale, the king is constantly irritable because his feet hurt. He can't find a comfortable pair of shoes! Everyone tries to find him a pair and they fail. Finally, his majesty gives up on the shoes and hires fools (court jesters) to make him laugh to forget his aching feet. The February Fool and March Fool try their best but leave it to the April Fool to soothe the king's temper...and his feet.

Reading Skills Activities

Sight Words

Words in the Environment. Reinforce words that came up in your teaching last month. Also, work with the following sight words: days of the week, color words, number words, labels on items in the classroom, names of the months, student's first and last names, names of classmates, weather words (sunny, cloudy, rainy, etc.), names of special classes such as art, music, gym, etc., any TV programs that are being viewed regularly. By this time children have built up quite an awareness of "words" in their environment.

Word Concentration Game. Do a form of the "Concentration" game. Make sets of color words and color names, and sets of number words and numerals, and sets of sight words and an accompanying picture. Students can play the games in pairs or in teams. For example, for numerals, put all of the numeral cards face down in a square. Put all of the number name cards face down in a pile. Children draw from the pile and point to a card in the square. Turn card over. Is it a match? If yes, student gets a point. If no, turn card over again, and it is the next person's turn. (Good exercise for strengthening memory span, because children should try to remember where the numerals are when they are turned back over.)

VARIATION: Play the "I'm thinking of a..." game but this time do it differently. Use this phrase, "I'm thinking of a color word that begins with the letter 'y,' and it's the color of the sun."

Word Bags. Make a set of picture cards and a set of name cards that represent labels in the classroom. Children reach in and get a card and keep it, and wait for the right match. Those with the most matching cards win.

Retelling Stories

Begin with familiar stories such as *The Three Bears, Red Riding Hood,* and *The Three Billy Goats Gruff.* Have the children write down the story in their own words and make pictures to go with the story. The children can retell their story aloud on the tape recorder.

VARIATION: Use flannelboard and cutouts for retelling, this time emphasizing the action.

The Storyteller. Make a storyteller costume. Collect a suit coat, eyeglasses with no lenses, scarf, top hat, gloves, or any other clothing desired. Turn out the lights except for the one over the storyteller.

A Rainy Day Book

Do one page per day, then put together the pages on Friday. Use 9″ × 12″ white construction paper. Draw with crayons and print the word with black crayon. Some picture suggestions are: umbrella, boots, clouds, raindrops, rainbow. Staple the finished pictures together or use a paper punch and tie together with thick yarn or ribbon. OPTIONAL: Watercolor the pictures with a wash of blue, light purple, or light black to indicate a dark, rainy sky.

Letter Recognition

Special Letter Days. For this month's basket, work with special letters that your particular group needs extra help with. There could be a variety of letters represented. Children can vote on a favorite letter day for each week and on that special day, bring in something for the "letter table."

Special treats for the letters of the alphabet serve as reinforcers. Go through the ABCs with the students, and elicit some food names. For "treats" here are some suggestions: A–almonds; B–blueberry muffins; C–carrots; D–donut holes; E–egg salad; F–fruit salad (graph it); G–grapes; H–ham salad; I–ice cream; J–juice; K–ketchup; L–lemonade; M–marshmallows; N–nuts; O–orange; P–pizza; Q–quince jelly; R–raisins; S–salami; T–tacos; U–ultra-good fruit; V–vegetable; W–watermelon; X–"x-tra" good pudding; Y–yogurt; Z–zucchini.

Dress-Up Day. Have students dress up to celebrate their very favorite alphabet letter. Make headbands with appropriate ears for letter variations, and/ or make face masks from paper plates.

Sentences

April Fool! Have the children listen carefully to see whether a sentence is fact or foolish. Some examples are: A big green firetruck will visit our classroom today for snack time. The weather forecaster said we will see purple snow falling from the sky today.

Foolish Sentences. Write foolish sentences on the board and direct children's attention to them. How can they be changed to make them factual? (For example, "Today Tuesday is," and "We gym have today," etc.) Have students verbally make up foolish sentences about the weather, school, Easter, or your class.

Authors and Illustrators

There has been an "explosion" in the field of children's literature and today we are fortunate to have many, many people who are highly regarded in their profession, writing and illustrating good books for children. As books are read to children, read the title AND the name of the author and illustrator. Also, look at the endpapers of the book. To whom is the book dedicated? What type of media is used for illustrations? Choose certain authors to explore with children, and have them work in the same medium, if the developmental level of the children permits. Be sure to let parents know of good children's books that would make fine presents.

Maurice Sendak. Over a one-week period, explore *Where the Wild Things Are*. Have the children draw a picture of Max and his boat, and a wild thing. The children can crosshatch (see the book's style) the picture.

Make "wild thing headbands" with bright-colored horns and act out the story. Read *Chicken Soup with Rice*. Make a cutout of a boy and crosshatch him. Make one of the arms moveable with a paper fastener. Paste a spoon in one hand and a bowl in the other. Serve chicken rice soup for the occasion. Read *Seven Little Monsters*. Children can make monster bookmarks on oaktag. Laminate them. Read *Pierre* and make lion puppets on a stick and act out the story. Obtain movie, "Really Rosie," from the library and show it to the group.

Ezra Jack Keats. Over a one-week period, read such books as *Peter's Chair, Whistle for Willie, Hi Cat!, Goggles,* and *Pet Show.* Keats worked with collages—torn and cut paper stuck onto a background sheet to build pictures. He used vivid colors, dark faces, wallpaper for interesting textures. For *Jennie's Hat,* make a huge bulletin board of a little face at the bottom and a great BIG hat. Have children cut out items from magazines that relate to spring. Collect a box of items such as cupcake papers, ribbon, yarn, aluminum foil, tissue paper that can be twisted. Have children "decorate" the giant hat with the items so that the hat becomes a big collage. Staple real ribbon bands on the sides of the hat and tie a big bow under Jennie's chin. Also, put a bird nest (paper or real) on the hat.

Leo Lionni. Over a one-week period, make torn paper mice for *Frederick* and *Alexander and the Wind-Up Mouse.* After reading *The Biggest House in the World,* have the children cut a spiral shell and paste it onto a 9″ × 12″ sheet of construction paper. Paste a strip of fringed paper along the bottom for grass. Draw a snail's head. Cut a yellow sun and paste it in the sky. For *Swimmy,* trace and cut out a black fish shape. Use a hole puncher to make the eye. On white 9″ × 12″ manila paper, make a green and blue watercolor wash, and then glue Swimmy in this ocean.

Eric Carle. Over a one-week period, read *The Very Hungry Caterpillar.* Retell it and illustrate it with felt cutouts. Illustrate it as a big class book, using colorful tissue paper that the children cut and glue on with rubber cement. (Be sure you help the children with this.) Read *The Grouchy Ladybug* and trace and cut out ladybugs from construction paper. Make ladybug necklaces out of paper and wear them for good luck. For *The Mixed-Up Chameleon,* place an 18″ × 24″ sheet of paper on the floor for each child. The children can do the outline of the chameleon in black crayon and color in with other crayons.

Children Become Authors/Illustrators. Children can make their own books working in small groups. Some can write their own, and some can dictate the text. Wallpaper makes excellent covers, and books can be stapled. The book can be about any topic and should include a title page, author/illustrator name, dedication, and pictures and text on each page. Students can share their books with the class. Also, they can share the books with school personnel. Have them take a Reaction Sheet along (see Reproducible Activity Pages) so that adults can make nice comments about the books. (Invite other teachers into the classroom so that children can sit in their laps and read their book aloud to them.)

Math Skills Activities

Manipulatives

Umbrella Math. Make up a kit of construction paper umbrellas and raindrops. Put problems on umbrellas (For example, "2 + 1 =") and answers on raindrops. Children can match them.

Math for a Rainy Day. Place a real umbrella up high enough so that children can touch the handle but not the ends of the spokes, and place math supplies underneath it. Make a sign for the umbrella that reads "Math for a Rainy Day." Use commercial materials or teacher-made materials such as geoboards, measuring rods, cubes, wooden blocks, clips, counting beads, math games, and other commercial materials. This attractive spot will attract

children during free choice time and give them additional "hands on" practice with manipulative materials.

Measuring

Growing Plants. Put lima beans in a glass jar between the edge and a piece of paper toweling wrapped around the inside. Keep water in the bottom of the jar to keep the toweling moist. Observe the plant growth. Draw from sample. Then plant and measure growth in inches.

VARIATION: Using big trays, plant tomato plants, marigolds, green beans, nasturtiums. Notice the difference in the seeds. Graph their growth.

Planting Herbs in Cups. Plant herb seeds in a styrofoam cup. When the seedling appears, child can take home the cup with a recipe attached showing that the herb can be used in salad or casserole dishes. Try planting seeds such as dill, parsley, sage.

More with Graphs

A graph is a picture that gives us information in an instant, and it is a valuable teaching tool. In April, in addition to graphing growing plants, you can graph favorite shapes, birds seen in the schoolyard, favorite author/illustrator, favorite part of *Where the Wild Things Are,* favorite book, favorite season that Frederick talks about, favorite Leo Lionni sea creature, favorite Ezra Jack Keats character.

Problem Solving

Seed Addition/Subtraction. Practice addition and subtraction facts using dry beans on a brown background. OR, fill a jar with a mixture of seeds and have students categorize them by biggest/smallest and then most/least.

Popcorn Estimation. Using popcorn seeds, measure 1 cup. Will it make 1 cup when popped? Estimate the number of cups that 1 cup will make. Then make up a rebus math strip about the 1 cup of popcorn seeds that was equal to ____ cups of popped corn. Is the same true for colored popcorn seeds?

More "Seedy" Problems. Why did some plants grow and some not grow? Try some experiments, and after one week check the plants to find out the answers. For example, ask, "Why didn't these plants grow? We planted them in good soil and watered them daily and put them on a shelf in the closed cupboard?" (No light.) AND, "Why didn't these plants grow? We planted them in good soil and put them in a sunny window?" (No water.) "Why didn't these plants grow? We put them in a cup, watered them daily, and put them in a sunny window?" (No soil.) THEN, hopefully, "Why did these grow?" (Water, sun, good soil.)

Counting by 10

Rote Counting. Make a chart with numerals from 1 to 100 so that children can gain practice in rote counting. Make all of the tens a different color, so that they are easily identifiable by children (10, 20, 30, 40, etc.).

A Sense of Ten. Put kraft paper on the floor and lay out things in rows of 10, such as 10 pine cones, 10 pencils, 10 leaves, 10 shoes, and so on, so that the children get a sense of "10." You can also make up bundles of 10 straws so that the children can take the bundles apart and count from 1 to 10 and KNOW that there are 10 in the bundle when it is put back together.

Estimation, Counting, and Graphing

Jelly Bean Math. Fill a medium-sized see-through jar with colorful jelly beans. Children can estimate the number of beans. Record the estimate after each child's name on a colorful egg shape. When all have made an estimate, dump the jelly beans into a clean plastic bowl. Using cellophane gloves children can separate the different colors into various smaller bowls.

Children can estimate again! How many black jelly beans, red ones, green ones, etc.? They can write their estimations on colored paper to match up with the colored beans. Have children work in pairs to count the number of each colored set of beans. Record the count and check the estimations. Add them all together to get the correct grand total.

Mix all of the jelly beans back together again, and with plastic gloves place a small handful into small plastic bags, so that each child has a set. Use a paper towel to cover desk or table workplace and have children separate their jelly beans by color. Next, graph them in a vertical line. How many of each color? Name the most and the least. Eat two of each. Has anyone eliminated a color? Eat two more of each. Now, has anyone eliminated a color? More subtraction

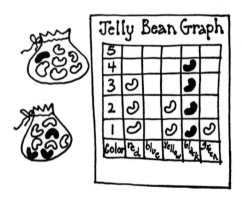

work can be done with the jelly beans, or by this time it might be just the right time to enjoy the rest of them.

Easter Bags. Children like "Easter Baggies." Use small plastic bags (double), put commercial Easter grass in the bottom, and a handful of colored jelly beans. Tie with a twister, and yarn or ribbon. Distribute them to children as they are leaving so that they can go home and practice their estimation and graphing with the jelly beans just like they did in class.

Numbers to Grow On

From the weighing/measuring done at the beginning of the year, weigh and measure again, and make growth comparisons. How much taller are we—show the difference on a yardstick. How much more or less do we weigh—show the difference on the scale pointer.

Age by Years and Months. Talk about age by years and months, such as 5 years and 7 months, 6 years and 1 month, and so on. How many more months to go until you reach the next number?

Measuring Body Parts. Use pieces of yarn and make comparisons. Measure head circumference and compare. Measure length of arm, leg, waist, chest, etc. Children enjoy doing this and making the comparisons. (See Reproducible Activity Pages.)

Other Skill Areas Activities

Easter

A Festival. This is a spring festival to celebrate the return of the warm sun to the earth. Just as the earth puts on new clothes (leaves, flowers), so, too, do people wear new clothes and flowers in their hair and hats. This custom has been carried out for many centuries. As a symbol of the renewal of the life of the sun, eggs were decorated and colored, and were given as gifts. Some people say that since rabbits are born in the very early part of spring, they have become a part of the celebration of "new growth" and "new life." And thus we have the Easter Rabbit who delivers colorful eggs.

Make Easter Baskets. Get some green plastic baskets that hold the fresh fruit at supermarkets. Children can weave ribbon in and out of the small squares. This is also an excellent eye-hand coordination exercise. OR, cut off the tops of milk cartons and rinse bottoms well. Allow to dry. Wrap colored purple or yellow paper around cartons, and have children decorate them with crayons. OR, a styrofoam cup with purple or green grass can be decorated and used for an Easter container. Use pipe cleaner handle.

Passover

Passover is an important Jewish holiday that is celebrated about the same time as Easter, and lasts for eight days. It is the holiday of independence, and special dinners and retelling of the story of the exodus of Jews from Egypt under their leader, Moses. Stories are told again and again to pass down traditions. Discuss "traditions" that children celebrate at this time of year, and stories that are told again and again by their family, relatives, or neighbors.

April Fool's Day

April Fish. Did you know that in France, on April 1, children try to fasten a paper fish on a friend's back? The victim is then an April Fish. Make fish shapes, place a word on each, and place them on the backs of five children. They have to guess who or what they are. Mix up the fish shapes, and place the same ones on the backs of five different children, and they have to guess who or what they are. It becomes more easy for children to guess as this is repeated.

Dress-Down Day. Use April Fool's Day for a "dress down day"—when children can come to school in play clothes. Use April Fool's Day as a day when children are wearing something "crazy"—socks that don't match, shoes that don't match, earrings that don't match, an inside shirt over an outside shirt, etc. All sit in a circle and just observe each other in order to discover what is foolish about the clothing.

Let's Be Foolish! To be foolish means to be rather silly and not have much sense. Let's pretend our thumb is stuck to our elbow and see how long we can remember to keep it there. As soon as someone removes thumb, that person is "it" and has to think of some foolish position for everyone to try. (Some suggestions: holding onto one strand of hair; standing on just one foot; holding right ankle with left hand; keeping one eye closed.) Children will come up with many suggestions.

Self-Concept

Kindergarten teachers are working on this all year long, every day, with positive reinforcement. Studies show that self-concept is "learned" from significant others—and teachers certainly fall into this very important category for the young, growing child. Carl Jung, the famous psychoanalyst, said, "The curriculum is so much necessary raw material but WARMTH is the vital element for the growing plant and for the soul of the child." It is an awesome responsibility!

"All About Me" Booklets. The pages can contain information about height/weight, self-portrait that shows color of hair and eyes, favorite food, favorite _____, pet, what they will look like when they're older, what career they'll be involved with.

Body Tracing. Children can trace their body shapes and color them in with facial features and clothing. Cut them out. Pin the children's tracings on the bulletin board or tape them along the wall. Have a catchy title such as "The Bunch from Room 21" or "The Gang's All Here." The children can print their names and attach them to the outlines. Use the "cartoon bubble" and have children dictate what they would like passersby to know about them—information about family, pets, hobbies.

A Talent Show. Have a talent show in which children can do something special, such as read a poem, paint a picture to share, dance, sing, tell a riddle, do a magic trick, and so on.

Creative Art

Here are several recipes to use in creative art activities.

SOAP "CLAY"

Materials: 2 cups soap chips or detergent

½ cup water

Whip with beater. Stir in more soap until mixture is like dough. Dip hands into water before using. This can be molded and dried. Less soap, whipped to the consistency of meringue, can be used in a cookie press or pastry tube, and can be used as decorations on other dough.

SAWDUST "CLAY"

Materials: 3 cups sawdust

1 cup wallpaper paste

Add water gradually until mixture is like biscuit dough. Mold, and allow to dry.

Uncooked Salt Dough

Materials: 2 cups salt

1 cup cornstarch

1 cup water

Mix dry ingredients together well first. Add water and (optional) 1 teaspoon alum or salad oil. This will keep in a plastic bag for about two weeks.

Plaster of Paris. Add dry plaster to water until consistency is rich and creamy. Stir well. Pour into mold (pie tin, small milk containers) or onto paper toweling. Can be used for hand prints, or can be decorated with items pressed into the mixture as it is "setting up." Can also be molded and used for modeling with fine tool. Dry tempera paint can be added for color, or it can be painted when dry.

Paste Materials

1 cup flour	3 tablespoons alum (optional)
1 cup sugar	2 cups hot water
2 cups cold water	2 drops oil of cloves

Mix dry ingredients with cold water and then add hot water. Cook in double boiler for ½ hour and add oil of cloves. Makes 1 quart.

Papier-Mâché

1 cup flour

2 cups hot water

2 teaspoons liquid glue

few drops oil of cloves

Make a creamy paste with flour and cold water, then add hot water and other ingredients. (Tear newspaper into small bits and pieces. Let soak for 24 hrs. in pail of warm water. Stir occasionally. Squeeze out excess water. Add the paste to the mashed paper and shape as desired. Let dry.) This material is light but durable.

Children can mold animals and face masks. Allow 1 to 2 days for drying. Paint with tempera paint. Other decorations can be glued on.

Make Your Own Paint

1 cup liquid starch

6 cups water

½ cup soap powder

Food coloring

Dissolve soap in water and mix with starch. Add coloring. (This would be a good review for mixing primary and secondary colors—red (primary) and yellow (primary) = orange (secondary), and blue (primary) and yellow (primary) = green (secondary). Let children predict: What happens if we mix red and blue? Red, yellow, and blue?

Peanut Butter Play Dough (You Can Eat It)

Peanut butter

Honey

Powdered milk

Start by mixing globs of peanut butter with powdered milk. A few tablespoons of honey will hold it all together. Recipe amounts are flexible depending upon needs.

Finger Paint. Commercial finger paint or powdered tempera mixed with water. For variety, children can paint on Formica tabletop area or countertop area. To make a "permanent print" of this, place a large sheet of paper over the top of the finger painting. With hand, press gently and evenly over entire paper. Remove sideways by lifting top and bottom corners gently. Allow to dry. HINT: Finger paintings are lovely when framed.

Muffin Crayons (Used Crayon Recipe)

Used crayons

Muffin tins

Muffin tin foil liners

Keep extra crayons in coffee cans. When they become too little to be useful, separate the colors. Make sure all paper has been removed. Place all reds in one section, all blue in another, etc. (It's fun sometimes to place a mixture of colors in one.) Place muffin tin in warming oven until crayons melt. The "old" crayons will form a "new" large crayon— muffin size, for creative drawing.

Collage materials

Bits of scrap paper

Material scraps

Liquid glue

Background paper

Encourage children to place the items on the background paper before they glue them on. Change the materials from time to time.

Outdoor collage materials

Background heavy paper or cardboard

shells

twigs
wheat
cattails
seeds
dried flowers
weeds

A collage of outdoor materials can be left natural or spray painted OUTDOORS for a different effect. (For example, orange and red for autumn, green and yellow for spring.)

Name

A TIME FOR PLANTING

Someone planted seeds from the packets below and they've grown into beautiful flowers. Look at each seed packet in the top row and then draw a line to the matching pot of flowers in the bottom row. Next, count the number of flowers in each flowerpot and write the correct numeral on the side of the pot. Color the seed packets, the flowers, and the flowerpots. Use bright, spring colors.

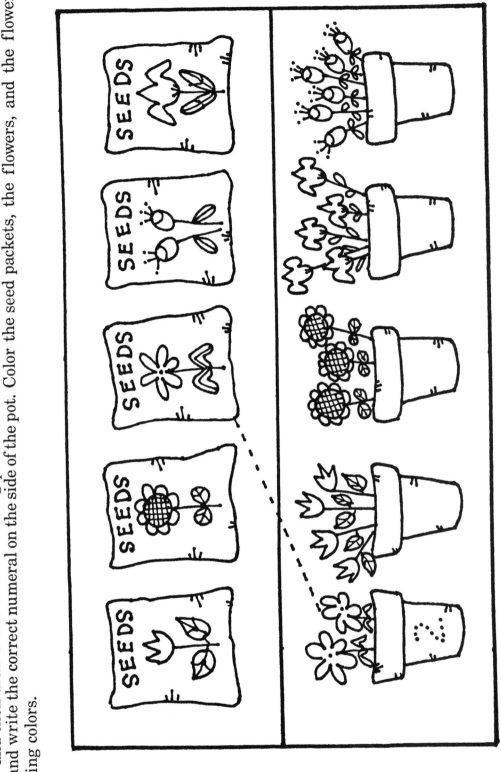

FLASH CARDS FOR NUMBER AND COLOR WORDS

These flashcards will help you practice your color words and number words. Cut the cards apart on the black lines. Work by yourself or with a friend. Mix the cards up so that when you turn a card over, it's a surprise. As you turn each card over, say the word. If you aren't sure what it is, ask an adult or a friend who can read these words. Keep the flashcards in an envelope with your name on the front.

red	yellow	one	two	three	four
blue	green	five	six	seven	eight
brown	purple	nine	ten	eleven	twelve
orange	black	zero	Number Words	Color Words	I can read!

Name _____

THE BIRDS ARE BACK!

These birds are flying back to their home after spending the winter in a warmer place. The first bird has a 10 on its chest and the last bird has 100 on its chest. Can you fill in the numerals that should be on the chests on the other birds? Remember to count by 10s. Color the picture. There are _____ birds in this picture.

Name _____

MATCH THE DECORATED EGGS

Someone has been busy decorating these Easter eggs. Look closely at the eggs in the first row. Draw a line from the eggs in the first row to the matching eggs in the second row. Decorate the eggs with your crayons or markers.

A WATERING CAN ALPHABET

Spring is here and the flowers are beginning to grow. Be sure to keep them watered. To use this watering can, you first have to trace over the lowercase letters that are there for you and fill in the missing letters. Remember that you must write LOWERCASE LETTERS.

Name _____

RAINY DAY NUMBERS

April showers bring May flowers! These clouds are dropping rain on the umbrellas below. Count the number of raindrops under each cloud and draw a line to the umbrella with the matching numeral. Color the pictures in rainy day colors.

Name _____

A DUCK BUNNY

Color one side of this animal to be a duck and the other to be a bunny. Cut out the duck bunny.

This part can be a duck bill or bunny ears.

This part can be a duck tail or bunny feet.

This part can be duck feet or a bunny tail.

Name _____

MEASURING ME!

You've really grown since school started in September. Measure yourself and record the information on this chart. Use a piece of string and a yardstick and ask a friend to help you. First, measure around your head, above the ears. Put your finger on the string where it meets the other end. Hold tight! Put the string on the yardstick with one end at zero. What number is the other end of the string closest to? Record that number on the line.

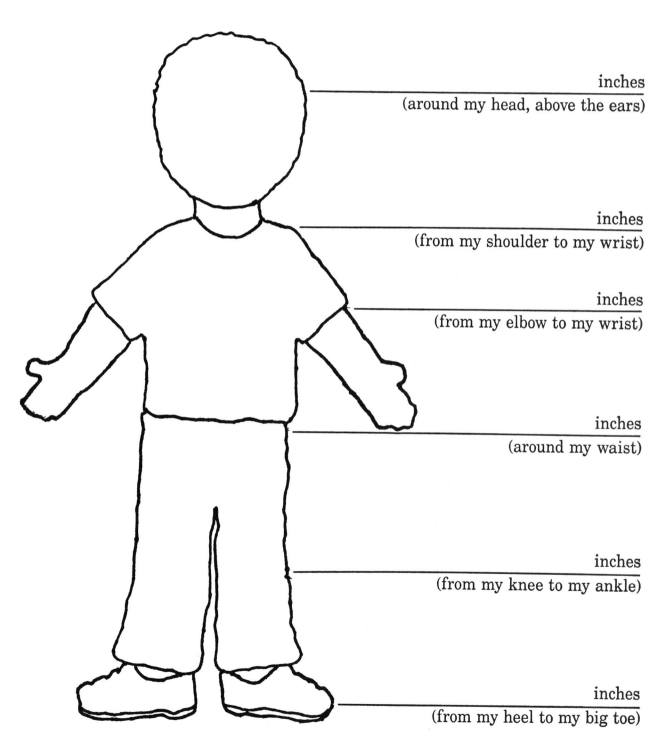

_____ inches
(around my head, above the ears)

_____ inches
(from my shoulder to my wrist)

_____ inches
(from my elbow to my wrist)

_____ inches
(around my waist)

_____ inches
(from my knee to my ankle)

_____ inches
(from my heel to my big toe)

Name _____

THE JELLY BEAN JAR

This jar is full of jelly beans. Look at the jelly bean code below and color each of the beans correctly. Then look at the number on each bean in the jar and color each one according to the secret code.

THE EGG BOOK

This is the story of how a little chick hatched from an egg. "Once upon a time there was an egg. The egg began to crack. Before you knew it, a little chick was pecking at the egg and poking its head out of the shell. Finally, the little chick jumped out and said, 'Happy spring!'" This book is shaped like an egg. Color the pictures and then cut the pages out on the black lines. Put the pages in the correct sequence and staple one side.

The
Egg Book
by
_____

Name _____

MAKE YOUR SPRING HAT

It's Spring! That means you need a new hat. Decorate your hat with animals, flowers, sports items, or your very favorite things. Cut out the hat. Staple ribbons on strings at the two "X" spots, and tie it around the back of your head. Have a Spring parade!

This can be reproduced on heavy paper and students can glue on feathers, and pieces of bright cloth.

Name _____

This little book tells some things about me. I helped to make it with my pencil and crayons. Then, I cut the pages apart on the black lines. Next, I stapled them together. I can read it to you.

A Shower of Good News About

(name)

I look like this.

My two favorite colors

My Height

My Age

Name _____

Make your pictures within the rainy day symbols. For a picture of your family, just make the faces. Cut the pages apart on the black lines. Staple them together for an eight page book, or a two page book.

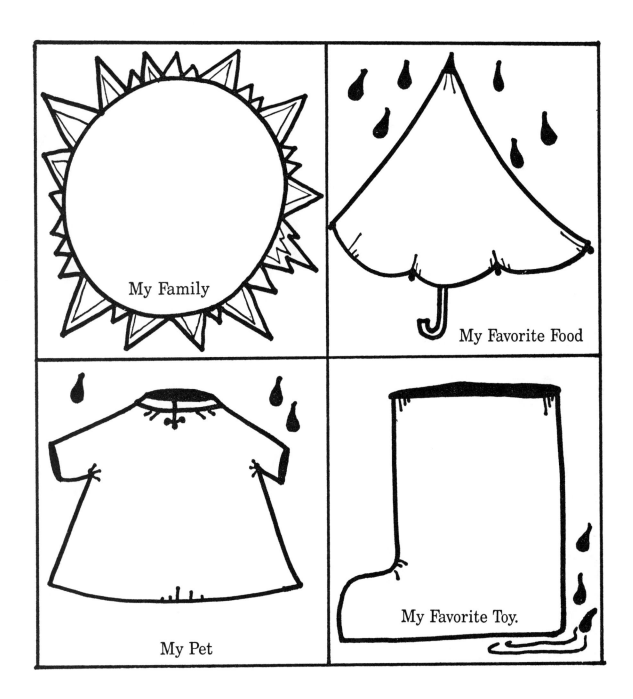

AN EASTER EGG TALLY

Every time the Easter Rabbit decorates ten eggs, he puts one egg in this basket. That helps him to keep track of his eggs. You can help. Write the numerals *by tens* on the eggs. How many does he have in total? Put the numeral in this box.
Be sure to decorate each egg with a different color and design. Make the basket look pretty too!

Name _____

MAKE A BUNNY NECKLACE

Color these three rabbits so that they look bright and healthy. Paste them onto a piece of oaktag and cut them out. Glue on a cotton tail. Make a paper punch circle at the "X." String them onto colorful yarn. Wear them as a necklace.

Name _____

TEDDY BEAR RESPONSE FORM

Hi! May I read this book to you? Thank you!

This is a Reaction Sheet. Please be patient with me. I hope you like my story. Please fill in the space below.

Name	School Position or Room Number	Supportive Comments

SPRING SHAPES

Now that Spring is here, you are spending more time outdoors. Take a good look around. Squint your eyes so that you can see just the outline shape of many things. Then, using your crayons, finish these shapes by making them into signs of spring. (For example: tree, house, bird, flower, animal.)

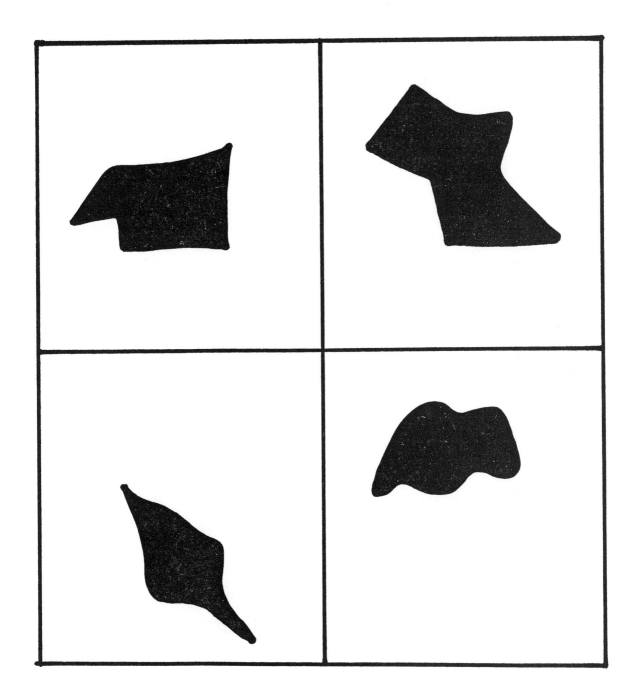

Compare your finished shape items with those of your classmates. How many different things did people draw using the same "starter" shape?

MAY AND JUNE

My, How You've Grown!

Basic Skills Review

Reading and Writing

"My, How I've Grown" Booklets • 287

Sentences

Rebus Sentence Review • 288
Chalkboard Sentences • 288

Language Development

The Final Curtain • 288

Letter/Sound Review

The Teddy Bears' Picnic Reunion • 289
Games to Play at the Reunion • 289

How quickly this school year has gone by! It hardly seems possible that the children who entered school in the fall are now ready to move along to the next grade level. It is important to reassess each child one last time so that you will have current information to pass along to next year's teacher. You will see that some children have grown steadily all year while others may have gotten a slow start but took off and learned quickly once the activities were under way. Still others are struggling with the concepts and skills presented during the year, and those are the ones you will need to evaluate very carefully. So keep learning alive in your classroom until you "ring down the final curtain"!

Recommended Children's Books for May/June

It's So Nice to Have a Wolf Around the House by Harry Allard, pictures by James Marshall (New York: Doubleday & Co., 1977). A very old man and his very old pets—a cat, a dog, and a goldfish so old that he prefers to float—decide to advertise for a house companion. Cuthbert Q. Devine, a charming wolf disguised as a German shepherd dog, answers the ad. He wins everyone over but one day the newspaper headlines contain startling headlines about a wolf wanted for robbery. What now?

The Summer Noisy Book by Margaret Wise Brown, pictures by Leonard Weisgard (New York: Harper & Row, 1951). Little Muffin, a black puppy, falls asleep in the back seat of a car and as it travels from city to country he is aware of a wide variety of sounds along the way that he can identify as he snoozes. But then Muffin hears a very loud noise way up in the sky that he can't identify.

The Very Hungry Caterpillar by Eric Carle (New York: Collins Publishers, 1979). A number tale about a caterpillar who eats his way through the days of the week and a great deal of colorful food until he finally rests, spins his cocoon, and emerges as a lovely butterfly. There is a small hole in each page to show where the caterpillar has eaten, and this appeals to young children who like to poke their fingers through them as they repeat the counting. The illustrations are big, bright, and appealing.

What's Good for a Six-Year-Old? by William Cole, illustrations by Ingrid Fetz (New York: Holt, Rinehart & Winston, 1965). This is a fast-paced book with lots of ideas of what six-year-olds like to do. Just ask Paul, or Rose, or David, or Ann, or many more children. Each child comes up with a variety of ideas and it's all done in rhyme. Mom has some input too.

Q Is for Duck by Mary Elting and Michael Folsom, pictures by Jack Kent (New York: Houghton Mifflin/Clarion Books, 1980). An alphabet guessing game that holds appeal for children who are familiar with the alphabet. It's playful, and children can join in the fun. (The formula goes like this: "B is for Dog. Why? Because the dog barks.")

Going Barefoot by Aileen Fisher, illustrations by Adrienne Adams (New York: Thomas Y. Crowell Co.,

1960). A little boy, waiting for June to arrive so that he can go barefoot, reviews for the reader, in rhyme, all of the animals that go barefoot all year round.

The Reason for a Flower by Ruth Heller (New York: Grosset & Dunlap, 1984). A beautiful picture book that visually and verbally takes the reader from birds and bees to pollen, seeds, plants and flowers, herbivores, and to flower sizes, smells, and uses. Children will read this again and again—an excellent teaching book.

My Grandpa Retired Today by Elaine Knox-Wagner, pictures by Charles Robinson (Chicago: Albert Whitman & Co., 1982). Margery's grandfather, a barber, is retiring and Margery is the only child who gets to attend his grown-up farewell party at the shop. His friends "retire" the barber's chair with him, and arrange to have it shipped to his home. Some of the mixed feelings of Grandpa's major change are sensed by Margery as he works it out.

Better Move On, Frog! by Ron Maris (New York: Julia MacRae Books, a Division of Franklin Watts, 1982). A frog sees lots of holes and wants one for his own. But, every time he goes to a hole IN a tree, or a hole UNDER a building, or a hole in the SIDE of a hill, he finds that it's already taken. Nature helps the frog to find its own place.

The Boy Who Could Make His Mother Stop Yelling by Ilse Sondheimer, illustrations by Dee deRosa (New York: Rainbow Press,

1982). When little Danny looks up, he perceives his mother as being a very, very big, tall lady. Also, he says she has two voices—a soft one for baby brother, and a big lion voice for him. What is he doing wrong? And what does he do that makes her stop yelling?

Reading Skills Activities

Basic Skills Review

At the end of the year it is the perfect opportunity to review the essential concepts covered during the preceding months. Pull out the letter and number games that you made during the teaching of those skills and use them to review with the children as well as to reevaluate each child. Skills and concepts to be covered should include:

Recognition of capital and lowercase letters
Recognition of numbers to 30
Identification of letter/sound correspondence
Recognition of long and short vowel sounds
Identification of high-frequency words
Ability to add simple number sentences
Ability to subtract simple number sentences
Ability to sort, classify, and pattern
Ability to graph objects
Ability to form letters
Ability to listen
Ability to follow directions
Ability to get along well with peers
Ability to express thoughts verbally

Reading and Writing

"My, How I've Grown" Booklets. Make booklets by folding 8½″ × 11″ paper and adding a construction paper or wallpaper cover. Staple the books at the left side. Have the children write "My How I've Grown" on the cover. Inside the booklet, the boys and girls can draw illustrations and write about

the favorite things that they have learned this year. Encourage them to spell words phonetically or give assistance as you feel is needed. Some ideas for the books might be: a picture of me at the end of the year; a picture of my class at the end of the year; a picture of my favorite part of the classroom; a picture of the school; a picture of my best friend; a picture of my favorite story; a picture of my favorite project; a picture of my favorite season; a picture of my favorite field trip; a picture of what I learned that I thought was most important; a picture of my favorite school helper; a picture of what I'd like to learn next year. The children can share the books with one another, with school helpers such as the principal, the secretary, the nurse, the custodian, or anyone else that will listen, or perhaps with the first grade teacher for next year.

Sentences

Rebus Sentence Review. Have a list of high-frequency words where the children can see them, perhaps on chart paper or on the chalkboard. Ask the children to say the words with you as you point to them just to review. Give the boys and girls large pieces of construction paper and ask them to write their own rebus sentences using some of the words, their own pictures, and remembering the punctuation marks at the end of of the sentences. Hang these all around the room and encourage students to stand by their sentences and read them to the class. Those children who are still having difficulty with the high-frequency words can simply draw pictures and talk about the pictures in complete sentences.

Chalkboard Sentences. Write rebus sentences on the chalkboard and call on children to come up and read the sentences to the class. Ask them how they might change one or two words or pictures in the sentence to make an entirely new sentence.

Language Development

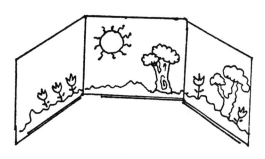

The Final Curtain. A fun way to check growth in oral language development is to have each child present a very short puppet show for the rest of the class. They can make background scenery by folding a piece of 12″ × 18″ oaktag into three sections and then unfolding so that the oaktag will stand on the floor or a tabletop. Meet with each child or have each talk to a friend to plan what their show will be about. They might use markers or crayons to color in the background. The characters for the story can be colored and cut from oaktag and taped to a tongue depressor so the puppeteer can lean over the top of the backdrop to make the characters move. Review with the boys and girls how every good story has a beginning, a middle, and an end. Talk about the stories that they have enjoyed most and why they believe those particular ones are so good. ("Is it the action in the story?" "Is it the way the characters talked in the story?" "Is it because there were surprises in the story?") Encourage the children to plan their stories in their head and then talk it through with a friend. Invite school helpers or children in other grade levels or parents to come and watch the final curtain puppet show.

Explain to the children that the words "the final curtain" mean that the show is almost over—and that's what this school year is, too.

Letter/Sound Review

The Teddy Bears' Picnic Reunion. Invite all of the teddy bears back for a last hurrah. The bears can wear their favorite letter pinned to them when they return and as everyone sits in circle, the bears can each tell what they liked best about the school year. Read or tell the story about the teddy bears' picnic again and ask different children to retell it. Have each child bring a sack lunch from home and ask the bears to join the class for a picnic at school. Each bear might get a certificate for completing kindergarten and a special sticker and a bear hug for being such a good bear all year long. Together, write an experience story about a little bear who went to school, asking each child to contribute a sentence. Duplicate the story and send a copy home with each child. Leave enough room for them to illustrate a part of the story.

Games to Play at the Reunion. At the picnic you might have teddy bear races, teddy back (like piggy back) races, jumping contests, honey eating contests, backwards rolling contests, a hokey pokey game, and other games that involve both children and bears.

Math Skills Activities

Numbers

Number Facts Books. Make various sizes of books and let each child pick one that appeals to them. Some might be tall and skinny books, others might be square books, or tiny books. The children can write NUMBERS on the front of the book and inside write a simple number sentence on each page. They should then draw sets of objects on each page that illustrate the number sentence. For example, there might be a set of two birds and a set of four birds on a page that says, "2 + 4 = 6." Some children may still need manipulatives to work out the problems.

Taking an Inventory

Classroom Inventory. The boys and girls can be a great help in doing the end of the year inventory and it can be a good way to check math skills. Make a sheet of rebus questions about the classroom—How many _____ ? _____. How many _____ ? _____. How many _____ ? _____. The sheet should reflect your particular classroom and include things that are special to your room and your children. When everyone has completed the worksheet, sit in circle and talk about how many of each thing everyone found. There will probably be some differences of opinion and you will need to have someone count to be sure of the correct answer.

Statistics

End-of-the-Year Statistics. Talk with the children about how we can learn many things and solve problems by compiling information. Make a worksheet that would reflect the following information and encourage everyone to work together to compile the information:

- How many new students joined our class during the year?
- How many students moved away during the year?
- How many people lost teeth during the year?
- How many teeth were lost during the year?
- How many sunny days did we have this year? (Information from monthly weather graphs)
- How many rainy days did we have this year?
- How many cloudy days did we have this year?
- How many new babies were born to our families this year?
- How many new pets did we get this year?
- How many new books did we buy for our library this year?
- How many new games did we get for the classroom this year?
- How many people grew taller this year?
- How many people learned to tie their shoes this year?
- How many people learned to count to 100 this year?
- How many people had new teeth grow in during the year?
- How many people brought their teddy bears to school?

rainy days   sunny days   babies born

Time

Although many children will not understand the concept of telling time, it is good to at least introduce the subject. Be sure the children are introduced to both digital clocks and standard face clocks.

Making Paper Clocks. Make paper clocks by writing the clock numerals around the edge of the paper plate and attaching two paper hands with a paper fastener. Introduce clock words such as hands, face, minute hand, hour hand, second hand, and digital. Have the children sit in circle with their clocks and give them a time to make on their clocks. Knowing the hour and half hour are appropriate for the children.

Special Times. Write special times during the school day, such as music time, story time, and gym time on the chalkboard and have the children duplicate that time on their paper plate clocks. Also write down times that might be important at home, such as breakfast time, bedtime, and dinner time.

A Giant Clock Game. Use a large sheet of roll paper to make a giant clock face with numerals. Make two large hands from cardboard, being sure that one is longer than the other for the minute hand. Choose two children to stand in the middle of the clock and make sure that they know which one is holding the hour hand and which one is holding the minute hand. The other children can suggest times (hour and half hour) and the two hand-holders will make the time on the giant clock.

Other Kinds of Time. Talk about other kinds of time—days, weeks, months, years, centuries, work time, leisure time, play time. Make a chart that lists time words. Included might be watch, alarm clock, hourglass, egg timer, sundial, grandfather clock.

Money

An introduction to money is a good ending activity for the year. Bring in real coins and bills so that the children can see the markings and actual color of the coins.

Let's Play Store. Turn the playhouse into a store and ask the children to bring in empty boxes and cartons that might be used to pretend that there is buying and selling going on. The boys and girls can take turns being the storekeepers and the customers. Mark each of the objects to be bought with a very simple price—3¢, 6¢, etc. If possible, use real money for the purchases.

A Circle Game. In circle, compare the sizes of coins and also their worth. Children find it interesting that the largest coins are not always worth the most money. Have the children order the coins from largest to smallest and then again from the coin worth the most to the coin worth the least.

A Visit from a Banker. Invite a banker to visit the class and talk about his or her job. Before the visit, help the children write questions that they might like to have the banker answer.

Other Skill Areas Activities

May Day

May Day is celebrated on May 1 and is a tradition from the country of England. On this day the people of England celebrated the coming of spring by decorating homes and churches with flowers, choosing a May king and queen, and by dancing around a Maypole that was wrapped with ribbons.

May Baskets. Make May baskets from paper cups with a pipe cleaner handle or from berry baskets from the grocery store with a pipe cleaner handle. Fill the baskets with tissue paper flowers on construction paper stems. The flower blossom can be a rectangle of tissue paper, scrunched, and glued to the stem. In England, the baskets were left on the doors of unsuspecting friends and neighbors. The "givers" would hide where the receiver wouldn't see them and watch as they found the basket.

Introduce the country of England as you talk about May Day. The English love pageantry, ceremonies, tea, soccer, cricket (an outdoor game similar to baseball), and castles.

A Tea Party. Have an English tea party. The children can fix toast and honey and enjoy a cup of warm tea.

The London Bridge. Sing and play "London Bridge Is Falling Down." Talk about how the London Bridge really did fall down. There have been three London bridges; the first one lasted the longest—622 years.

VARIATION: Borrow some books from the library that have pictures of other English traditions and landmarks, such as Big Ben, Windsor Castle, the Royal Guardsmen, double-decker buses, Buckingham Palace, and London Tower.

English Words. Learn some English words and their American translations:

lorry (heavy truck)   petrol (gasoline)
lift (elevator)   taa (thanks)
queue, cue (wait in line)   cheerio (goodbye)
boot (trunk of a car)   brolly (umbrella)
bonnet (hood of a car)   biscuits (cookies)

Mother's Day and Father's Day

The day that we honor our mothers, Mother's Day, falls in May and our special day for fathers, Father's Day, comes in June. In talking with the children, help them think of special jobs that they can do for mom and dad on these days for remembering the people we love. They might even make a coupon for a present that would entitle mom to a day off from dishwashing or dad a day off from taking out the trash. Gifts of service are rewarding both to the giver and the receiver.

Summer Safety

Rules. Summer is a time when people are outside and active. Help the children brainstorm some summer safety ideas and write them on an experience chart. The safety ideas might include rules for the swimming pool, a plan for a tornado safe place, safety tips for riding long distances in a car, rules for being careful on playgrounds, and walking in the neighborhood.

Safety Pictures. Have the children draw safety pictures of themselves observing a safety rule in the summer.

VARIATION: Make a safety mural that includes neighborhood houses and children observing safety rules.

Summer Learning Packets

It is helpful for children to have learning materials to work on at home during the summer to reinforce the skills that they have learned during the school year. To make a summer packet, fold a piece of 12″ × 18″ construction paper in half and staple the sides so that the materials can slip down into the pouch. You might include:

- math sheets for reinforcing counting, addition, subtraction, graphing
- letter formation sheets
- phonics sheets
- bingo game cards with letters on them to identify
- number word and color word sheets
- number formation sheets

- rebus story books
- rebus sentence sheets
- calendars for each summer month with a task to do each day (count the flowers in your yard, jump up and down 25 times, tell your dad that you love him, say the Pledge of Allegiance to the flag, count backwards from 20, recite a nursery rhyme, write down the names of your favorite zoo animals, count the number of teddy bears in your house, etc.).

Name _____

SUMMER SUBTRACTION

You can practice subtracting with these summer things. Each box has a number sentence written beneath it. The first numeral in the sentence tells how many things are in the box. The second numeral tells you how many to cross out. You write the numeral that tells how many things are left. Color the objects.

3 - 1 = 2

5 - 2 =

7 - 3 =

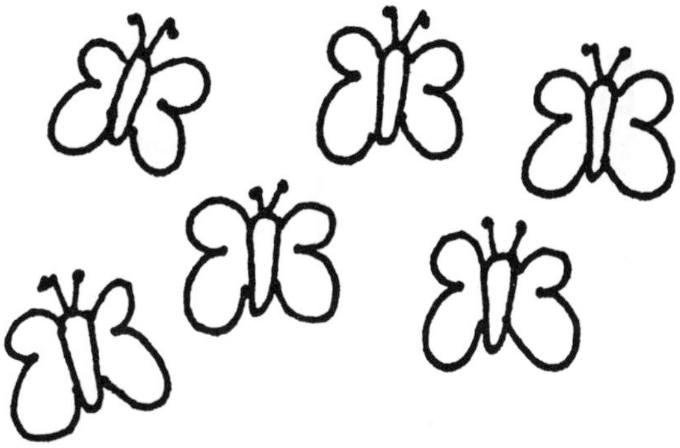

6 - 4 =

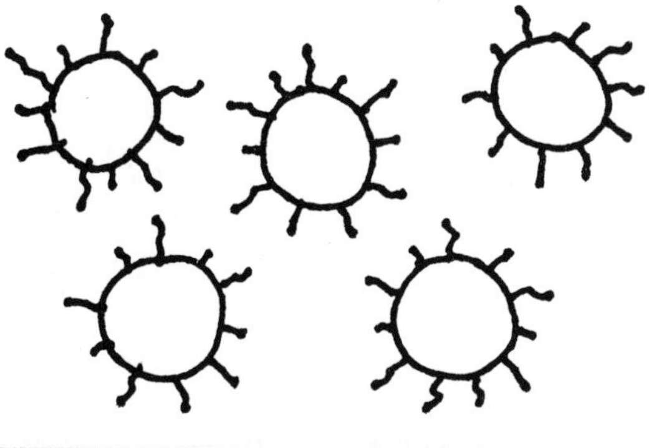

5 - 0 =

6 - 2 =

Name _____

RAINY DAY NUMBERS

April showers bring May flowers! These clouds are dropping rain on the umbrellas below. Count the number of raindrops under each cloud and draw a line to the umbrella with the matching numeral. Color the pictures in rainy day colors.

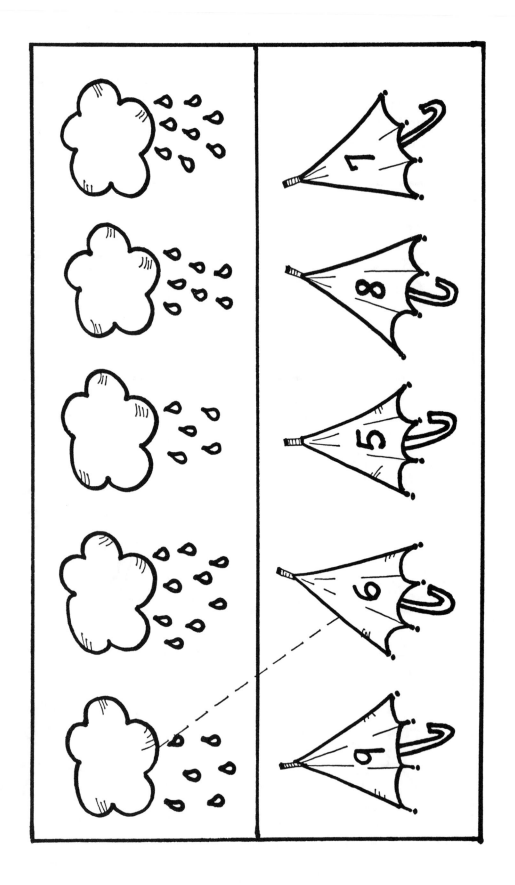

THE THREE PIGS BOOKLET, page 1 of 2

This little booklet tells the story of the three pigs and you can read it. Color the pictures and cut the pages apart on the black lines. Put them together in the right order. Read the booklet to a friend.

THE

THREE

1

Name _____

2

A 🐷 is in a 🏠 .

The 🐺 will go to the 🏠 .

Will the 🐺 go in ?

He will go in.

3

A 🐷 is in a 🏠 .

The 🐺 will go to the 🏠 .

Will the 🐺 go in?

He will go in.

4

Name ______________________

THE THREE PIGS BOOKLET, page 2 of 2

A  is in a .

The  will go to the .

Will the  go in?

He will go in.

5

The  will go to the 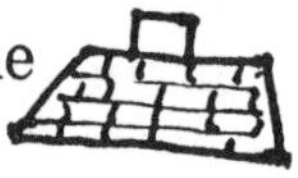.

He will go in the .

He will not go in the .

6

WORDS

a	he	to
is	will	the
in	go	not

7

The End

8

Name ______________________________

AN ALPHABET BOOK, page 1 of 5

We have been learning about the alphabet all year long—now it's time to make an alphabet book of your very own. Think about the alphabet books that we have read this year. Each one was different but each one talked about the letters of the alphabet. On the little pages below, decide what you can draw that will represent each letter. Try to sound out the word for each letter thing that you draw and put that in the little box, too. You're going to be an illustrator! Cut the pages apart on the black lines and staple them together in the correct order. Check your work by singing the alphabet song to make sure the pages are where they should be.

MY

ALPHABET

BOOK

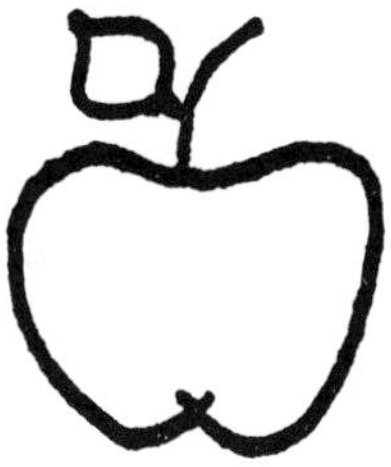

Name ____________________

Aa is for ____________________

Bb is for ____________________

Cc is for ____________________

AN ALPHABET BOOK, page 2 of 5

Dd is for ____________________	Ee is for ____________________
Ff is for ____________________	Gg is for ____________________
Hh is for ____________________	Ii is for ____________________

Jj is for _____

Kk is for _____

Ll is for _____

Mm is for _____

Nn is for _____

Oo is for _____

Pp is for _____

Qq is for _____

Rr is for _____

Ss is for _____

Tt is for _____

Uu is for _____

Vv is for _____

Ww is for _____

Xx is for _____

Yy is for _____

Zz is for _____

The
End

Name _____

A SUMMER CONCENTRATION GAME

Each of the boxes below contains a summer picture. Color each picture and cut the boxes apart on the lines. To play the summer memory game: Lay the cards face down and turn over two cards at a time. If the cards match, you may keep them. If the cards don't match, turn them back over. Your turn is over. Try to remember where each picture is hidden as the other players take their turns. The person with the most matches wins the game.

summer		fun	
			summer
	fun		

Name _____

This is the story of Goldilocks and the Three Bears and you can read it. Color the pictures and cut the pages apart on the black lines. Put them together in the right order. Read the booklet to a friend.

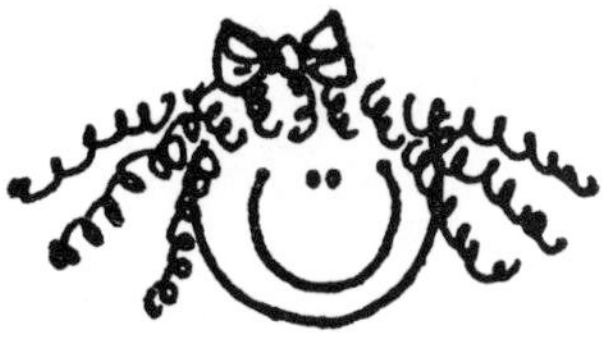

and the

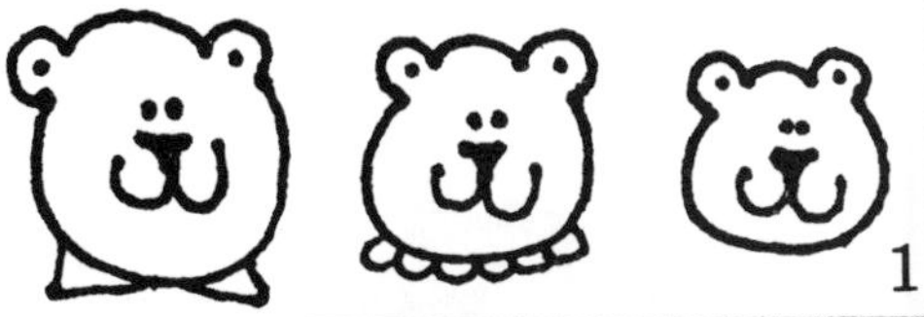

1

Name _____

2

The

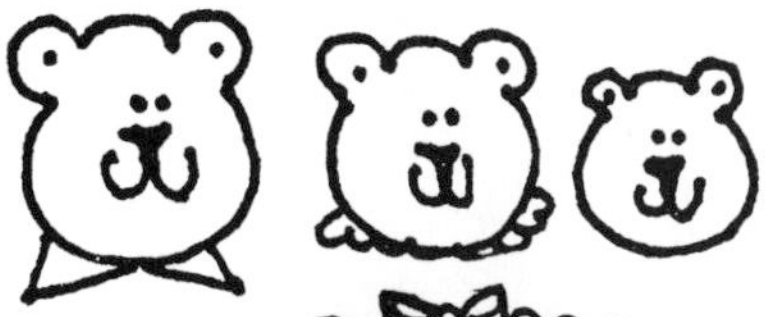

go.

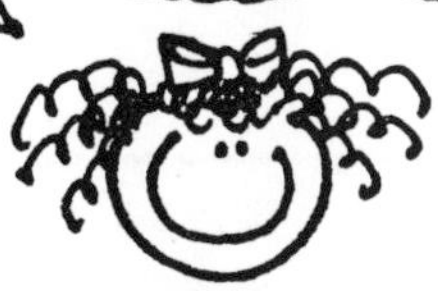

will go in the

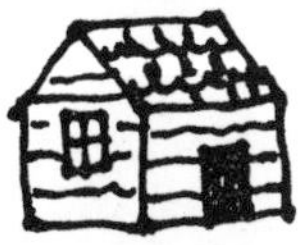

3

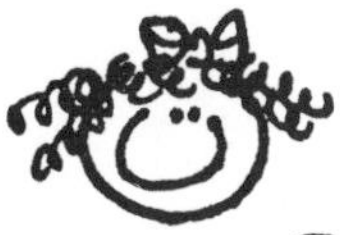

will not go in

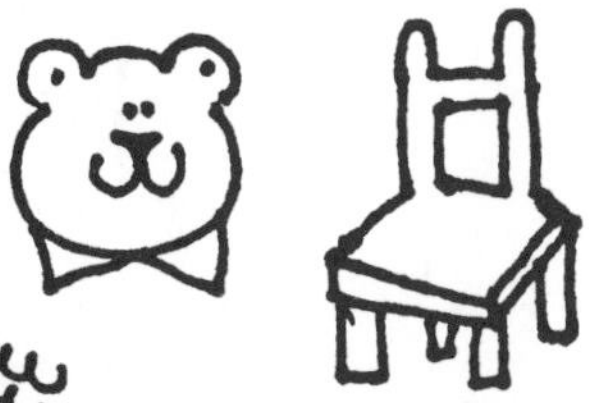

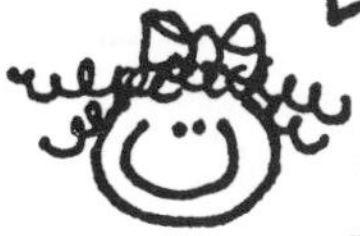

will not go

in

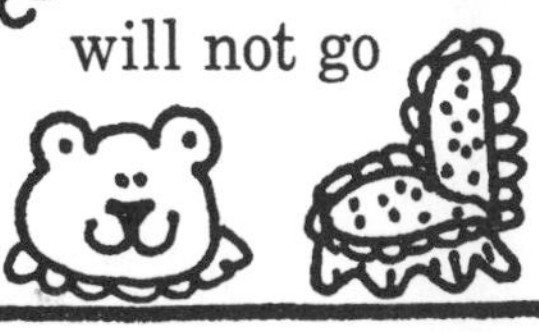

4

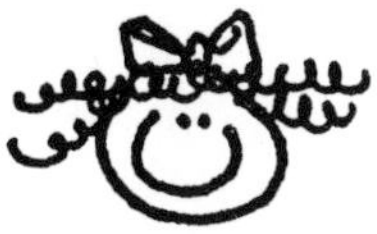

will go in

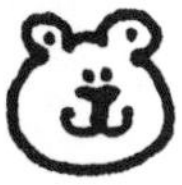

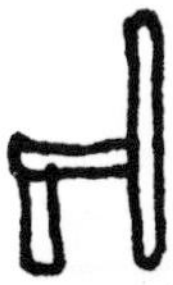

It

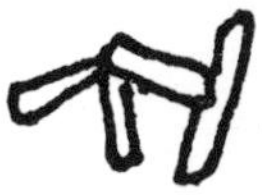

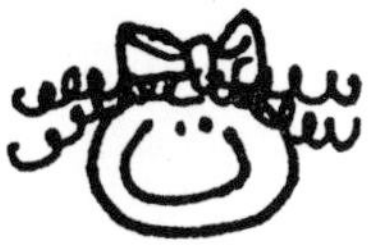

will not

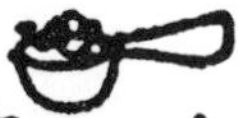

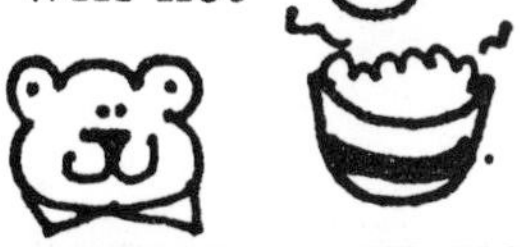

5

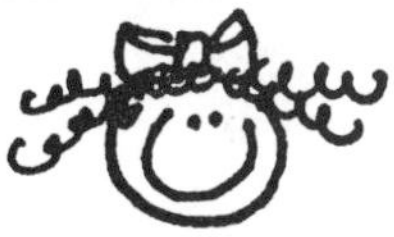

will not

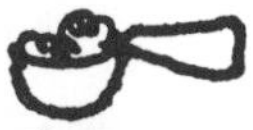

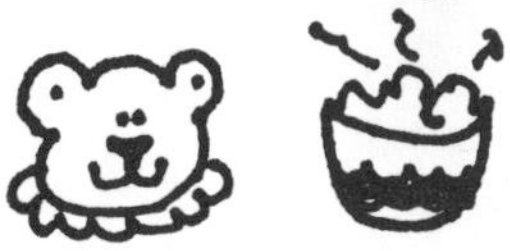

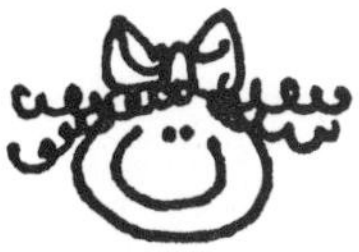

will

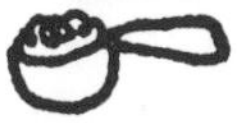

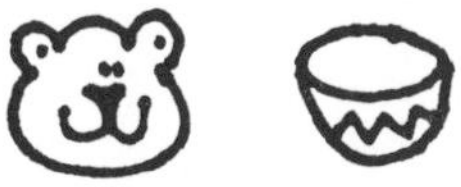

6

7 will not go in

will not go in .

8 will go in .

The go in the .

9 They see the

and the

and the .

10 will go!

11 Words

the	in	they
go	not	see
will	it	and

12 The

End

Name _____

GROWING FLOWERS

These flowers are growing in a row and each one is in the right order. The first flower has the numeral 20 in its center. Fill in the missing numerals in the other flowers. Color the flowers in warm colors for summer.

Name _____

GRAPHING INSECTS

Look at the insects in the box. There are four different kinds. Count how many there are of each kind. Graph that number by coloring in the correct number of boxes above each insect.

5				
4				
3				
2				
1				

A PIECE OF THE PIE

This apple pie will taste yummy. Color it lightly with a brown crayon. How many pieces have been cut? How many people could each have a piece of the pie? Is each piece the same size? How could you find out if each piece was the same size? How many pieces would be half of the pie? Cut ⅙ of the pie to eat!

WHAT COMES NEXT?

The objects in the boxes below are in patterns. For example, the first box has the pattern—tree, butterfly, tree, butterfly. What will come next in the pattern? Finish the ball–umbrella pattern and the snail–balloon pattern. Each row should have FIVE pictures in it. Color the patterns in this way:

green   yellow

red   orange

blue   purple

SUMMER SIGHTS

These boxes are filled with things that you might see in the summer. Look at each box and count the number of objects in it. Then find the matching number word and draw a line to it. The first one is done for you.

two

one

seven

five

three

four

nine

eight

six

zero

Name _____

ALFIE'S SUMMER IDEAS

Activities for every other day!

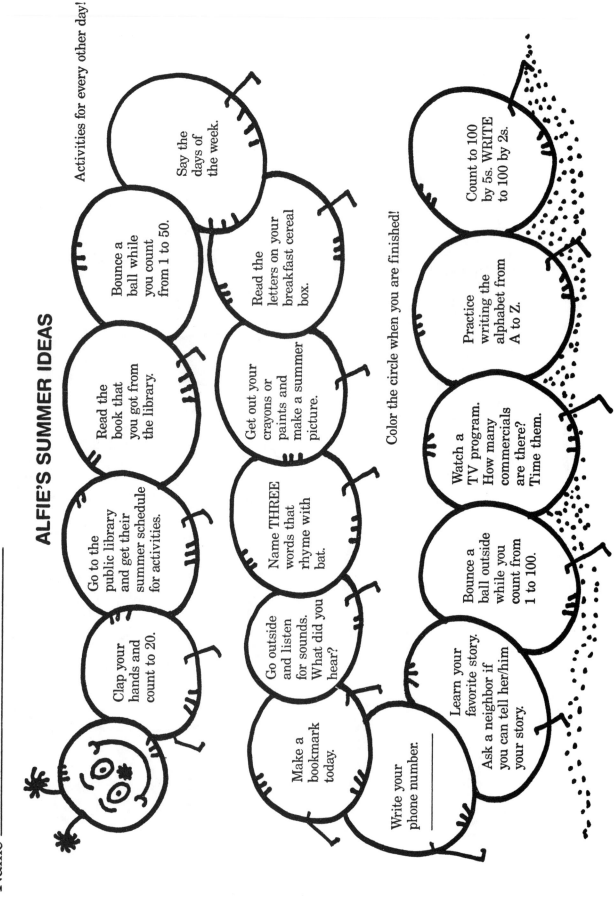

Color the circle when you are finished!

Clap your hands and count to 20.

Go to the public library and get their summer schedule for activities.

Read the book that you got from the library.

Bounce a ball while you count from 1 to 50.

Say the days of the week.

Read the letters on your breakfast cereal box.

Get out your crayons or paints and make a summer picture.

Name THREE words that rhyme with bat.

Go outside and listen for sounds. What did you hear?

Make a bookmark today.

Write your phone number. _____

Learn your favorite story. Ask a neighbor if you can tell her/him your story.

Bounce a ball outside while you count from 1 to 100.

Watch a TV program. How many commercials are there? Time them.

Practice writing the alphabet from A to Z.

Count to 100 by 5s. WRITE to 100 by 2s.

KEEP LEARNING WITH ALFIE

Activities for Every Other Day!

Color the circle when you are finished.

Make your very own Alfie!

Ask Mom to read the comics to you.

Visit the library for story time. Get a book.

Draw a circle, a square, a triangle, and a rectangle.

Count the number of windows in your house. Write it down.

Write a letter to a friend.

Plan a play for the neighborhood. You can act out a favorite story.

Practice saying the Pledge of Allegiance to the flag.

Sing three nursery rhymes.

Drink a glass of water. Name four words that begin with "w."

Look at a map. Find your city. Find your vacation spot.

Sit down for 10 minutes with a book today. Read it.

Say the days of the week. Write them.

What are your 3 favorite holidays? Draw a picture to go with each one.

Take a can of vegetable soup out of the cupboard. How many letters or words can you say?

Say the 12 months of the year. Write them.

How many days are there until school begins?

Make your own story book about summer.

When you go to the store, look at the fresh veggies. How many can you name?

Make a list of things you will need for school.

Smile a lot today! School will begin soon!

Name _____

TELL IT TO ALFIE

Alfie wants you to write down six things that you can do to show that you are ready for school! Then do them, and keep doing them, so that you will "keep learning alive!"

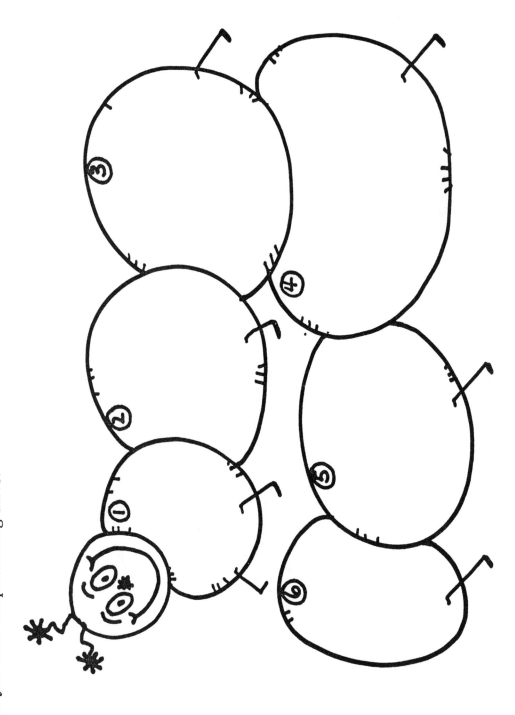